THE SHINING PATH OF PERU

Also by David Scott Palmer
PERU: AN AUTHORITARIAN TRADITION

THE SHINING PATH OF PERU

Second Edition

Edited by
David Scott Palmer
Boston University

ST. MARTIN'S PRESS
NEW YORK

Peru map courtesy of U.S. Department of State.

Ayacucho Emergency Zone map, courtesy of Amnesty International.

Parts of chapter 1, "Introduction: History, Politics, and Shining Path in Peru," taken from David Scott Palmer, "Peru: The Enduring Authoritarian Legacy," Howard J. Wiarda and Harvey F. Kline, eds., *Latin American Politics and Development*, 4th ed. Boulder, CO: Westview Press (1995), with the kind permission of the editors.

The first section of chapter 3, "Return to the Past," edited and revised from Carlos Iván Degregori, "A Dwarf Star," *NACLA Report on the Americas*, 24:4, December-January 1990-1991, pp. 10-16. Reprinted by permission of the North American Congress on Latin America.

Sections of chapter 8, "Shining Path's Stalin and Trotsky," taken from Gustavo Gorriti, "The War of the Philosopher King," *The New Republic*, June 18, 1990, pp. 15-22, and reprinted by permission of the editors of *The New Republic*.

First published in the United States of America 1992
Revised and updated second edition first published 1994

Printed in the United States of America
ISBN 0-312-10619-X (paperback only)

Library of Congress Cataloging-in-Publication Data
The Shining Path of Peru / edited by David Scott Palmer.— 2nd ed.
    p. cm.
  Includes bibliographical references (p.   ) and index.
  ISBN 0–312–10619–X (pbk.)
  1. Sendero Luminoso (Guerrilla group) 2. Peru—Politics and
government—1968-1980. 3. Peru—Politics and government—1980-
I. Palmer, David Scott, 1937- .
F3448.2.S54 1994
322.4'2'0985—dc20   94–25904
                                      CIP

Contents

Peru

— International boundary
–·– Department boundary
★ National capital
⊕ Department capital
┼┼ Railroad
—— Road

Callao is the capital of the Constitutional
Province of Callao which has the status
of a department but is too small to be
shown on this map.

0   100   200 Kilometers
0   100   200 Miles

Transverse Mercator Projection, CM 71°W

COLOMBIA

ECUADOR

Manta

Quito
Ambato

Guayaquil

Cuenca

Tumbes
TUMBES
Loja

Talara
Sullana PIURA
Piura

Paita

LAMBAYEQUE
Chiclayo

AMAZONAS
Chachapoyas

Moyobamba
Tarapoto
SAN
MARTIN

Yurimaguas

LORETO

Iquitos

Leticia
Benjamin Constant

BRAZIL

CAJAMARCA
Cajamarca

Santa
Lucia

Cruzeiro
do Sul

LA LIBERTAD
Trujillo
Salaverry

Pucallpa

SOUTH
PACIFIC
OCEAN

Chimbote
Huaraz

ANCASH

Tingo
Maria
HUANUCO
Huanuco

UCAYALI

Rio
Branco

PASCO
Goyllarisquizga
Cerro de Pasco

Huacho

JUNIN
Huancayo

MADRE DE DIOS

Cobija

Callao
LIMA
Lima

Huancavelica
HUANCAVELICA
Pisco

Ica
ICA
Nazca

Quillabamba
Ayacucho
AYACUCHO

CUSCO
Machupicchu
(ruins)
Abancay
APURIMAC

Cusco

Puerto Maldonado

PUNO

BOLIVIA

AREQUIPA

Juliaca

Puno

La Paz
Guaqui

Arequipa

MOQUEGUA
Matarani

Moquegua

Ilo

Desaguadero

Oruro

TACNA
Tacna

Arica

CHILE

Boundary representation is
not necessarily authoritative

Emergency Zone

Huancayo
HUANCAYO

JUNIN

TAYACAJA

Pampas

HUANTA

LA CONVENCION

Pichari

HUANCAVELICA

ACOBAMBA

Sivia

Luisiana

CUZCO

Huancavelica

Pucayacu

Acobamba

Tambo

Julcamarca

Huanta

San Miguel

HUANCAVELICA

ANGARAES

LA MAR

Rio Apurimac

Ayacucho

Castrovirreyna

HUAMANGA

Soccos

Ocros

CHINCHEROS

Totos

Chuschi

CANGALLO

Chincheros

Pacucha

Cangallo

Andahuaylas

Vilcanchos

Huancapi

Vilcashuaman

CASTROVIRREYNA

VICTOR
FAJARDO

Canaria

Sacsamarca

ANDAHUAYLAS

AYACUCHO

APURIMAC

LUCANAS

Puquio

Departments in bold capitals
(e.g. **AYACUCHO**); provinces in
light capitals (e.g. HUANTA).

Provinces called Huanca
Sancos and Vilcashuaman are
to be formed from districts now
in Cangallo and Victor Fajardo
provinces

PREFACE

This volume is the most comprehensive effort to date to understand the Shining Path phenomenon, which so unexpectedly has convulsed Peru as its citizens try to establish and extend full-scale procedural democracy under civilian rule. Fifteen individuals from the fields of journalism, academia, and development, from Peru, the United States, and the Netherlands, come together to provide their distinctive analyses and insights based on a wide range of experiences. All have carried out extensive field work in Peru from their respective disciplinary or professional perspectives, including but not restricted to Shining Path. All have published their work on Peru and on Sendero Luminoso; the chapters in this volume represent original distillations and syntheses of their research in almost every case. Each gives a window on Shining Path; while there is some overlap in the views provided, each also covers various features not systematically reviewed by the others. The overall result, we think, is more than the sum of its parts and provides the most complete survey of Shining Path to date.

However, this is not to claim definitiveness. The work of various serious students of Sendero, including Raúl González, Nelson Manrique, Enrique Melgar Bao, Michael Reid, Colin Harding, Henri Favre, and Lewis Taylor, among others, could not be included. Nevertheless, our individual and collective debt to them is manifest through the frequent citing of their work throughout this volume.

Our goal was to place within the covers of a single book as much information and analysis of the Shining Path of Peru as we could fit, so that one could come away with as complete a picture as possible of what is to many the most distinctive full-blown revolutionary movement the Western Hemisphere has ever seen. We believe that we have been quite successful in our effort. However, it remains for you, the reader, to make your own determination.

In putting together such a volume, one incurs many debts. I am particularly grateful to the contributors themselves, each of whom entrusted to me their draft chapters for editing and, in some cases, for translating and integrating. This turned out to be extensive in several cases, due mainly to new length restrictions imposed by the publisher after I had submitted the entire manuscript. Many contributors also endured my calls and faxes to track down elusive citations or to seek clarifications, a most unenviable chore which I suspect bordered on harassment at times. Although I made every effort in each aspect of the editing process to remain completely faithful to the chapter authors' research, findings, and intent, I take full responsibility for any errors or oversights which might remain.

For the Sarhua folk painting which graces the cover I am indebted to fellow erstwhile University of Huamanga colleague and long-time friend Luis Millones for the original inspiration and photograph, to Michael L. Smith for placing his copy at my disposal, and to Washington, D.C. artist Sally Ehrlich Hoffman for her superb photographs of the painting from which the cover was ultimately chosen.

The Andean Jurists Commission, the American Participants program of the United States Information Agency, and the Ford Foundation (through its support of the Terrorism in Context project at Wesleyan University) all made possible my trips to Peru while the volume was in progress. This permitted me to confer with contributors, conduct interviews, and gather research materials. I particularly value the friendship and confidence of Gustavo Gorriti and his family, whose assistance on these visits as well as during his Nieman Fellowship and Guggenheim Foundation residences at Harvard University made the whole enterprise possible — and worthwhile.

At Boston University Mary Catherine Harmon put most of the manuscript's pieces into recognizable form, while International Relations Department administrator Carole Chandler found ways to cover many of the inevitable overhead costs. Computer whiz Henry R. Crawford, also my nephew, successfully, even brilliantly, translated the multiple modes of the contributors onto the single disk from which the final book emerged, with the finishing touches added by Mary Catherine and Boston University's outstanding University

Information Systems office. At St. Martin's, editor Simon Winder and his assistant Laura Heymann helped things along at every stage in a manner both constructive and thoroughly professional.

In many ways this effort to understand more fully the complex contemporary reality of Peru goes back some thirty years — to my in depth initiation into Andean Peru as a Peace Corps Volunteer in Ayacucho from September 1962 to July 1964. I had the opportunity to teach at the University of San Cristóbal de Huamanga in 1962 and 1963 when it was still small and intimate (about 700 students and 40 professors), very pluralistic politically, and most conscious of its potential to transform the countryside with a wide variety of initiatives. Who could have guessed then what fellow professor Abimael Guzmán Reynoso and those who were to become his disciples (a number of them my students, acquaintances, and friends) would eventually do with this enterprise? Only much later did I learn that it was Guzmán himself who masterminded the removal of the Peace Corps from the University of Huamanga in November 1963, his first significant political victory there.

Ironically, this event exposed me to a very different Ayacucho reality, that of the remote and isolated Indian communities. Soon after leaving the university I directed for some five months a reforestation project with the help of the Peruvian Forest Service and Food for Peace, in the Víctor Fajardo province communities of Huancaraylla, Llucita, and Circamarca, a three-hour drive and four-hour walk from the city of Ayacucho. My experiences there, as well as those at the university, left an indelible mark on my own world view, one that looks toward the center from the periphery and evaluates Peruvian reality with that perspective. While I am not and cannot be a part of that periphery — though I was named officially a member of those distant Víctor Fajardo Indian communities by their residents — my profound concern for what is happening in present-day Peru comes largely from that vantage point. This perspective has only been reinforced by subsequent research and writing on the country over the intervening years, of which this volume is the latest effort.

In some ways Shining Path has taken up the banner of the periphery — understood in cultural, economic, and geographic terms — which neither I nor the Peruvian government nor the multiple public and private international development agencies made the time for or had the vision to do. Sendero's view of the New Peru is a utopian one which has the potential to attract many who have always struggled on the periphery. With my memories of sacrifice and struggle in the Ayacucho countryside still fresh, I am forced to respect the dedication and zeal of the Shining Path leadership as it tries to forge a new and more meaningful reality for peripheral Peru's long-suffering citizenry. However, Shining Path's obsessively destructive methods are abhorrent. Sendero believes that it alone knows what the citizenry needs, and wants to impose its solution at whatever costs over all obstacles — including the real needs and aspirations of the population itself. Shining Path's lack of respect for the very periphery it proposes to liberate ultimately will likely prove to be its downfall.

David Scott Palmer
Boston, Massachusetts
December 1991

PREFACE TO THE SECOND EDITION

When *Shining Path of Peru* first went to press in early 1992, Peru was struggling to pull back from the brink of disaster. It was not at all clear at that moment whether the country was going to make it. Even so, the thrust of the case studies in the volume — representing the cumulative experience of researching, writing, studying, and/or working in or on Peru totaling more than 200 years! — noted quite clearly and consistently the real limitations in Shining Path's ability to take full advantage of the Peruvian people's distress. We also pointed up the many limitations of Peru's government, and observed with much concern that the real losers in the country's late 1980s and early 1990s crisis dynamic were the long suffering Peruvian people themselves.

As we go to press again just over two years later, the changes have been dramatic. Sendero, bolder and more confident over the first eight months of 1992, has been forced onto the defensive since. Some, in fact, view Shining Path as a spent force soon to disappear from the Peruvian political landscape. The government, beleaguered and harassed and frequently viewed as its own worst enemy in its fight against Sendero, quickly and quite effectively turned the tables on the guerrillas. Only the distressed state of the Peruvian population remains constant. Improving its situation must be changed, too, and quickly.

The most significant events that this revised edition of *Shining Path of Peru* presents and analyzes are President Alberto Fujimori's *autogolpe* (self-administered coup) of April 1992, the capture of Shining Path's leader, Abimael Guzmán Reynoso, in September 1992, and the progressive reintroduction of a more centralized and authoritarian representative democracy over the course

xvi   *The Shining Path of Peru*

of 1993. I have largely rewritten introductory and concluding chapters to take into account these changes and their effects. I have also added to the introduction a substantial section on Peru's complex political history to help readers more fully understand the larger national context from which Shining Path emerged. While the other contributors were also invited to change their chapters as they thought appropriate, most concluded that their analyses and findings stood up well, and therefore chose not to do so. The overall conclusion of this revised edition is that Shining Path has been dealt some heavy blows by the combination of government initiatives and popular rejection, but is far from finished as a significant actor on the Peruvian political stage.

David Scott Palmer
Boston, Massachusetts
May 1994

CONTRIBUTORS

Ronald H. Berg is a program officer for the Latin American Scholarship Program of American Universities (LASPAU). He has a Ph.D. in Anthropology from the University of Michigan and has taught anthropology at Michigan and Notre Dame.

Carlos Iván Degregori is professor of anthropology at the Universidad Nacional Mayor de San Marcos and director of the Instituto de Estudios Peruanos. He received his anthropology degree from the Universidad Nacional de San Cristóbal de Huamanga, where he also served as a member of the faculty.

Ton de Wit and **Vera Gianotten** work for the Royal Tropical Institute, the Netherlands, in Third World development programs. They lived in Ayacucho between 1977 and 1983 working in a rural development program sponsored by the Dutch government.

Gustavo Gorriti is a free-lance journalist who wrote for Peru's leading weekly magazine, *Caretas*, and was the recipient of a Nieman Foundation Fellowship and a Guggenheim Award to pursue his research and writing on Shining Path. Forced into exile after the April 1992 *autogolpe*, he is presently Senior Research Associate at the North-South Center of the University of Miami.

José E. Gonzales is a journalist who has served as a professor in the Facultad de Ciéncias de Comunicación at the Universidad de Lima, as a political analyst for the Peruvian research institute APOYO, and as Latin America analyst for Baring Securities in New York. He is currently completing his Ph.D. at the University of California, Berkeley.

William A. Hazelton and **Sandra Woy-Hazelton** teach at Miami University (Ohio), where Sandra is deputy director of the Institute of Environmental Sciences and William is director of the International Studies Program.

Billie Jean Isbell is professor of anthropology at Cornell University and served as director of the Latin American Studies Program there.

Tom Marks teaches social sciences at the Academy of the Pacific in Honolulu, Hawaii, and is chief foreign correspondent for *Soldier of Fortune* magazine. He received his Ph.D. from the University of Hawaii.

Cynthia McClintock is professor of political science at George Washington University. During 1990-1991 she held the William Jennings Randolph Peace Fellowship at the U.S. Institute of Peace.

Luis Millones received his doctorate in history from the Catholic University of Peru. He has written extensively on Andean history and culture for the past twenty-five years.

David Scott Palmer is professor of international relations and political science at Boston University and director of the Latin American Studies Program there.

Michael L. Smith is a free-lance writer who resided in Peru for sixteen years and whose reporting has appeared in the *Washington Post* and *Newsweek*, among other publications. His writing for this volume was made possible by a grant from the John D. and Catherine T. MacArthur Foundation.

Gabriela Tarazona-Sevillano served as a criminal affairs prosecutor of the Ministry of Justice of Peru from 1984 to 1986 and is now a visiting professor of international studies at Davidson College (North Carolina). In 1989 she was a visiting scholar at the Hoover Institution.

ABOUT THE COVER

I know of three printed panels (*tablas*) from the Indian community of Sarhua in the heart of Andean Ayacucho that reflect on local politics and how they tie in with national issues. One of these, titled "Broken Promises," depicts local activities of national political parties. The central figure in this *tabla* is an obvious city slicker haranguing a bored peasant audience. The second *tabla*, titled "Born Under an Unfavorable Star," has as its main theme a group of peasants being dragged off to a waiting truck, along with other violent scenes, including one showing the unfortunate Indians being put in jail.

These two *tablas*, plus the one shown here, illustrate the collective despair brought about as a result of the ties between the community of Sarhua and the government of Peru, a despair that is a symptom of even more serious problems. The daily lives of these painters of Sarhua, southwest of the Pampas River in the poverty-stricken province of Víctor Fajardo, Ayacucho, have been profoundly disrupted. They were forced to abandon their lands and their loved ones due to the violence of the guerrilla war, and now must produce their *tablas* in their Lima workshops. Their migration to the capital is best described as flight, and it occurred just when rural-to-urban movement was decreasing after having reached flood levels in the late 1960s.

Created as ceremonial paintings, the *tablas* were originally rectangular (about four feet by five feet) and were placed on the inside of the roofs of new houses. Each panel depicted family scenes designed to strengthen the moral and religious aspects of the new home. The ghastly civil war that began in 1980 swept before it these Andean folk painters. In the tumult and poverty of Peru's capital city, encapsulated thirty years ago in the title of Sebastian Salazar Bondy's book, *Lima the Horrible*, their folk art has become their means of survival. By cutting up the original panels into small pieces with individual scenes and selling them separately, painters found they could increase their income. While the original quality and character of the *tablas* was retained, necessity forced the natives of Sarhua to begin to sell their own heritage.

The written text within the painted panel chosen for this book cover refers to the forced gathering of the community by outsiders with "machine guns, dynamite, and red flags," who oblige its monolingual Quechua-speaking members to listen to their "false promises," in Spanish, about social justice and a higher standard of living. I am certain that the words have been very carefully thought out by those who, by the mere fact of being from Ayacucho, are constantly considered by government authorities to be suspicious characters. Even so, it is indicative that of the three *tablas* noted, this is the only one titled in Quechua, "Onqoy," or sickness.

Many of the *tablas* painted in Lima have as their central theme ceremonies and activities related to folk medicine and folk healing practices. Just like the painters, traditional Indian medicine also moved down to Lima. Some of their specialists and their remedies have attracted a large and anxious clientele.

If the guerrillas are a sickness, what is the cure? The ancient chronicles tell us that when the Inca faced a problem that did not seem to have any solution, he called together all the local and regional gods (*wakas*) of the empire and asked their advice. Today, when a folk healer (*curandero*) gets no response from his local god (*apu*), he can get the *apu* to gather his peers and together they can look for the *onqoy* (sickness). Could this be what the *tabla* is telling us?

Luis Millones
Lima, Peru

1

INTRODUCTION:
HISTORY, POLITICS, AND
SHINING PATH IN PERU

David Scott Palmer

Peru's political history is remarkably rich, distinctive, and complex. It was the land of the Inca and the center of Spain's Empire in South America. The final decisive battle that assured the independence of Latin America from Spain was fought here, in Ayacucho, December 9, 1824. Stable elected civilian government came late as well, in 1895 with the "Aristocratic Republic." This experiment in limited liberal democracy was also shorter lived than most of its contemporary counterparts in the region. It was interrupted by a civil military coup in 1914, but definitively terminated by the elected president's own takeover five years later. Not until the 1980s did civilian democratic rule with successive elected governments return to Peru (ironically ending the same way on April 5, 1992!). Over the intervening years the military dominated Peruvian politics most of the time — as "watchdogs of the oligarchy" from the 1930s through the 1950s, and as progressive reformers in the 1960s and 1970s.

The Shining Path Challenge

Nothing in Peru's past, however, prepared the country for Shining Path (Sendero Luminoso, SL, or Sendero) with its Gang of Four Maoist prescriptions and ruthless political violence, which began and spread in the 1980s. From 1980 through 1993, such violence claimed over 30,000 lives and more than $24 billion in direct and indirect property damages (over half of Peru's Gross National Product). This organization, which calls itself the Communist Party of Peru (PCP) and which almost everyone else calls Shining Path, has been something of an enigma since its inception over twenty years ago. It has not followed the pattern of most Marxist movements that developed in Latin American universities. These were usually oriented more toward intellectual analysis and influence within academe than toward action and system transformation through violence. Shining Path did not develop in the country's major university in the capital city and spread outward, but rather in a small, newly refounded provincial university in a small, isolated, historic but impoverished department (state) capital. Almost alone among the left, it vehemently opposed the reform initiatives of Peru's first long-term military government (1968-1980). The military in power attempted to make substantial changes in the country's economic and social structures and consciously opened up spaces for the left to organize and grow.

The PCP organized and grew initially not during economic crisis and government retrenchment, but during an extended period of economic growth and government expansion (1963-1975), particularly in public education and rural development initiatives. It gained control of the provincial university where it began and used that power base to deepen and extend its activities and its influence (1968-1975). Then, however, Shining Path turned its back on that university when it lost subsequent elections there and made no serious attempt to regain its position. It constantly denounced the government but also used public resources and positions to advance its own agenda, particularly in teaching posts in rural and provincial public schools. It was expelled from the national Maoist movement in Peru and eventually became the preeminent Maoist organization itself. It formally began the armed struggle at the very moment that Peru was returning to civilian democratic rule with universal suffrage and a free press.

By pursuing its own agenda and its own timetable, by starting at the remote outposts of government rather than at its center, and by organizing slowly and methodically under the constant and firm hand of a single leader, Shining Path emerged during the 1980s as the most radical expression of Maoist revolution in the hemisphere. The Peruvian government was forced into a reactive response, in part because it did not take Sendero seriously for some time. This fact often enabled the guerrillas to continue to choose the time and place of their actions. Once the government did get involved, for some years it emphasized military initiatives, frequently excessive and sometimes indiscriminate. These harmed the civilian population the authorities were charged with protecting as much or more than they affected Shining Path. Such a military emphasis contributed to the extension and expansion of violence, particularly in the countryside, which often played into the guerrillas' hands.

A widening and deepening economic crisis — including rampant inflation, substantial decline in the production of goods and services, loss of jobs, and a virtual paralysis of government services by the end of the decade — reflected a succession of failed central government policies. The high cost of these failures in human terms, from growing unemployment, declining living standards, rising crime rates, malnutrition, infant mortality, and susceptibility to disease, such as the 1991 cholera epidemic, gave Shining Path new opportunities to gain at the government's expense.

The guerilla organization had exploited these opportunities until the dramatic and totally unexpected capture, without violence, of Sendero founder and leader, Abimael Guzmán Reynoso, on September 12, 1992. Evidence gathered at Guzmán's Lima hideout by the specialized police intelligence unit (National Counterterrorism Agency — DINCOTE) responsible for preparing and conducting the raid revealed that Shining Path was in the midst of planning a major offensive. October 1992 was to have been a month of violent attacks "to shake the country to its foundations." This was to have been followed by a year long violent commemoration of the 100th anniversary of the birth of Mao, beginning in December, designed to bring the government "to its knees" by the end of 1993.

The government's intelligence coup abruptly turned the tables. Collective anxiety throughout Peru turned to mass euphoria almost at once. Over the subsequent 18 months, over 3,600 guerrillas were captured or turned themselves in. Levels of political violence declined somewhat in 1993 (by 9 percent in incidents and by 25 percent in deaths) and more sharply during the first three months of 1994. In a dramatic turnabout, Guzmán himself sued for peace negotiations in a letter from prison to President Alberto Fujimori (1990-1995), made public on October 1, 1993. The government had ample basis after September 1992 to trumpet its progress against Shining Path and regularly did so. However, the repeated assertion that the guerrilla threat would be eliminated by the end of 1995 seemed grossly premature. While Peru's police and armed forces did succeed in largely putting out of business by the end of 1993 the country's other guerrilla organization, the Tupac Amaru Revolutionary Movement (MRTA), Shining Path retained a significant operational capacity. Ominously, the Sendero leadership never renounced violence, even as they sought peace discussions with the government. Instead their key figures wrote from prison of returning to the organization's longer-term strategy of regrouping and rebuilding for the eventual triumph of "the people's war" in the 21st century. Government triumphalism notwithstanding, indications point to Shining Path's continued presence in Peru for some time to come. It is certainly the case, however, that the serious threat Sendero posed to Peru's government as recently as July-August 1992 has been substantially reduced.

Peruvian Politics in Historical Context

To fully appreciate the Sendero phenomenon, it is necessary to provide a fuller understanding of the larger historical context of Peru. Although in many ways Shining Path has forged, even defined, its own history, the movement is also a product of Peru's past. Key among the factors shaping the political culture of Peru is the almost 300 years of Spanish colonial rule. The main elements of Spanish control were authoritarian political institutions and mercantilist economic institutions, both of which gave colonialists little experience in handling their own affairs. The carryover into the postcolonial period was greater in Peru than in other Latin American countries not only because control was imposed more consistently but also because of the nature of the independence movement itself. The belated struggle for independence was more a conservative reaction to liberalizing forces in Spain and elsewhere than a genuine revolution, and it was brought largely from outside. As a result, despite the introduction of some liberal organizations and procedures, Peru did not break with the colonial past after 1824.

Not surprisingly, authoritarian rule continued long after independence. No civilian president was elected until Manuel Pardo in 1872, although there were some enlightened military leaders such as Ramón Castilla (1845-1851, 1854-1862). Also continuing were neomercantilist economic policies as Great Britain replaced Spain as Peru's major trading partner and the source of most capital and investment. Of the local entrepreneurs who emerged in this context, most acted as agents for British interests. Peru did experience its first economic boom during this period, based on the rich deposits of guano on islands off the coast. The economic benefits were foreshortened, however, by the outbreak of the War of the Pacific (1879-1883).

The war forced the partial break with Peru's past that independence had not. Chile wrested from Peru the coastal department of Tarapacá, with its immense nitrate deposits, and occupied a large portion of the country, including Lima. Politically, this disaster demonstrated the weakness of existing institutions and contributed to the emergence of Peru's only sustained period of electoral democracy (1895-1919). Economically, the war left the country bankrupt. Because many of the country's basic resources were mortgaged, Peru became even more dependent on British interests. This coincidence of sharply increased economic dependence and liberal democracy set the pattern for a limited state (i.e., small budgets) and private enterprise (i.e., large foreign investment) that most Peruvian governments tried to follow until the 1968 military coup.

In addition, much of Peru's independent political life has been marked by a flamboyant leadership style that has tended to garner support on the basis of personal appeal rather than institutional loyalties and obligations. Many leaders have tended to place personal interests above obligation to any political party organization or even to the nation. As a result, most parties have been personalist vehicles, and most presidencies have involved tumultuous struggles among contending personalities, often ending in military coups.

Furthermore, until very recently a large percentage of Peru's population was not integrated into national economic, political, or cultural life. The Indian subculture of Peru, though in numbers predominant until the 1970s, has participated in national society only in the most subordinate of roles, such as peon, day laborer, and maid. The way open, historically, for Indians to escape repudiation by the dominant society was to abandon their own heritage and assimilate into Spanish culture. Among the most important changes in contemporary Peru is large-scale Indian immigration to towns and cities, where Indians feel that they — or their children — can become a part of the dominant culture: Catholic, Hispanic, Spanish speaking. In addition, the Constitution of 1979 gave illiterates — predominantly Indian — the right to vote for the first time in national and municipal elections.

Several elements delayed changes in Peruvian politics. Domestic elites were willing to retain strong foreign economic control. The military was largely dominated by the elite. Political leadership kept its personalistic and populist character. A non-Communist, mass-based political party absorbed most of the emerging social forces and the Indian cultural "barrier" slowed the flow of new elements into national society. As a result, the liberal model of limited state and open economy endured.

Peruvian political history may be divided into the following periods: consolidation (1824-1895), limited civilian democracy (1895-1919), populism and mass parties (1919-1968), reformist military rule (1968-1980), fully participatory formal democracy (1980-1992), and an authoritarian democratic combination (1992-present).

Consolidation (1824-1895)

Peru took much longer than most Latin American countries to evolve a reasonably stable political and economic system. Because Peru had been the core part of a large viceroyalty during the colonial period, it took some time just to define the country's national territory. The boundaries were roughly hewn out in 1829 (by the failure of Augustín Gamarra and José de la Mar to capture Ecuador for Peru), in 1839 (by the Battle of Yungay in which Andrés Santa Cruz lost his post as protector of the Peru-Bolivia confederation when defeated by a Chilean army), and in 1841 (by the Battle of Ingavi when Gamarra was killed in his attempt to annex Bolivia to Peru).

Once the boundaries were more or less settled, there remained the key problem of establishing reasonable procedures for attaining and succeeding to political office. Peru had at least fifteen constitutions in its first forty years as an independent country, but force remained the normal route to political power. Of the thirty-five presidents during this period, only four were elected according to constitutional procedures, and no civilians held power for more than a few months. Regional caudillos often attempted to impose themselves on the government, which by the 1840s was becoming an important source of revenue because of the income from guano.

Unlike much of Latin America during the nineteenth century, Peru was less divided politically by the conservative-liberal cleavage and more by the issue of military or civilian rule. By the 1860s partisans of civilian rule were beginning to organize themselves into the *civilista* movement. The War of the Pacific dramatically demonstrated the need for professionalization of the Peruvian military and helped provoke the formal establishment of the Civilista Party, as well as a number of more personalistic contenders. The eventual result was Peru's first extended period of civilian rule, starting in 1895.

The War of the Pacific also more firmly embedded Peru's tendency to depend on foreign markets, foreign entrepreneurship, and foreign loans. War debts of more than $200 million were canceled by British interests in 1889 in exchange for Peru's railroads, the Lake Titicaca steamship line, a large tract of jungle land, free use of major ports, a Peruvian government subsidy, and large quantities of guano.

Limited Civilian Democracy (1895-1919)

Peru's longest period of civilian rule began in 1895 under the "Authoritarian Republic." While the military reorganized itself under the guidance of a French mission, a coalition of forces from an emerging commercial elite gained control of the government. Embracing neopositivist ideals of renovation, modernization, and innovation, the civilians also advanced the classic liberal precept of a limited government primarily organized to serve the private sector. Their main political objective was the very modest one of keeping civilians in power. This effort implied fostering a civilian state and a civilian society by increased government expenditures for communications, education, and health. These were financed by taxes on rapidly expanding exports, by revenues from new foreign investments (largely U.S.), and by new foreign loans after Peru's international credit was restored in 1907.

Civilian rule was somewhat tenuous even at its height. The Civilista Party, although reasonably well organized, suffered periodic severe internal divisions. Other parties, such as the Liberal, the Democratic, and the Conservative, were personalistic and rose and fell with the fortunes of their individual leaders.

The civilian democratic interlude was undone by various factors. One was the severe domestic inflation precipitated by the international economic crisis accompanying World War I. Another was the growing unwillingness of elite-oriented parties to respond to an expanding array of political demands from new segments of the population who had not previously been involved in national affairs. To a certain degree, then, elites had problems in dealing with the longer-term political consequences of their own economic success. Also corrosive to civilian rule were the actions of some leaders themselves. In particular, Presidents Augusto B. Leguía (1908-1912; 1919-1930) and Guillermo Billinghurst (1912-1914) operated in self-serving and personalistic ways.

Billinghurst, once elected, eschewed Civilista Party support to make populist appeals to the Lima "masses." Although he was beholden to the commercial elite, Billinghurst did not try to work within the party or "the club" to try to bring about some quiet accommodation that might have avoided a confrontation. The elite's dismay eventually drew them to the military, which intervened in 1914 just long enough to remove Billinghurst from office. Leguía, after ruling constitutionally during his first presidency, ended once and for all the shaky civilian democracy in 1919. Rather than moving to work out differences with opposition elements in 1919, after he had won the democratic election, he led a successful coup and ruled without an open vote until being ousted himself in 1930.

Populism, Parties, and Coups (1919-1968)

The populism of this period took two forms: civilian, exemplified by Leguía, and military, best illustrated by General Manuel Odría (1948-1956). Both forms were characterized by efforts to stymie political organization and to encourage loyalty to the person of the president through special considerations for elites and by distribution of goods, jobs, and services to politically aware nonelite segments. Both forms were also marked by very favorable treatment for the foreign investor and lender; thus, they maintained already established external dependence relationships.

Civilian and military populism each had a number of important effects on the Peruvian political system. They permitted elites to retain control through their narrowly based interest-group organizations (the National Agrarian Society — SNA, the National Mining Society — SNM, and the National Industrial Society — SNI) and their clubs (Nacional and La Unión). When confronted after 1930 with Peru's first mass-based political party, APRA elites turned to the military to carry out their political will because they had no comparable party to which to turn. The military, for its part, found it could accomplish its own objectives by directly intervening in the political system rather than by working through political organizations. Thus populism, by discouraging parties, contributed significantly to continued authoritarianism and political instability.

Between 1914 and 1984, Manuel Prado (1939-1945; 1956-1962) was the only elected civilian to complete a term (the previous). Why he did so is instructive. He was of the elite and accepted by it. He did not try to upset the status quo. He gained the military's favor by supporting its material and budget requirements. He reached an implicit modus vivendi with APRA. In addition, he happened to be president during a period when foreign market prices for Peruvian primary-product exports were relatively high and stable.

The most important twentieth century political development in Peru before 1968 was the organization of APRA. Although founded in Mexico by exiled student leader Victor Raúl Haya de la Torre in 1924, APRA soon became Peru's first ideological and mass-based political party. By most accounts APRA was strong enough to determine the outcome of all open elections after 1931. Until the 1980s, however, the military ensured that the party would never rule directly. This was due to an enduring hostility resulting from armed confrontations between them in 1932 in Trujillo during which scores of military personnel and APRA militants were killed.

Although APRA has had a strong populist appeal through the years, the party's importance for Peruvian politics rested on its reformist ideology and its organizational capacity. With the exception of Lima, APRA absorbed most of the newly emerging social forces in the more integrated parts of the country between the 1920s and the 1950s, most particularly labor, students, and the more marginal middle sectors. The party's appeal to such sectors thus helped prevent the emergence of a more radical alternative. Furthermore, even though

APRA was an outsider for most of the period from its founding to 1956, it never overthrew the system. At key junctures the party leadership searched for accommodation and compromise to gain entry even while continuing to resort to assassinations and abortive putsches in trying to impress political insiders of its potential power.

Between 1956 and 1982 APRA became a centrist party willing to make almost any compromise to gain greater formal political power. In 1956 APRA supported the conservative Manuel Prado in his successful bid for a second term as president and worked with him throughout his administration in what was called in Peru *la convivencia* ("living together"). When APRA won open elections in 1962 but was just shy of the constitutionally required one-third, the party made a pact with its former archenemy, General Odría, to govern together. At this point the military intervened and ran the country for a year before facilitating elections, which its favored candidate, Popular Action's (AP) Fernando Belaúnde Terry, won. During the Belaúnde administration (1963-1968), APRA formed an alliance with Odría forces in Congress to attain a majority and block or water down many of AP's reforms. Although such actions discredited the party for many, APRA remained Peru's best organized and most unified political force.

The AP, founded in 1956 when APRA shifted to the right, brought reformist elements into the system just as APRA had done before. AP's appeal was greater in the *sierra* and south, where APRA was weak. Thus, the two parties complemented each other by region, and between them they channeled into the system virtually the entire next wave of newly mobilized popular forces.

In spite of APRA-Odría political obstructionism, important reforms were carried out between 1963 and 1968, including establishment of various new agricultural programs; expansion of secondary and university education, cooperatives, and development corporations; and reinstitution of municipal elections. For all intents and purposes the extremist threat to Peruvian institutions, which broke out briefly in 1965, remained stillborn. But the opposition majority in Peru's Congress often blunted initiatives or refused to fund them. The U.S. government, anxious to assist Standard Oil Company's settlement of the investment expropriation dispute between its Peruvian subsidiary, International Petroleum Company (IPC), and the Peruvian government, withheld for more than two years Alliance for Progress funds badly needed by the

Belaúnde administration to help finance its reforms. Growing economic difficulties in 1967 and 1968 eroded public confidence, and a badly handled IPC nationalization agreement sealed Belaúnde's fate. On October 3, 1968, with a bloodless coup, the armed forces began long-term, institutionalized military rule in Peru.

The Military *Docenio* (1968-1980)

"The time has come," stated the new military regime's first manifesto, "to dedicate our national energies to the transformation of the economic, social, and cultural structures of Peru." The underlying themes of the military's major statements during the *docenio* (twelve-year rule) included a commitment to change, national pride, social solidarity, the end of dependency, a worker-managed economy, and "a fully participatory social democracy which is neither capitalist nor communist but humanistic." Past governments had declared their intention to change Peru, but this one was prepared to act. True enough, the civilian government from 1963 to 1968 had been a reformist one, and in many ways it set the stage for continued change after the takeover. What was surprising, given Peru's history of military intervention on behalf of the elites, was that the 1968 military coup occurred primarily because the civilian government had failed to carry out fully reform initiatives, not because it was succeeding in doing so.

An explanation lies in changes occurring over a number of years within the military. These prompted most of the officer corps, at least within the army, to conclude that the best protection for national security was national development. In their view, civilian politicians and political parties had failed to meet the development challenge in the 1960s. Many officers concluded that only the military, with its monopoly of legitimate force, was capable of leading Peru toward this goal. Helping to forge this reformist perspective were several factors: the officers' educational experience after the mid-1950s in the pro-development Center for Higher Military Studies (CAEM); a short but intense campaign against pro-Castro guerrillas in 1965; U.S. military training from the 1940s through the 1960s; the U.S. government's decision in 1967 not to sell jet fighter planes to Peru; and a vigorous army-led civic action program after 1959.

Once in power, the military called itself revolutionary but practiced reform. Almost without exception, the 1968-1975 policy initiatives were based on the twin assumptions of continued economic growth, with improved distribution of this growth, and the willingness of economic elites to accept incentives to redirect their wealth toward new productive activities. The military's policies were not based on redistributing the existing pie.

Significant changes occurred. One of the most important was the rapid expansion of state influence and control. New ministries, agencies, and banks were established; basic services were expropriated, as were some large foreign companies in mining, fishing, and agriculture, with compensation and reinvestment incentives; and state enterprises or cooperatives were established in their place. Important areas of heavy industry were reserved for the state, new investment laws placed various controls on the private sector, and government employment mushroomed. At the same time Peru pursued the objective of enhancing development by diversifying its external relationships in order to reduce the country's economic and political dependency. Another major initiative was a large-scale agrarian-reform program, which effectively eliminated large private landholdings. About 360,000 farm families received land between 1969 and 1980, most as members of farm cooperatives. Commitment to cooperatives illustrated the regime's concern for popular participation at various levels. Neighborhood organizations, worker communities, and both production and service cooperatives proliferated after 1970, as did various coordinating bodies. All of these changes represented substantial adjustments in past practices, and for a time appeared likely to succeed.

Three major factors led to the regime's undoing, however. First and most fundamentally, success was premised on continued economic growth, which stopped after 1974 when economic difficulties began to multiply rapidly. In part such difficulties were caused by overly ambitious projects and miscalculations of resource availability, somewhat due to the military's desire for perquisites and equipment. With domestically generated resources not available as expected, the military government turned to foreign loans, often short-term ones, to keep up the momentum. This policy produced a severe resource crunch by 1977-1978, the first of what became in the 1980s endemic debt crises in Latin America, and partly explains Peru's recurring economic problems to the early 1990s.

Second, those in power failed to consult openly and as equals with the citizens, the presumed beneficiaries of the reforms. This neglect contributed both to popular resentment and mistrust and to a number of inappropriate and counterproductive policies. Third, the illness after 1973 of the head of state, General Juan Velasco Alvarado, contributed to a loss of the institutional unity of the armed forces themselves, which his dynamic and forceful leadership had helped to instill. The eventual result was a mixture of old and new programs in yet another overlay, increasingly ill-financed, confusing to the citizens, and ultimately unsuccessful.

An August 1975 coup led by General Francisco Morales Bermúdez and supported by the military establishment gently eased out the ill and increasingly erratic General Velasco and ushered in the consolidating phase of the *docenio*. With the exception of the agrarian reform, initiatives were quietly abandoned or sharply curtailed. By 1977 mounting economic and political pressures prompted the military regime to initiate a gradual return to civilian rule. The resulting Constituent Assembly election in 1978 represented another political milestone, for they included participation by an array of leftist parties, which garnered an unprecedented 36 percent of the vote — even though APRA won the most seats. The Assembly itself was led by Haya de la Torre, another first. These elections marked the beginning of significant involvement in the system by the Marxist left. The Assembly produced the Constitution of 1979, which set up national elections every five years and municipal elections every three years beginning in 1980. One irony of the elections was that they returned to the presidency the same person who had been so unceremoniously unseated in 1968.

The Civilian *Docenio* (1980-1992)

This time Belaúnde's AP was able to forge a majority in Congress, in coalition with the small Popular Christian Party (PPC), and won the first plurality in the municipal elections as well. But events conspired once again to make life difficult for the governing authorities. Inflation continued to increase; from 60 percent in 1980 it exceeded 100 percent by 1984. The recession deepened so that in 1983 the GNP actually declined by over 10 percent, and real wages eroded during Belaúnde's second administration (1980-1985) by over 30 percent. World market prices for Peru's exports — copper, oil, sugar, fish meal, minerals — remained low or declined even further. Devastating weather accompanied the arrival in 1982 of the El Niño ocean current. Crops and communications networks in the northern half of Peru were destroyed because of rain and flood while in the south crops withered as a result of drought. Given such unfavorable economic developments, the foreign debt burden became even more onerous — from $8.4 billion in 1980 to over $13 billion by 1985. International Monetary Fund (IMF) agreements provided new external resources and debt refinancing but also imposed restrictive domestic economic policies, which sparked much controversy. Belaúnde ultimately hedged on these requirements, thus provoking a breakdown in the IMF agreement and leaving a substantial burden for the next civilian administration of Alan García.

Another unanticipated problem for the civilian government was the growing violence associated with the guerrilla activities of Shining Path. Originally based in the isolated south-central sierra of Ayacucho and headed by former professors and students from the University of Huamanga there, Shining Path advocated a peasant-based republic forged through revolution. The group's ideology was Marxist-Leninist, based on the principles of Mao and José Carlos Mariátegui, a leading Peruvian intellectual of the 1920s who founded what became the country's original Communist Party of Peru. After some fifteen years of preparations — which included study groups, control of the University of Huamanga, leadership training in China, and work in the Indian peasant–dominated local countryside — Sendero launched its people's war on the very eve of the May 18, 1980 national election.

The Belaúnde administration did not take the increasingly violent group seriously for almost three full years. Only then did the government declare the Ayacucho area an emergency zone and send in the military. Although the government committed itself to providing economic aid to the impoverished region as well, little was actually done before 1985. By the end of Belaúnde's term over 6,000 had perished in the violence, most in 1983 (1,977) and 1984 (3,587); human rights violations had skyrocketed (more than 1,700 reported "disappeared" in 1983 and 1984 alone); and over $1 billion in property damage had occurred. A new guerrilla group had appeared as well, the Lima-based MRTA, which contributed to spreading the perverse legitimacy of political violence (though it never accounted for more than about 10 percent of reported incidents).

These difficulties substantially weakened popular support for Belaúnde and for the AP in the 1983 municipal elections; in the 1985 presidential vote, the AP candidate was routed, gaining only 6 percent of the total. The largely Marxist United Left party (UI) garnered 23 percent for its candidate, and a rejuvenated APRA, with the youthful (thirty-six) Alan García as its standard bearer, won with 48 percent.

The García victory was doubly historic: After a fifty-five year struggle, APRA had finally gained both the presidency and a majority in both houses of Congress. In addition, for the first time in forty years an elected civilian president handed power over to an elected successor (only the second time since 1912). The 1986 municipal elections also saw substantial APRA gains, including, for the first time ever, the mayorship of Lima. García's forceful, nationalistic leadership put the international banking community on notice that Peru would be limiting repayments on its debt (now over $14 billion) to 10 percent of export earnings. This contributed to long overdue domestic economic growth at rates of 9 percent in 1985 and 7 percent in 1986. But the recovery ran out of steam in 1987, and the economy was further shaken by the surprise presidential announcement that year nationalizing domestic banks.

Although the bank nationalization attempt ultimately failed, the second half of Garcia's term was an unmitigated disaster. Peru suspended virtually all foreign debt repayments, so international credit dried up. Inflation skyrocketed to 1,722 percent in 1988, 2,600 percent in 1989, and 7,650 percent in 1990. The economy declined by more than 20 percent during this period. Political violence, which had ebbed between 1985 and 1987, surged anew. By the end of the García government (1985-1990), casualties exceeded 20,000 and direct and indirect damages, $14 billion. Total foreign debt with arrearages was over $23 billion. Not surprisingly, García's popularity plummeted from an 80 percent favorable rating early in his term to single digits near the end.

While rumors abounded of a possible coup, military spokespersons committed their institutions to uphold civilian rule. Parties across the political spectrum competed aggressively for support in the November 1989 municipal elections and the April 1990 presidential and congressional vote. In early 1989 IU divided badly, squandering an historic opportunity. From virtual oblivion Peru's right reemerged, centered on the capacity of novelist Mario Vargas Llosa to galvanize popular concern over President García's failures. A new coalition, the Democratic Front (FREDEMO), was formed among conservative and centrist parties, including former President Belaúnde's AP, perennial conservative candidate Luis Bedoya Reyes's PPC, and Vargas Llosa's new Liberty Movement. To the surprise of many, FREDEMO captured a plurality of mayorships in the 1989 municipal elections.

However, Shining Path also used the elections to step up its campaign of violence and terror by killing over 100 candidates and local officials and intimidating scores of others into resigning. As a result, about 25 percent of Peru's 1,800 district and provincial councils could not carry out their elections at all. The total valid 1989 municipal vote was sharply reduced.

In the run up to the April 1990 national elections, Vargas Llosa was shown to be the heavy favorite by opinion polls. Many were stunned when another political newcomer, National Agrarian University rector Alberto Fujimori, came from less than 2 or 3 percent in the polls a month before the vote to finish second with 24 percent (just behind Vargas Llosa, with 26 percent). Fujimori won easily in the June 1990 runoff, which is required of the top two contenders when no one gets an absolute majority. His victory was explained as the electoral expression of popular frustration with politics as usual. There was also the sense that Vargas Llosa was too removed from the economic hardships suffered by most Peruvians and had become too closely identified with the politicians of the right.

Once in office, President Fujimori launched almost immediately an economic shock program even more severe than that proposed by Vargas Llosa during the campaign. He argued that economic recovery could not be secured until Peru's economic mess had been straightened out and the country's international credit standing restored. In the short run, however, his drastic measures dramatically accelerated inflation, further reduced domestic economic activity (-8 percent in 1990), and pushed several million more Peruvians below the poverty line (to some 12 to 14 million, or 60 to 70 percent of the population). Congress went along for the most part, even though Fujimori's party grouping, Cambio 90, held only about one-quarter of the seats. So did most Peruvians; Fujimori's level of support in opinion polls remained consistently well above 50 percent.

By early 1992, such drastic measures were beginning to produce the desired results. Inflation was sharply reduced (134 percent in 1991). International economic reinsertion was on the verge of being accomplished after monthly payments to the international financial institutions (IFIs) were resumed, along with regular and extensive negotiations, in late 1990. Signs of economic recovery also began to appear. Beginning in October 1991, the United States increased bilateral economic assistance and initiated its first substantial military aid in over twenty years. The Peruvian Congress was becoming somewhat more restive and assertive, particularly with regard to human rights issues, but did authorize emergency executive branch decree powers and approve most of the results. Public support had flagged somewhat, from over 70 percent to the mid-50s, but still remained high by international standards. While political violence continued to be a serious problem (3,745 deaths in 1990 and 3,044 in 1991), government forces also had some successes against both Shining Path and MRTA. Given this overall essentially positive panorama, few were prepared for President Fujimori's April 5, 1992 declaration "temporarily suspending" democracy in Peru.

The *Autogolpe* and Its Aftermath

This *autogolpe*, or coup against oneself, drew immediate and almost universal international condemnation. Fujimori, with armed forces support, dissolved congress, the judiciary, and the general accounting office, and began to rule by decree. The United States immediately suspended all assistance save humanitarian and counter-drug aid. It also used its influence to ensure postponement by the IFIs of Peru's economic reinsertion as well as of new aid by most of the dozen countries making up the Peru Support Group. The Organization of American States (OAS) deplored democracy's suspension in Peru and provided international monitors to oversee and validate its reinstatement. Fujimori agreed immediately to electoral restoration on a one-year timetable, which was accomplished with national elections for a new, smaller, one house congress *cum* constitutional convention in November 1992 and municipal elections in January 1993.

The result was a substantially different political dynamic. The traditional parties were largely marginalized, the political process was much more concentrated in the presidency, and Fujimori now had a congressional majority. Furthermore, Alan García, Fujimori's *bête noire,* was forced into exile after the *autogolpe* and lost his leadership role in APRA as democratic procedure was being restored in 1993. The new constitution was narrowly approved (52-48 percent) in an October 31, 1993 referendum. It recentralized government authority, set the bases for privatization and economic liberalization, provided the death penalty for terrorism, and allowed for the immediate reelection of the sitting president. As the *autogolpe* turned out, then, it worked very much to President Fujimori's advantage.

However, the April 1992 suspension of democracy easily could have proven to be a colossal disaster. International economic assistance suspension postponed economic recovery in Peru by at least a year. The populace lost access to the political system through their elected congressional representatives. Shining Path moved quickly to expand violent activities and recruitment, and began to discuss openly revolutionary victory in the 1990s.

What saved Fujimori's authoritarian gamble was the careful police work of a small, specialized antiterrorist group (DINCOTE) in the Ministry of the Interior, formed under García, which paid off with the dramatic capture of Shining Path leader Guzmán and key lieutenants in September 1993. Several hundred other guerrilla operatives were rounded up in the weeks to follow, thwarting what was to have been a massive Shining Path offensive to close out the year. To be sure, tougher anti-terrorist decrees issued in the aftermath of the *autogolpe* permitted rapid trials in military courts and life terms without parole for some two hundred key figures. However, the sheer good fortune of capturing the bulk of Shining Path leadership, more than any other development, legitimated the *autogolpe* and gave the Fujimori government the political space, at least temporarily, to pursue its presidentially directed agenda.

Windows on Shining Path

Historically revolutions advance as much because of governments' failures as due to the insurgents' successes. The Peruvian government of the 1990s was more vulnerable because of the shortcomings of its predecessors, from the military regime's reformist overreaching to the succeeding elected civilian government's populist shortsightedness. When Alberto Fujimori succeeded to the presidency of Peru in 1990, he moved immediately to try to reduce this vulnerability by taking drastic measures.

The economy, in shambles, was the first and most immediate challenge he had to confront. His response was the economic "shock" program of August

1990, which by raising prices and removing many subsidies while holding wages down, impoverished millions virtually overnight. However, it also reduced inflation dramatically within months (from 7,650 percent in 1990, to 139 percent in 1991, 58 percent in 1992, and 39 percent in 1993), and eventually restored economic growth (to just over 7 percent in 1993, the first net growth year since 1987). Continuing economic liberalization, including substantial privatization and continuing increases in foreign investment, indicated that Peru's long delayed breakthrough to economic growth would continue in 1994. Such drastic measures, even when they involved considerable hardship for many Peruvians, continued to be supported by the majority.

Another major challenge from the outset of the Fujimori administration was responding effectively to Shining Path. Here, too, the beleaguered Peruvian government managed to stem and even reverse the tide, in spite of the negative consequences of the April 1992 *autogolpe*. Sendero's weaknesses, always present, were highlighted by government successes against them in 1992 and 1993.

Among other problems, popular support was lacking, mistakes were made by the insurgents as well, and the base organizations were still weak, particularly among urban labor. In addition, an inherent tension always existed between the centralized decision making of the organization's central committee, on the one hand, and the requirement of a certain autonomy of action by the party's regional commanders and their cadres, on the other. Guzman's capture and the roundup of key Sendero figures, beginning in September 1992, only exacerbated this problem. Ideology, strong and uncompromising in Sendero hands, guided recruits but also led on numerous occasions to counterproductive activities against the very peasants and workers the guerrillas claimed to represent. Through the information and analysis provided, chapter by chapter, in the body of this volume, the strengths and weaknesses of Shining Path are presented, as are those of the society and system of Peru that the guerrillas have been working to overthrow.

In chapter 2, "Taking the High Ground," journalist Michael L. Smith points out that Sendero Luminoso (SL) developed in the interstices of the exceedingly complex Andean society — between urban and rural, Indian and non-Indian, *gamonal* and *peón*, community and cooperative, community and community, the less and the more poor. Geography sets the original parameters in Peru with its remarkably diverse climates based fundamentally on altitude, latitude, soil composition, and access to water. The population differentiates accordingly and, in most cases, requires access to zones outside its habitat to maintain itself and have at least some prospect for improvement. Ayacucho, where SL began, is a microcosm of the extraordinary diversity of the Andes, and particularly of its poverty.

Sendero leader Abimael Guzmán Reynoso and his cohorts, all from outside the region, saw this reality daily and responded to it in both ideological (Maoism) and practical (work the cracks of society and recruit from them) terms. Whatever Sendero's pretensions nationally and internationally, its origins and early evolution were based in Ayacucho: poor, provincial, isolated, Indian. Guzmán and other outsiders at the University of San Cristóbal de Huamanga adapted to that medium and developed an ideology and strategy related to it, simplistic and erroneous to outsiders, galvanizing and liberating to many at the interstices, especially the first-generation Quechua-Spanish speakers who made up the bulk of the student body during the 1960s (65 to 75 percent). The Sendero view seemed to some of them to explain their predicament and offered a way out on terms developed within the university (and by their respected professors), which most had sacrificed much to attain.

In the first section of chapter 3, Peruvian scholar and anthropologist Carlos Iván Degregori notes that SL originated and developed in the reinforcing authoritarian contexts of Andean peasant-*misti* or mestizo elite relationships, student-professor relationships, and Marxist ideology. It was led by *mistis* and was made up of the first generation of "children of the deceived" to attend the university and be exposed to Marxism as an explanation of reality and as an organizing principle for upward mobility. The Andean Ayacucho roots gave Sendero its distinctive perception of Peruvian reality as province against capital and contributed to its isolation from the left in Peru and elsewhere.

The result of these factors in combination for Sendero was a totalitarian vision of a single proper course that must be imposed from the top down. In this vision local organizations such as peasant communities, labor unions, and neighborhood associations were to be disregarded or destroyed and replaced by the party's own "generated organisms." The party represented the only solution, and its "Andean Maoism" could prevail only by force, wiping the slate clean, in effect, in order to build the new society as determined by the party leadership. "Sendero explains and is explained by a return to the past."

In the second section of chapter 3, Dutch development workers Ton de Wit and Vera Gianotten argue that Sendero's rise was largely a function of the failure of the center to take the periphery seriously on a number of levels. The reformist military government (1968-1980), which carried out a substantial agrarian reform, could not bring itself to allow the reform's presumed beneficiaries among the peasantry to claim the power the national leadership had promised. Shining Path grew within a provincial university and an isolated highland department through the 1970s and even into the 1980s after the armed struggle was declared because no one — not the central government, political parties, the military itself — took the movement or that part of the country very seriously. High levels of conflict among Ayacucho's many peasant communities kept levels of horizontal organization very low and facilitated Sendero's entrance, as did the many community studies in Ayacucho carried out by university students.

These same students were frustrated in their efforts to improve their economic and social status through education, and often became susceptible to recruitment. The government's tenuous presence in much of the periphery melted before the Sendero onslaught, and many residents of the department's capital of Ayacucho remained indifferent to their rural compatriots' plight. The racial divide among white, mestizo, and Indian appeared to be the decisive factor that kept the center from responding effectively and kept the periphery paying a disproportionate human toll in the ongoing struggle. The 1990 election of Alberto Fujimori represented the poor majority's rejection of both Sendero's radical solution and the national institutions of government and party, which still did not seem to understand what needed to be done — "full citizenship, proper incomes, and security and protection."

Chapter 4 presents a summary analysis of anthropologist Billie Jean Isbell's work over more than two decades in the rural Ayacucho community of Chuschi and the Pampas River valley. Shining Path carried out the first action of its self-declared armed struggle in May 1980 in Chuschi, and subsequently pursued a number of activities there and in the surrounding area. Actions punishing corrupt local officials or philandering husbands, trying and killing cattle thieves, or communal planting on the University of Huamanga's experimental farm were all greeted with considerable enthusiasm. During this period Sendero gained control of some nine communities in the Pampas River valley.

But when Sendero organizers abandoned community residents during a government military attack after the residents were made part of a Shining Path people's army/militia (without guns), the insurgents lost their momentum in the area. Subsequent efforts to organize communities forcibly into arrangements not related to their local production structure or activity cycle, to shut off access to local market days, and to impose new planting procedures all failed, and support for Sendero waned. As violence increased in the area with the large-scale entrance of Peruvian military forces, most communities cast their lot with the government rather than with Sendero. Chuschi went so far as to request and receive in 1983 a permanent police garrison based in the community.

Shining Path failed in the Pampas River valley because it did not understand the complexities of the communities and their sense of time and space and because it tried to impose a set of procedures and controls that appeared to the communities simply to replicate the same structures of domination most were trying to escape. Sendero badly underestimated the peasants' awareness and sophistication. Peasants concluded that the government, not Shining Path, was in a better position to respond to their needs. The violence and disruption, while severe in many communities of the valley, provoked locally driven changes, such as authorities who are more educated and bilingual, which could turn out to benefit the communities in future relations with the outside world. The rapid expansion of fundamentalist Protestant churches in such communities as Chuschi and Quispillacta may also have served to draw significant portions of the communities' residents toward alternative religious solutions to their problems than the religion of violence of Shining Path.

In chapter 5 anthropologist Ronald H. Berg shares his insights on the community of Pacucha and the surrounding area of Andahuaylas, which he has studied since Sendero began to be active in the region. The province of Andahuaylas, Apurímac Department, adjoins the Department of Ayacucho and shares with it many linguistic and cultural characteristics, but had a much stronger network of haciendas mixed in with the local peasant communities.

When implementation of the military government's agrarian reform was long delayed in the region, poorer peasants organized, with some outside help, and invaded many of the large private holdings. This locally driven reform was overturned by force in 1974-1975 by belatedly active central authorities who imposed a cooperative structure with outside, often corrupt or incompetent administrators. Wealthier peasants moved in to occupy the space left by the departing large landowners, often by establishing small stores in the communities.

When Shining Path began to be active in Pacucha and surrounding communities in 1981 and 1982, there was a reservoir of potential support for it in the area. Government forces responded ineptly, reinforcing the province capital, Andahuaylas, and leaving the rural hinterland open except for occasional ill-planned forays. As a result, Sendero was able for a time to operate relatively freely in most of the province's countryside. Actions were directed primarily at the hated cooperatives and the wealthy peasants/shopkeepers, and contributed on balance to maintaining a certain level of sympathy for Sendero on the part of many peasants in the communities. Furthermore, deteriorating economic conditions forced down the wages on which many peasants depend, and continuing lack of access to land for economic security pressed them further. These local realities of the peasant economy also served to maintain sympathy for Shining Path.

In the rapidly escalating violence of 1983-1984, when Andahuaylas became part of the Ayacucho area emergency zone, brutal and often indiscriminate military/police actions served as much to reinforce sympathy for Shining Path as to thwart the movement's further advance. In much of rural Andahuaylas at least, SL was perceived as the lesser evil. Where local organizations of political parties or the church were better established and more deeply rooted, as in Puno, Sendero had a much more difficult time gaining sympathy or support.

Peruvian journalist José E. Gonzales has made numerous research trips to the Upper Huallaga Valley (UHV), where some 65 percent of all the coca leaf used in the manufacture of cocaine worldwide is grown and where insurgents have operated since the mid-1980s. In chapter 6, he argues that there is no way to separate the drug production and trafficking problem from the guerrilla problem in the UHV. They were inextricably intertwined, and actions affecting one inevitably had an impact on the other. Events in the valley after Shining Path first entered suggested that concentrating primarily on the drug side of the issue adversely affected the tens of thousands of peasant families there who make their living growing coca and drove them to seek Sendero protection. This problem was unwittingly created by U.S. government assistance in an eradication and interdiction effort in the area. Only when a substantial Peruvian military force with a decisive commander moved against Shining Path in the UHV without directly disrupting the peasants' livelihood, as occurred in 1984-1985 and in 1989, was the guerrilla-peasant alliance of convenience (at least from the peasants' perspective) threatened or broken and central government authority in the area reestablished.

However, rivalries between the military (primarily concerned with the guerrilla problem) and the police (primarily concerned with the drug production and trafficking problem) reduced the effectiveness of the government in the UHV. When the police post at Uchiza was attacked and overrun by a large Sendero force in March 1989, the military did not come to its aid. When an army general moved effectively against Shining Path in the valley between April and November 1989, he was regularly undercut by police sources who suggested that he and his forces were receiving financial support from the traffickers. The peasants want to earn a living and have demonstrated that they will support whoever makes that possible, politics aside, even if the option is crop substitution. The UHV became a centerpiece in Sendero's strategy, both for the financial support it provided to help maintain its guerrilla apparatus and for the potential it offered to gain a solid base of peasant support. Central government, on balance, remained tentative and indecisive in spite of the significance of the UHV as a regional testing ground for the battle of Peru through 1992.

Michael L. Smith's second contribution to the volume analyzes Sendero's urban strategy in the Lima community of Ate Vitarte. He notes in chapter 7 that Sendero's leadership recognized that its armed struggle could not be victorious until it had a significant base of support in urban areas among the working class, and that it had long worked toward that goal. The Lima organization (Metropolitan Committee) of Shining Path, for example, had always had the same standing in the hierarchy of regional-based party units as the Principal Regional Committee in Ayacucho, and, during some periods from 1983 onward, the number of incidents attributed to Sendero in and around Lima equaled or even surpassed those in any specific rural area. Because SL head Guzmán was obliged for health reasons to spend most of his time on the coast in Lima, the Metropolitan Committee also developed a massive support and protection system. In fact, one of the surprises associated with Guzmán's September 1992 capture — in Lima — was the total absence of any armed guard. The conclusion drawn was that the Shining Path head had become overconfident after years of success in eluding government authorities.

Developments in the Ate Vitarte illustrate Sendero's urban strategy: to identify key figures, assist, co-opt, intimidate, or kill them; to mount active support services for strikes, from soup kitchens to leadership to cadres to mount violent attacks; to discredit existing organizations and leadership; and to mount fully integrated land invasions. SL activities form part of a long-term strategy to neutralize left- wing party grass-roots organizations by exploiting both the fissures between them and their problems with their national leaderships; to make the state and its activities seem impotent or counterproductive; to paralyze production in the industrial center of the country (the Central Highway area of Lima and environs) by inhibiting reinvestment and employment by placing company workers on a permanent strike footing; and to gather the momentum necessary in a strategically vital area (in and around Ate Vitarte on the Central Highway) to be able to choke off flows of electricity, food, and water to the capital. Sendero's urban strategy was slowly building momentum against a rather ineffective state and against a divided and hesitant legal left until the dramatic reversals of late 1992 and 1993 starting with Guzman's capture.

In chapter 8 Peruvian journalist Gustavo Gorriti, who has been writing about Sendero since it initiated the armed struggle in 1980, discusses two of SL's leading figures. He observes that Shining Path is unique among revolutionary parties in that the cult of personality has dominated the organization before rather than after taking power. This makes for a much more disciplined and ordered group in which a single dominant line can be imposed more effectively. Guzmán was a very dedicated and intelligent student from a lower middle-class background and an irregular family situation who advanced by dedication and self- discipline rather than natural brilliance. When he went to the University of Huamanga in Ayacucho in 1962, he applied these same approaches and became a dominant figure in the classroom and in party positions.

His leading role in the party cannot be underestimated, and his ability to adopt the tenets of the Chinese Cultural Revolution (1966-1976) without destroying his own organization in the process was quite remarkable. His leadership ensured that the internal discussion in the party was resolved in favor of the line he supports — toward the armed struggle from 1976 onward and toward urban as well as rural actions in the 1980s. Those who opposed too strenuously were rejected and humiliated. However, if they were deemed of some potential future service for the party, Guzmán brought them back in very subordinate roles.

Sendero's Trotsky was Luis Kawata Makabe, who made a major contribution with his proselytizing lectures but who lacked the discipline Guzmán felt necessary. As a result, Guzmán personally drummed him out of the party. Kawata subsequently suffered indignities from fellow Sendero compatriots in prison and was eventually brought back in with a very minor role — in Germany. Guzmán not only makes no apologies for the cult of personality but sees it as an indispensable component of the pursuit of victory in the armed struggle. It is at once both Sendero's greatest strength and its greatest weakness, as became clear after Guzmán's capture with the organization's temporary loss of direction.

Peruvian lawyer Gabriela Tarazona-Sevillano notes in chapter 9 that the organization of SL was a combination of a strong, centralized command structure directed by a small national central committee led by Abimael Guzmán, or Presidente Gonzalo as he called himself, and a set of six regional committees with substantial independent authority covering most of the country. In principle, this setup permitted the formulation of grand strategy and long-term planning at the center by the national leadership as well as responses in specific areas based on differing local situations as determined by the regional leadership most familiar with them. There was both central coordination and direction and considerable regional autonomy.

The expansion of Sendero activities over time required the introduction of additional coordinating bodies to facilitate communication between the center and the regions, including the distribution of resources derived largely from the payments and "taxes" on drug production and trafficking activities in the Upper Huallaga Valley. These coordinating efforts also included ties to the grass-roots popular support networks, from legal defense to assistance for SL prisoners and their families to help for various student, women, peasant, neighborhood, and worker organizations. These different networks of Sendero incorporate a hierarchy of support, from sympathizers to activists to militants to commanders to the leadership "cupola." Members move up the ranks as needed and as they demonstrate their capacity to further Sendero's goals, often by specific acts of violence.

Women play significant roles in the organization at all levels. "Special squads" are trained to carry out specific terrorist actions and always have backups. Growth of the organization and its units over time attested to its success at one level, but also brought with it a number of problems, from coordination difficulties, to greater opportunity for government intelligence windfalls, to large-scale movement of militants out of their "home" regions to areas where they were less effective, to greater disagreement on the best approach. Sendero's organization has been one of its greatest strengths, but it became increasingly vulnerable as it expanded. By the end of 1992, at least sixteen of the nineteen central committee members had been captured or killed, and operations of five of the regional committees severely disrupted. A new central committee was constituted in early 1993 under the leadership of surviving member Felipe Ramírez Durand, with concerns focused primarily on damage control and organization rebuilding.

Military journalist Tom Marks argues in chapter 10 that Sendero is best understood as an insurgency — that is, "a political campaign backed by threatened or actual violence." Purposive action and leadership may be more helpful in understanding the movement than structural factors such as centralism, racism, or the class system. It is not a peasant rebellion but an insurgency directed by mestizos, which uses terror selectively and purposefully to generate legitimacy in areas of operation. Selective terror is combined with recruitment and infrastructure expansion at the local level through overt popular committees and support bases, on the one hand, and a covert party structure with its cells, on the other. Terror helped Sendero get established; recruitment and infrastructure then gave the movement a life of its own.

By keeping terrorist actions selective, they maintained effectiveness at the local level and could gain or keep popular support by showing what happens to traitors or local officials or rich peasants. This made it in the interests of the local population to give their support to Sendero. Recruitment and an alternative organizational infrastructure then gave tangible form and legitimacy to this support. The same rules do not apply to government forces, which must hold to a higher standard if their objectives of retaining or expanding the legitimacy of democratic forms and procedures are to be accomplished. Sendero basically uses political means to achieve political ends, with force when necessary. The similarity of Sendero's approach with Viet Cong strategy in rural Vietnam before the large-scale introduction of North Vietnamese forces is striking.

In chapter 11 American political scientists Sandra Woy- Hazelton and William A. Hazelton focus on Peru's large Marxist left. The unprecedented expansion of the legal, mostly Marxist left from the late 1970s onward poses a major obstacle for Shining Path in its violent quest for power. This electoral left has been strongest in local governments, neighborhood organizations, and labor movements, but has also had significant representation in Congress. Shining Path has found it very difficult to develop its strategy in areas and organizations where the legal left is strong. These left groups have been specific targets of Sendero as the insurgents tried to increase their influence.

At times the left has played into SL's hands, particularly in 1989 and 1990 when it divided into several parts, fielded multiple candidates for the presidency and for Congress, and came out with a reduced national vote and representation. At the local level, however, the left retained considerable influence, which could be the basis for a new effort to form a unified left in the 1990s, and, united or not, serves to continue to block Sendero's advance in many areas. Both the 1989 municipal elections and the 1990 national elections, however, showed a disturbing pattern of increased null and void ballots and abstention in many of the areas where Sendero was the most active. This suggested that Sendero's threats were having more of an impact, or that more of the populace in these zones of conflict were becoming discouraged with the democratic process, or both. A strong and organized legal left in the 1990s will be a major factor in keeping the political space on that side of Peru's ideological spectrum closed to Sendero.

Chapter 12, by political scientist and longtime Peru watcher Cynthia McClintock, puts Shining Path into the larger context of theories of revolution. She notes that the historical examples of successful revolution in Latin America are few in number and do not give a clear picture for understanding the Shining Path insurgency in Peru. The key strands of theories of revolution include: (1) the nature of the government in power; (2) the nature of society, especially its reduced capacity to respond to citizen needs; (3) the world context, whether permissive or not; (4) the ability of the revolutionary organization to offer benefits to presumed beneficiaries as rational utility maximizers; and (5) ideology.

Sendero's ideology serves as both motivation and explanation for revolution in Peru. The key components of the ideology appear to be identical with those of Mao: (1) Society is semifeudal; (2) Violence is central to revolutionary process both as a strategy and as experience; (3) Maoism alone is truth; (4) The peasantry is the key to the revolution. Thus for SL, claims by other Marxist groups in Peru to be vanguard elements are totally invalid, and other so-called Communist countries are corrupt revisionist opportunists.

When one compares Peru's reality with Shining Path's analysis, the latter is lacking on all counts. Peru is largely urban and literate and does not have large landowners due to the military government's extensive agrarian reform from 1969 to 1975. Peru's situation in the 1980s is quite distinct from that of China and its revolutionary period in the 1930s and 1940s. Democratic procedures and practices are widespread in Peru and are generally supported by the population. But it is also true that successive elected regimes performed poorly and opened up a regime legitimacy crisis that contributed both to Fujimori's victory in 1990 and to his 1992 *autogolpe*. The Peruvian government, while formally democratic again in the course of 1993, was also more personalistic, more centralized, and more dependent on military support. While most Peruvians find SL ideology archaic and its tactics abhorrent, for some the ideology provides an explanation for their difficult circumstances and empowers them. Because U.S. policy toward Peru focuses more on the drug problem and human rights issues than on the guerrilla threat, the world context could be considered as permissive for Shining Path's advance.

In the concluding chapter I focus on the disparate strands of Shining Path as viewed from the various "windows" of the individual authors. They show, not surprisingly, that Sendero's capacity and its approach vary considerably from area to area and over time. Cumulatively, however, they indicate the great degree to which SL's revolution is identified with its leader — founder, organizer, strategist, intellectual, ideologue — "the sun around which the planets revolve." In Sendero's case, revolution *is* leadership, defining reality, setting the terms of the combat and pushing for a response that justifies and legitimates the definition rather than the other way around. Shining Path defines the setting in ways that make revolution the only possible outcome, and then wages revolution on its own terms. Thus the insurgency itself becomes the independent variable, not dependent on social, economic, or external factors.

This is not to say that context is not important for the movement's growth and orientation — it certainly is. Context includes a provincial university at a historic moment; a poor, overwhelmingly Indian region isolated in the Andes; an inappropriately conceived and applied agrarian reform in an area of great need; expanding educational opportunities and stagnant employment prospects; the opportunity to train in China during the Cultural Revolution; and a succession of civilian governments at the center unwilling and/or unable to respond appropriately to the needs of the population at the periphery (geographical, economic, social, cultural, and political). Shining Path and its people have been very much affected by such contextual factors. These have served more to prepare the organization and its leadership to seize the initiative, however, than to explain why Maoist revolution started in Peru, or why it started where it did. On its face, the moment was clearly inauspicious — in the midst of an enthusiastic and robust nationwide democratic reawakening. But Sendero actions turned that moment to its advantage, not the reverse, in a triumph of ideology over reality.

The combination of context and revolution as leadership also contributes to our understanding of Shining Path's significant shift in strategy after the Fujimori government succeeded in breaking into the core of the guerrilla organization in late 1992 and 1993. Guzmán, in letters and videos from prison, where he is serving a life sentence without parole, recognized the authority of President Fujimori for the first time in October 1993. He also acknowledged the superior counterinsurgency tactics of the government and requested peace discussions. In other communications, however, both Guzmán and other important jailed Sendero leaders refused to renounce the armed struggle and declared their commitment to long-term rebuilding designed to achieve eventual victory in the next century. Given the consistency of Shining Path's statements regarding its ultimate goal, the leadership's conciliatory gestures toward the Peruvian government seemed to be a calculated tactical maneuver. The short-term Sendero objective was to restore contact among the SL leaders in prison with those still at large in order to guide the organization's rebuilding process. Political violence was consciously subordinated for the time being as well to help achieve the larger goal.

President Fujimori, for his part, encouraged Guzmán to write and speak from prison through a channel directly controlled by the president himself. The government also facilitated some contacts among the imprisoned leadership as well as some communications between them and their colleagues outside who were responsible for Sendero's day to day operation. The ultimate goal of the Peruvian government was to divide and weaken the guerrilla organization further by helping to sow dissension among Shining Path militants. The shorter term objective, however, was to bolster support for President Fujimori, both in favor of the 1993 Constitution (successful, although the vote was much closer than had been expected) and for a likely 1995 campaign for a second consecutive term in office (not permitted under either the 1933 or the 1979 Constitutions). Many recognized this official approach as a high risk one that might enable Sendero to turn its present weak position to advantage. Instead of contributing further to Shining Path's destruction, the government strategy could blow up in its face. This would be the result if the Peruvian government itself turned out to have helped Guzmán and his imprisoned colleagues regain their leadership role over a revived Shining Path.

Even if this scenario should actually develop, the odds were overwhelmingly against an eventual Sendero victory. Most would-be social revolutions fail; Shining Path probably will also. The few that have succeeded usually have done so not because of the brilliance of their strategy and tactics but because the governments they were fighting collapsed. In other words, revolutions rarely succeed, but governments sometimes fail. This seemed a real possibility in Peru in the 1989-1992 period. Successive civilian governments had not handled well either the Sendero challenge or the country's growing economic problems. Political violence had ebbed substantially between 1985 and 1987 but increased markedly thereafter. The government confronted its worst resource crisis since post–War of the Pacific days, so most social programs dried up just when they were most needed. Under these circumstances, the staying power of the Peruvian government against the Sendero challenge at that critical juncture was all the more remarkable. While there were several factors involved — including the election of an "antipolitical" president; forceful and successful action against runaway inflation; and Sendero extremism, ideological rigidity, and hubris — the turning point in the government's favor came with the 1992 captures of Guzmán, other key leaders, and many of Sendero's computer records.

As of mid-1994, the Peruvian government had Shining Path on the ropes. However, the knock out punch was yet to be delivered. The frequent announcements of Sendero's death may well prove premature, as they have in the past following significant government successes. Each time Shining Path managed to reassess its position, regroup, and adjust its strategy and tactics to come back as an even more formidable adversary. It was still possible, though less likely than just two years earlier, that SL could beat the odds and succeed after all. However, it would do so by running against the grain of revolutionary theory and practice once again. That is to say, a Sendero victory would be unlikely to result from the collapse of the Peruvian government or society or from an upsurge of popular support. Rather, it would come about primarily through Shining Path's superior strategy and tactics for waging revolution. Whatever the ultimate outcome, Sendero's epitaph has yet to be written.

2

TAKING THE HIGH GROUND: SHINING PATH AND THE ANDES

Michael L. Smith

In November 1988, guerrilla units of the Communist Party of Peru (PCP-SL), better known as Shining Path (SL or Sendero), laid the final crossbeam in an Andes-spanning strategy. They knocked down a vital power line between Lima and the Mantaro hydroelectric plant in the Central Sierra. When the state electricity company moved to repair the downed pylons, Sendero quickly blasted others. SL also sabotaged the rail line between the mining center of Cerro de Pasco and Lima. Sendero columns moved viciously into the peasant communities and agrarian cooperatives in the countryside around Huancayo, the breadbasket of the national capital.[1]

Lima tottered on the verge of social and economic disarray. Already reeling from Peru's worst depression, the city and most of the coast sputtered on rationed electrical power and rotated blackouts and brownouts for six weeks. The troubled government of President Alan García Pérez (1985-1990) declared a state of emergency in Junín, joining seven other departments under military control. Across a broad swath of Andean sierra and Amazon jungle, roughly 750 miles long and 200 miles wide, the civilian government recognized that it could not maintain a semblance of authority and order.

The department of Junín is not an isolated backwater, as is Ayacucho, where Shining Path threw its first dynamite stick at public office in 1980. The marketwise peasants in the Mantaro River valley have often been raised as examples of the healthy confluence of Indian, mestizo, and creole racial currents. The region is a pivotal transport and commercial nexus for the Central Sierra and Amazon jungle. Its mining and metallurgical companies provide substantial export earnings and tax revenues to the government. The hydroelectric complex on the Mantaro River supplies Lima and the coast with much of its electrical power.

Since Sendero started its insurgency in 1980, the conflict has cost over 23,000 deaths and damages in excess of $20 billion. Government figures put Sendero's strength as a fighting force at three thousand men and women. Independent sources double that number to six thousand. Sendero has relied on labor-intensive methods of organization for logistics, propaganda, and recruitment. It has consistently maintained the political and military initiative, deciding when, where, and how it strikes. It has operated with an absolute economy of force. Although it has made mistakes in the past, they have never compromised the general thrust of its strategy. With control over the Upper Huallaga Valley (UHV) and its thousands of coca growers, Sendero gained access to financial resources that it had never dreamed of before 1987.

This chapter addresses a central question: What sort of conditions are necessary for an insurgent movement to be successful in an ethnically, culturally, and politically heterogeneous and fragmented society like Peru? In other words, why has Sendero been able to expand beyond its original stronghold in the south-central Andes, in Ayacucho and Huancavelica? Most of the literature examining Sendero has focused on the early phases of the insurgency and the peculiarities of the region.[2]

Seven Propositions to Explain Sendero

The seven propositions to be discussed are not mutually exclusive and are all interrelated and intertwined. They will be substantiated by a discussion of some of Sendero's practices in rural areas, drawing on firsthand experience of grass-roots communities caught in the conflict as well as other resource material.[3]

Proposition No. 1: Sendero bases its strategy on an understanding of the interplay between Andean society, politics, geography, and ecology.

The Andes rise 6,000 meters or 19,700 feet above sea level, separating the other two geographic determinants of Peruvian reality, the Pacific Ocean and the Amazon jungle basin. The Andes comprise about a third of Peru's territory. The extreme variables of altitude, temperature, moisture, and other factors make the Andes a highly risky, hostile, and complex environment for human beings. Out of a possible 103 ecological zones in the classification made by Joseph Tosi, Peru's 1,284,640 square kilometers or 797,761 square miles have 83. For the modern nation-state of Peru, this mountain mass poses major problems for development and integration in a single society.

At an altitude of 3,5000 meters or 11,480 feet above sea level and higher stretches the *Andean bridge*.[4] The Suni-Puna ecological levels stretch for nearly 1,600 kilometers or 2,560 miles along the upper reaches of the Andes, a corridor of relative uniformity within geographic complexity. Over the past decade, it has provided Sendero with a preferred field of military operation.[5] These Andean ecological floors have always privileged organizations willing to work with labor-intensive methods, abnegation, patience, discipline, and long-term strategies.

Another element in the Andes is that it has been a refuge region for Peru's underprivileged Quechua- and Ayamara- speaking Indians. Three ecological floors — Suni and Puna, plus the Quechua floor immediately below them (2,300 to 3,500 meters or 7,546 to 11,480 feet above sea level) — hold 40 percent of the nation's total population and 60 percent of its rural population. Suni and Puna (3,500 meters or 11,480 feet and above) hold 10 percent of total population and 17 percent of rural population.[6] As of 1989, there were 4,140 recognized peasant communities located in the sierra.[7] The communities in the Andes sustain themselves with a pastoral and farming economy, plus other secondary activities, such as crafts, trading, and services. Almost by definition, the zone is marginal and impoverished, removed from the modernizing influences of the national economy. By concentrating on this region, Sendero is working from the top down geographically but from the bottom up in political, social, and economic terms.

However, Andean space does not limit itself horizontally. Interconnection down the slopes, both to the Pacific coast and to the Amazon jungle, is important for access to key resources and other markets. The Quechua ecological floor (from 2,500 meters or 8,200 feet to 3,500 meters or 11,480 feet), has been pivotal in the management of Andean space. It is more productive for farming and holds more population. The Quechua zone lies mainly in the intermountain valleys.

Sendero has consistently used the jungle as a refuge and a connection to other regions. In the Apurímac Valley, Sendero first came into contact with coca growers, producing both for legitimate consumption and drug trafficking. SL has been much more involved since the mid-1980s with coca growers in the Upper Huallaga Valley. The coast also provides alternative escape routes and a ready source of recruits in times of crisis.

Some analysts have questioned whether SL's dogmatic interpretation of Maoism is a viable political option. For instance, why carry out a rural revolution (the classic formula of the countryside laying siege to the city) when the society is fast moving in an urban direction? This strategy may seem out of step with a modern Peru, but the point is irrelevant. The Andes are still a huge physical space with strategic value for a guerrilla organization obsessed with sustaining an autonomous revolt.

Sendero's operational priority in the Puna and neighboring regions does not give it enough military and political weight to win its war. Nevertheless, it is a perfect place both to wait for the decadent capitalist system to collapse, as Sendero has been predicting for the past twenty years, and as a staging area for the final assault on power. In a cold-hearted analysis of costs and benefits, this region had little importance for the Lima government. It did not warrant the investment of political, economic, military, and human resources to maintain effective control there. However, in late 1988, Sendero drove home the strategic importance of the Cerro de Pasco-Huancayo zone by cutting the power supply and rail transport to Lima.

Proposition No. 2: In practical terms, Sendero's frame of reference works within a local or regional setting.

The overriding question is how Sendero can operate within a geographical space that is so complex and diversified. This fragmented landscape shapes the populations living there. The sociologist José Matos Mar has characterized Peru politically as an archipelago.[8]

The complex Andean geomorphology and ecology have a direct bearing on agricultural production and other economic activities. Minute changes require an intensive management of microspaces, land, and water usage. Conflict and cooperation are constants among individual production units and the collective mechanisms for managing these production zones that may span several Andean ecological levels. Such micromanagement has an impact on survival strategies, local labor pools, and ties with urban and rural markets. Smaller scale production imposed by the Andes makes capitalist markets less efficient and less profitable.[9]

These economic implications also have repercussions on local politics. Local histories of conflicts and tensions, frequently unregistered outside oral traditions, and strong local identity blend with a culture of opposition. Frequently, the minutiae, codes, and rules of this political reality are imperceptible to outsiders. The crucial transitional stage has been when these microunits try to mesh with broader regional and national phenomena, predominately urban in nature.[10] In the past, the crucial element in consolidating Andean space and society into broader entities has been articulating and linking up these political building blocks.[11]

For lack of a more adequate term, I call this concept Andean ecopolitics. It aims to capture the nuances and subtleties of Andean society and culture. When analyzing national political and economic trends, it is necessary to keep in mind that their impact on the microsetting has unique, varied implications.

Although Sendero has earned a reputation for being ideologically dogmatic and fanatical, it is highly versatile in fitting its strategy and tactics to the demands of Andean ecopolitics. Sendero itself expressed this concept subconsciously when it called the current revolutionary phase "The War of Little Wars" in its pamphlets — a thousand little wars spread across the Andes.[12] Each skirmish is fought on its own terms, without the adversaries necessarily being aware that war has broken out.

The inhabitants of these ecopolitical microsettings do not necessarily adhere to Sendero's ideology and politics, but rarely can they challenge them openly. Instead, residents employ a centuries-old range of survival strategies.[13] The locals view Sendero's intrusion against the backdrop of their own agenda.

Without resorting to SL documents, we can find a short list of enemies. A quick examination of Andean folk tales, songs, and traditions shows who oppresses and humiliates the peasant. The oppressor is not an abstract regime but the priest, the schoolteacher, the judge, the police officer, the engineer, or the government bureaucrat.

Proposition No. 3: Sendero plays off friction within the interface between urban and rural worlds.

Sendero exploits a host of factors to leverage groups or individuals into revolt. These forces include racial and ethnic hatred, class and generational differences, the lack of employment prospects, ideology, and radicalized political and military practices.[14] The issues and differences are frequently imperceptible to outsiders. The exact mixture of these ingredients varies from place to place. The shared battleground is, however, the urban-rural interface, the space "between capital and provinces, between the city and the countryside, between Andeans and creoles."[15]

I am not speaking in simplistic, black-and-white dichotomies — an "official Peru" and a "profound Peru" (to use the terms of Peruvian historian Jorge Basadre) or isolated backward peasants versus a cosmopolitan, modern Peru. The continuum between the urban and rural worlds is complex, ambiguous, multifaceted, and elastic. It can even change over an annual calendar and through periods of boom and bust.

The growth of provincial urban centers, especially provincial and district capitals, marks a major difference between Sendero's strategy and Peru's previous guerrilla conflict in 1963 to 1966. Better transport, expanded state services, and larger commercial volume mean that locals are now used to seeing newcomers in their towns. Sendero units often move back and forth between rural and urban modes. Columns may break into smaller units and blend into the urban flux of traveling merchants, students, and market-day peasants. Sendero's cadres are exceptionally well equipped for working it both ways. Several analysts have described Sendero's following as "de-peasant-ized youth."[16] In other words, rural youth are no longer satisfied being peasants but cannot find adequate employment or opportunity in urban Peru.

Three issues of conflict in the rural-urban interface deserve special mention: the state in its most parochial guises; capitalist markets; and the issues of land, water, and other scarce production factors. These provide the wedge Sendero uses to open the cracks in rural societies and garner quick support.

The State

Despite the advances of representative democracy in the past decade, the local power structures are still in place in the countryside. The old *gamonal* system finally fell to pieces with the reforms of the military government of General Juan Velasco Alvarado (1968-1975).[17] Through expanded bureaucracy, control of government revenue, and centralization of decision making, the state came to substitute for the social control exercised by the former landowners. With the return to civilian rule in 1980, national parties had to depend on local power groups (former landowners, merchants, and other provincial urban intermediaries) to provide the final links to the rural sectors. Elections have become a periodic lottery in which the state booty is raffled off. Local power groups can then benefit from control of patronage and state expenditures. This fuzzy boundary between personal interests and the state frequently blends with a backlog of local conflicts and tensions.

Since the mid-1960s, the state's expansion has not, paradoxically, resulted in a stronger presence. Due to the periodic retraction of state revenue and shifting priorities, programs rarely have long-term viability. In local residents' eyes, they end up as pork-barreling and patronage sops to restricted groups of followers. The presence of state institutions has set off a process of social differentiation, heightening urban-rural conflicts. But the state has also grown progressively weaker and become increasingly incapable of meeting its minimal duties, such as collecting taxes, educating young people, and dispensing justice. By late 1989, it even seemed incapable of defending itself.

The Capitalist Market

Capitalism and the broadening scope of the market economy have imposed new, daunting challenges in rural areas. Sendero has chosen to center its efforts in mercantile spaces where noncapitalist, communal production modes clash with an encroaching urban market.[18] These are the most remote markets in the commercial chain.

A survey of five rural markets in the department of Cusco showed that prices were 50 to 200 percent higher than in the Cusco retail market.[19] These markups are in part due to the distance and difficulty in reaching weekly markets, but peasants are aware of these price discrepancies. In addition, market prices do not allow peasants to recover production costs, let alone earn a profit.[20] There are enormous markups on prices paid in the field for produce and the final prices in urban centers. It should therefore come as no surprise that peasants may conclude that capitalism is devoid of virtues.

The same distributors of urban goods are also purchasers of peasant products, personalizing the defects of the capitalist mercantile market. In Cusco and Puno, many merchants and shopkeepers are former hacienda owners who have retreated to the urban centers. They still harbor hopes that they can regain control of the land. The economic dislocation of the late 1980s has had dramatic effects. The Ayacucho peasant federation complained that in 1988, a sack of potatoes bought a box of matches.

However, these points should not lead to the conclusion that peasants want to isolate themselves from the market. Aside from selling and buying farm produce, they regularly seek temporary employment, sell handicrafts and utilitarian goods, barter, seek marriage and bloodbrother matches, and forge social alliances. Markets also serve as intermediaries between different ecological floors. A peasant's survival depends on keeping links through local markets.

Sendero's practice of organizing armed strikes and threatening and harassing merchants and truck drivers (important intermediaries) tries to alter the conduct of commercial intermediaries. But peasants vehemently opposed Sendero's effort to close down the markets completely, so SL shifted its ground to attack those who accumulated capital through the markets.

Even during periods of economic growth, such as 1986 to 1987, Sendero can make inroads. The central government distributed benefits unevenly among the groups demanding a share, based on proximity to urban centers, regional priorities, or political favoritism, thereby incurring resentment that Sendero could exploit.

Land, Water, and Scarcity

Landownership has undergone huge changes in the past two decades. The 1969 Agrarian Reform distributed land and set up new production units, but kept rural power concentrated in a few hands (the cooperative leaders) and sustained the marginal role of peasant communities within these new enterprises. The rural associative enterprise or cooperative incorporated former hacienda employees, workers, and peons as well as neighboring peasant communities. However, the communities rarely received a fair share in the ownership and management of the cooperative's land.[21] The former haciendas concentrated the best farm and grazing land, water, and access to markets. Where there are cooperatives, there were haciendas before. Sendero finds in and around the cooperatives a motherlode of rancor and pent-up conflicts waiting to be mined.

The past decade, however, has seen a second land redistribution after the collapse of the associative enterprises. The redistribution's causes were the government's erratic agricultural policy, often against the rural producer, natural disasters (drought and excessive rains), the inefficiency of cooperative management, and the presence of Sendero itself. According to recent land-ownership figures, cooperatives dropped from 4.0 million hectares in 1979 to about 900,000 hectares in 1988. Of the landholdings of more than 50 hectares, individuals hold 88 percent.[22] This process of breaking up cooperatives into smaller holdings has been arbitrary, prone to abuses, chaotic, and without a clear legal framework.

From a local viewpoint, this process intensifies local tensions. Without a redistributive goal to favor communities and landless peasants, land restructuring benefited the local system of power and those who happened to be employees or peons of the former haciendas. Nor does Sendero necessarily need large landholdings to enforce its land reform. In Cajabamba (Cajamarca), there are cases of Sendero forcing holders of five hectares to give up two to poor peasants.

Proposition No. 4: Sendero's fetish for violence serves as a compass in navigating the waters of Andean ecopolitics.

Within a local context, Sendero's interpretation of class struggle seems to boil down to personal vendettas or blood feuds, but depersonalized behind the fetish of violence. Like a shark scenting blood, Sendero is almost instinctively drawn to conflict.

What has struck many observers is Sendero's use of violence against a wide range of victims and targets. It has hit at institutions that even radical Marxist groups accept, such as rural development projects, where it has slaughtered cattle and destroyed seedbeds, and the Catholic Church. Sendero shows no respect for grass-roots organizations because, from its viewpoint, they are pillars of the old order, tinged by the old power relationships. By patching the system or setting up survival networks (soup kitchens or communal development programs), these organizations are merely propping up the government by reducing social tensions.

For Sendero, violence has been a constant, the dynamo of history.[23] In Peru, as Sendero sees it, the struggle of the proletariat and peasantry was hampered by its disjointed, sporadic nature, lacking a central command to give it firm direction. False allies, infiltrated into the masses, continually betrayed the underclasses. These traitors are the reformists and pseudorevolutionaries who propose patching up the capitalist system.

Within Sendero's worldview, during the past 1,200 years of Peruvian history, since the appearance of a strong centralized state, the administration of death has been a monopoly of a minority. The state has exercised this monopoly through the system of justice, the slow starvation of economic exploitation, or outright repression through the armed and police forces. Abimael Guzmán Reynoso, Sendero's founder and ideologue, said that the capitalist system condemns "60,000 infants a year to death before the age of one." In comparison, the "quota of blood" necessary for the revolution is a small price for installing a more egalitarian system, he adds.[24] Sendero's assertion of its capacity to administer capital punishment demonstrates that it is an alternative power.

Sendero needs this power to turn peasant communities irrevocably against the state. Otherwise, the communities will fall back on the old game of submissive resistance. The peasants will say meekly, "Yes, sir," with their heads humbly inclined toward the ground. The next day they will repeat the same to the police, the ruling party, the church, and anyone else who comes to offer something to the communities.

This use of force is all too familiar to peasant organizations. Sierra hacienda owners, or *gamonales*, used many of these "authoritarian and vertical structures, based on the use of the most primary violence," into the 1900s.[25] New political agents on the Andean scene have adopted these same practices. Local communities often know who Sendero militants or sympathizers are but will not inform on them to the police. The common expression, "The party has a thousand eyes and ears," forewarns potential informers that Sendero will find them out. Sendero punishes the crime of being a stool pigeon with death.

Sendero's presence also sets loose a dynamic that makes the local elites more dependent on the police and the armed forces, the most repressive side of the state. Perhaps no other factor can alter the local scene more than militarization. It sweeps aside the local power structure and forces a realignment in terms of armed force. It reduces the chances of generating a broader consensus for formulating a more democratic approach.

Proposition No. 5: Sendero's aim is to disorganize politics.

Samuel Huntington once wrote, "In the modernizing world, he controls the future who organized its politics."[26] Sendero turns this statement on its head: He controls the future who *dis*organizes its politics. Through its tactics of intimidation, harassment, and acts of selective terrorism, Sendero is undercutting both the fragile supports of the establishment and the potential for future rivals emerging from local societies. Sendero is snipping the ties between the rural and urban power networks by eliminating or neutralizing the figures who move the conveyor belts between the two circuits.

When Sendero is sizing up a new field of operation or community, it asks a simple question: "Who is the most hated figure in the community?" The winner of this reverse popularity contest turns up dead a few days or weeks later. The other side of this survey of the local networks is that Sendero also asks who are the most respected leaders, including catechists, grass- roots leaders, and teachers. Sendero courts, badgers, and harasses them to cooperate, remain neutral, or leave.

A facet of this strategy is to boycott all elections, disrupt campaigns and pollings, assassinate candidates and authorities. The campaigns are a crucial period in which local power networks realign, striking fresh partnerships between urban and rural groups. Frequently, security forces and the ruling parties aid Sendero in discrediting the electoral process. During the 1987 municipal elections in Huanta province, Ayacucho, for example, the army aided and abetted dubious voting practices, such as forbidding the use of indelible ink to prevent repeated voting. The argument was that Sendero would cut off the fingers of those peasants showing signs of casting a ballot.[27]

Proposition No. 6: Sendero fills the vacuum it has created with three elements: a militarized party apparatus, armed violence, and an iron-clad ideology.

Sendero addresses a crucial problem in Peru — how to integrate a fragmented society trapped in a zero-sum game. Peruvian society seems to be caught in a situation in which no single group holds sufficient power to be able to break through the social, political, and economic bottlenecks. Sendero takes the most radical tack, clearing the table and starting anew. It says that there is nothing redeemable in the status quo and the first task is to destroy the old order militarily. Sendero has devised its party apparatus and ideology to serve those purposes. Sendero does not have to define what kind of society it will construct after its victory because it believes that the new material conditions themselves will dictate the new state and society.

Because of the major role played by the PCP-SL, it is necessary to sketch its central elements. First, it is characterized by the single-minded subordination of the party, its cadres, and its resources to its military and political goals. This militarization of the party has permitted Sendero to demonstrate a close, measurable relationship between objectives, actions, and results.

Second, it has a vertical, authoritarian structure and cell organization that has been almost impossible to infiltrate or break. The party leadership is a stable, permanent war staff, held in strategic reserve. This provides long-term planning, "strategically centralized and tactically decentralized," and constant evaluation of the immediate situation.[28] A unique trait is that this authoritarian structure allows regional and even column leaders operational autonomy.

Third, the party leadership has carefully constructed a motivating myth, personified and exalted in Abimael Guzmán, the former philosophy professor of the University of Huamanga now known as President Gonzalo. The extension of this myth is Gonzalo Thought, the application of Marxism-Leninism-Maoism to Peruvian reality, and the calling of the Peruvian Communist Party to be the germ of a worldwide Maoist revolution.[29]

Fourth, there is an absolute rejection of all organizations that do not subordinate themselves to the militarized party. In sacrificing short-term gains that might be attained by forming complicated alliances, Sendero has reduced the threat of infiltration.

Fifth, since its inception as a party, Sendero has resourcefully exploited nonpolitical mechanisms to advance its cohesion, recruitment, and appeal. These mechanisms are copaternity, kinship, initiation bonds, blood brothers, peer pressure, and other relationships.[30] In provincial settings, these mechanisms can be even stronger than ideology or political conviction.

Sendero espouses a virulent brand of Marxism, acquired by its historical leaders' exposure to the Chinese Cultural Revolution in the 1960s and early 1970s. What it may lack in sophistication, it makes up for in cut-and-dried formulas that explain everything from world power politics to personal psychology. It has been flash-frozen for mass consumption. During a crisis period of values and ethics, as Peru is now experiencing, Sendero offers an unswerving moral code and set of values. Its ideology works within a historical timeframe that spans decades and even centuries and, thus, is not easily disoriented by periodic crises. Indeed, it expects them. Ideology is important because Sendero has to bind together all its "little wars" across the country. It has to build up identities between the Huallaga coca grower and the reclusive peasants, between the urban youth and the burned-out union militant.

Proposition No. 7: Sendero's pedagogical roots and experience give its ideology and praxis a utilitarian, didactic approach that belies its dogmatism.

Sendero's roots in education date back to Ayacucho in the 1960s. Many analysts described Sendero as a radical, elitist faction emerging from the University of Huamanga. Yet Sendero also had a more egalitarian and broad-based patrimony. It stretched from the humble one-room rural school in hundreds of hamlets to the urban secondary schools. In the city of Ayacucho in 1970, a quarter of the population of 43,000 were secondary and university students. Many of these students came fresh from rural settings and were finishing their studies in the city. Ayacucho city was a ready-made laboratory in popular education and a privileged space of encounter between urban and rural worlds.[31]

Guzmán hatched Sendero's pedagogical formula in those formative days and has varied it little since then. Indeed, this educational plateau has allowed Sendero to spread out from Ayacucho to other parts of the Andes — almost anywhere there is a blackboard and benches.[32] The message is internally coherent, exhaustive in explaining a wide universe of experience, and simple to understand, especially when contrasted with the dysfunctionality of the official curriculum in the public school system.[33] Though repetitive and prone to rote memory methods, it aims at a target public trapped between an illiterate and semiliterate level of awareness.

There has been a steady decline in Peruvian public education since the early 1970s. In real terms, the government was spending less on education in 1985 than in 1963 even though enrollment had tripled.[34] Another manifestation of this breakdown was in the sharp drop in the quality of education of the teaching profession, for providing both employable skills and valid explanations of what was happening in the country.[35]

In the midst of this crisis, the public education system's curriculum has undergone a major revision of historical interpretation in the past twenty years. A recent investigation shows how the pre-1970 version of Peru's history, based on a static interpretation of historical events and individuals, lost acceptance among teachers and students. A new curriculum, not officially sanctioned, took root, incorporating advances in Peruvian social sciences strongly influenced by Marxist concepts. Elements of this "critical idea" include blaming imperialism for Peru's backwardness, the inability of the ruling classes to defend the national interest, the danger of losing Peru's cultural patrimony due to aping American customs, and the utopia of the Inca empire as a period of self-sufficiency. These elements can play into the hands of Sendero, especially when combined with other assets of popular Marxism prevalent in Peru.[36]

Sendero's pedagogical nature complements its ideological and military characteristics. As a "revolutionary apprenticeship," it is a prerequisite and a culmination of armed struggle. It also imposes a timeframe that may span decades, even generations. Though Sendero has shown effective methods of indoctrination, it still requires time to absorb, educate, and prepare new members of the organization. The real liberating experience comes only through war itself. Therefore, Sendero is not an apparatus that can rapidly expand its membership rolls.

Conclusion

The Andean bridge has always had a bearing on military strategy in Peru. During the pre-Columbian era, the Wari and Inca empires dominated the

Andes through control of the upper levels. The continentwide War of Independence against Spain came to a conclusion in Ayacucho. The War of the Pacific (1879-1883) between Chile and the allied forces of Bolivia and Peru and its aftermath of twenty years of civil strife in Peru brought the crucial battles to the Andean heartland. What is unique about Sendero is that it has set off on this Andean jihad without first having a slice of power and resources. It is also striking to see this strategy played out on the Peruvian map with almost Prussian precision. Despite the technological advances of warfare this century, Sendero has reasserted an Andean preeminence in this conflict.[37]

Measured by its expansion over the past ten years, the Peruvian Communist Party — Shining Path and its military and political organizations — have to be judged without analog. Its followers have welded together ideology and political praxis, military tactics and long-term objectives by adapting them to the niches of Peruvian society, especially its Andean segment. It is this chapter's central contention that Sendero has an Andean functionality which has been crucial to its expansion. In fact, the peculiarities of the Peruvian case seem to carry as much weight as universal criteria used in analyzing insurgency movements. By the end of the 1980s, it was difficult to determine how much of Sendero's expansion was due to effective guerrilla strategy and how much to the breakdown of governance. In any case, Sendero had positioned itself to take maximum advantage of the circumstances. It should be self-evident that Sendero has gained a foothold on Peru's troubled political stage and will remain a destabilizing factor in the coming decade.

Notes

1. Nelson Manrique, "Sierra Central: La batalla decisiva," *Quehacer*, 60, August-September 1989, pp. 63-71. Also, Rodrigo Sánchez, "Las SAIS de Junín y la alternativa comunal," *Debate Agrario*, No. 7, July-December 1989, pp. 85-101.

2. The first crop of studies on Sendero include those of Carlos Iván Degregori, David Scott Palmer, Lewis Taylor, Henry Favre, Billie Jean Isbell, Ronald Berg, and Cynthia McClintock. The serious journalistic writings of Raúl Gonzalez, José Gonzales, and Gustavo Gorriti also form part of this material. The first comprehensive study on

political violence came from a Special Senate Committee on the Causes of Violence and Alternatives for Pacification in Peru, published as *Violencia y pacificación* (Lima: DESCO and Comisión Andina de Juristas), 1989.

3. Field work for this study was carried out in Ayacucho, Cajamarca, and Puno from 1987 to 1989. Further interviews and research took place in Lima. I discussed preliminary drafts of this chapter in several Lima research centers and with individual scholars. Comments and criticisms were invaluable in focusing, clarifying, and refining the propositions.

4. I will be using the nomenclature developed by the Peruvian geographer Javier Pulgar Vidal. He divides the Andes into eight natural regions based on altitude with variations due to climate (mainly levels of moisture and temperature), flora and fauna. The two Amazon categories (rupa-rupa and omagua) and the categories of coast (chala) and lower slopes (yunga) are of minor importance for this study. See his *Geografía del Perú: Las ocho regiones naturales* (Lima: PEISA, 1987). Also Olivier Dollfus, *El reto del espacio andino* (Lima: Instituto de Estudios Peruanos, 1981) and Instituto Geográfico Nacional (IGN), *Atlas del Perú* (Lima: IGN, 1989).

5. Almost without exceptions, campesinos say that Sendero columns come from "above," the higher altitudes of the Andes. Testimony from Cajamarca, Huaraz, Huancayo, Ayacucho, and Puno. In the Communist Party of Peru-Sendero Luminoso's 1986 document *Desarrollar la Guerra Popular sirviendo a la Revolución Mundial*, the Central Committee says that the aim of its Great Leap Plan since 1984 was "occupying the Sierra, the historic axis of Peruvian society and its most backward and poorest part, to convert it into the great theater of revolutionary war" (p. 36).

6. Efraín Gonzales de Oliarte, *Economía de la comunidad campesina: Aproximación regional* (Lima: Instituto de Estudios Peruanos, 1984), pp. 38-39.

7. Pulgar Vidal, *Atlas del Perú*, p. 210. This figure refers to communities registered with the government. When existing but unregistered communities are added, the total is estimated to be around six thousand. Peasant communities should not be seen as a retreat to archaic modes of production. They are not static entities. The growth in the number of officially recognized communities over the past decade is due to four factors: the collapse of associative enterprises (cooperatives) and their replacement by communities; their continued viability as an instrument spreading the risks of producing in a precarious environment; incentives for communities under the García administration (grants and zero-interest loans); and efficient support from the Register of Peasant Campesino Communities in the Ministry of Agriculture. Under Peruvian agrarian law, the peasant community has a precise legal standing.

8. José Matos Mar, "El pluralismo y la dominación en la sociedad peruana, una perspectiva configurativa," in José Matos Mar et al., *Dominación y cambio en el Perú rural* (Lima: Instituto de Estudios Peruanos, 1968), pp. 24-59.

9. Enrique Mayer and Marisol de la Cadena, *Cooperación y conflicto en la comunidad andina: Zonas de producción y organización social* (Lima: Instituto de Estudios Peruanos, 1989).

10. See Telmo Rojas, "Límites y posibilidades del desarrollo microregional" in Fernando Eguren et al., eds., *Perú: El problema agrario en debate* (Lima: Universidad Nacional de San Cristóbal de Huamanga and Seminario Permanente de Investigación Agraria,

1988), pp. 386-391. Rojas gives a provocative survey of class and group structure within rural societies and how they function.

11. Gavin Smith, "The Fox and the Rooster: The Culture of Opposition in Highland Peru," *This Magazine*, 19, April 1985, pp. 9-14.

12. Partido Comunista del Peru (PCP), *Desarrollemos la guerra de guerrillas* (March 1982). "Develop Guerrilla Warfare!" (in the imperative voice) is the correct translation.

13. The Ayacuchan anthropologist Rodrigo Montoya says that Andean culture contains a "structural hypocrisy" in which the peasants consent to the domination of the government or other power groups but, at the same time, try to obtain the maximum benefits from the relationship. This concept also applies to all outside influence. Peasants have to keep all their options open, just as they strive to gain access to a maximum number of ecological niches. Rodrigo Montoya, *La cultura quechua hoy* (Lima: Mosca Azul, 1987), p. 13.

14. Although Sendero's guerrilla war has clear ethnic and racial overtones, the Andean populace does not fit neatly into pigeonholes. Luis Lumbreras points out that there are "white" ethnic groups, such as the Morochucos of Pampa Cangallo (Ayacucho) who have light-colored eyes and hair, speak Quechua, and feel peasant. In other regions, such as Cajamarca, peasants have lost indigenous linguistic and racial features but still think and act like peasants and feel bound to the earth. The *mistis*, the dominant class in the Andes, may speak Quechua, share cultural traits, and have Indian or mestizo physiological characteristics, but it falls on the other side of the racial-class divide. Luis Lumbreras, "Segregación racista y marginalidad clasista," 1990, ms.

15. Carlos Iván Degregori, *Sendero Luminoso: Los hondos y mortales desencuentros y lucha armada y utopia autoritaria* (Lima: Instituto de Estudios Peruanos, 1986), p. 8.

16. Henri Favre, "Sentier Lumineux et Horizons Obscurs," *Problèmes D'Amérique Latine*, 72, 2ᵉ trimestre, 1984, pp. 23-28.

17. *Gamonal* is an Andean term for landowner or hacienda owner. Following the collapse of effective government after the 1879 to 1883 War of the Pacific, the central government ceded broad powers to local landowners. This power was frequently used to take land away from campesino communities, pushing them back to the most unproductive land. The gamonal, however, also served as intermediary between native groups and authority. This system, known as gamonalismo, began to decline in the 1940s.

18. Efraín Gonzales de Oliarte, *Economías regionales del Perú* (Lima: Instituto de Estudios Peruanos, 1982), pp. 236-237.

19. Gerardo Lovón, "Crisis y precios en la región," *Sur*, November-December 1988, pp. 23-26.

20. Salomón Beisaga, "Costos de producción y precios de garantía," *Sur*, August 1988, pp. 15-16.

21. The Peruvian agrarian reform (1969-1979) set up several ownership schemes, most of them based on the cooperative. In the sierra, the government tried to incorporate campesino communities into the cooperative scheme but rarely met with success. The military also tried to set up social property companies, another mode of ownership, mainly in Puno. For purposed of simplicity, I will call them all cooperatives.

22. *Amauta*, June 22, 1989.

23. "Violence is a universal law without exception; [revolutionary violence] is what permits us to resolve the fundamental contradictions with an army and through the people's war." Guzmán interview, *El Diario*, July 24, 1988, p. 15.

24. Ibid., p. 27.

25. Nelson Manrique, *Yawar Mayu: Sociedades terratenientes serranas, 1879-1910* (Lima: Instituto Francés de Estudios Andinos and DESCO Centro de Estudios y Promoción del Desarrollo, 1988), p. 183.

26. Samuel Huntington, *Political Order in Changing Societies* (New Haven: Yale University Press, 1968), p. 461.

27. Interviews with several observers of municipal elections, November 1987, Ayacucho. In addition, the army convoked peasant "civil defense committees" for their weekly flag raising ceremony and then marched them directly to the voting booths. Observers overheard officers telling peasants to vote for the American Popular Revolutionary Alliance (APRA) party. In the countryside, more blatant practices were reported.

28. PCP, *Desarrollar la guerra popular sirviendo a la revolución mundial* (Lima: Ediciones Bandera Roja: 1986), p. 37.

29. Jesús Manuel Granados, "El PCP Sendero Luminoso: Aproximaciones a su ideología," *Participación y Socialismo*, 37, March 1987, pp. 28-31.

30. Sendero's original leadership in Ayacucho drew on a tight network of interconnected families and marriages, bordering on political incest and nepotism. More recent evidence comes from a study of Sendero inmates in Peruvian prisons. Once a person has been drawn into the organization or jailed on terrorism charges, Sendero's support organizations, People's Aid and the Committee for Political Prisoners, concentrate on winning over relatives and friends. Frequently, whole families join the party. In rural areas, other types of bonds, such as sharing a common hometown or clan membership, also enter into play. Interviews by the author in Canto Grande maximum security prison, 1988-1989, and press reports.

31. Norman Gall, *Reforma educativa peruana* (Lima: Mosca Azul, 1976), pp. 39-51. The text was originally published as "Peru's Education Reform," *American Universities Field Staff, West Coast South America Series*, 21:3-5, 1974.

32. This observation is based on extensive interviews with University of Huamanga educators and participants during the early period.

33. Juan Biondi and Eduardo Zapata, *El discurso de Sendero Luminoso: Contratexto educativa* (Lima: Consejo Nacional de Ciencia y Tecnología-CONCYTEC, 1989), p. 44.

34. Gonzalo Portocarrero and Patricia Oliart, *El Perú desde la escuela* (Lima: Instituto de Apoyo Agrario, 1989), p. 188, 234-236.

35. See Hernando Burgos, "Maestros: La última clase," *Quehacer*, 58, April-May 1989, pp. 32-66.

36. Portocarrero and Oliart, *El Perú desde la escuela*, pp. 104-120.

37. For two interesting studies highlighting the strategic importance of the Andes, see John Hemming, *The Conquest of the Incas* (London: Penguin, 1983), and Nelson Manrique, *Las guerrillas indígenas en la guerra con Chile* (Lima: Centro de Investigación y Capacitación (CIC) and Editora Ital Perú S.A., 1981). Sendero has studied armed conflicts in the Andes, especially the peasant guerrilla resistance to Chilean troops in the Central Andes. The army has found copies of Manrique's book on several fallen Sendero militants.

3

THE ORIGINS AND LOGIC OF SHINING PATH: TWO VIEWS

RETURN TO THE PAST[*]

Carlos Iván Degregori

On the night of May 17, 1980, the eve of Peru's first presidential elections in seventeen years, a group of youths broke into the town hall in the small Andean town of Chuschi. They took ballot boxes and voting lists, and burned them in the town plaza. The incident was lost in the avalanche of election news. Over the following months, while the press reported the theft of dynamite from a few mines, isolated bombs began to go off here and there. No one paid much attention until the end of that year, when the situation acquired a folkloric if sinister dimension: Early risers in Lima began to find dead dogs hung from

[*]Edited and revised from Carlos Iván Degregori, "A Dwarf Star," *NACLA Report on the Americas*, 24:4, December-Janaury 1990-1991, pp. 10-16, with permission.

traffic lights and lamp posts. They were adorned with signs that read "Deng Xiaoping, Son of a Bitch."

The Communist Party of Peru, known as Shining Path (SL or Sendero), points to that remote May 17 as the beginning of the "People's War." In the years since then, Sendero has emerged as the most important armed movement in contemporary Peruvian history. No one attached much importance to the first skirmishes because in 1980 Shining Path was a small regional organization that had not played any role in the great social movements that shook the country between 1976 and 1979 and forced the military government (1968-1980) to withdraw to the barracks.

Beginnings

Sendero was born in the Andean department of Ayacucho, one of the nation's poorest and most backward, where until midcentury bankrupt landowners persisted in the serflike exploitation of "their" Indians. Ayacuchans, however, did not have their backs turned to the modern world; they migrated by the thousands and flocked to schools to escape their misery and oppression.[1] Their desire for education was so great that, unlike other Andean departments, the principal social movement in Ayacucho between 1960 and 1980 was not for land but in defense of free education, which the military government tried to cut back in 1969.

Ten years earlier, in 1959, San Cristóbal de Huamanga University in Ayacucho, the only school of higher education in the region, reopened its doors. (Founded in 1677, it had been closed since 1885.) The tiny regional committee of the Peruvian Communist Party (PCP) operating in Ayacucho took off soon after, when a group of professors signed up. The committee chair was a young philosophy professor named Abimael Guzmán Reynoso, today the supreme leader of Shining Path.

Soon Guzmán, together with his most faithful followers, formed a clandestine Red Faction within the PCP, which was to be the forerunner of Shining Path. In January 1964 the PCP split into a pro-Soviet faction and another that was Maoist. The Red Faction aligned itself with the latter, and in a few years it gained influence in the student federation and among the faculty. It also helped set up a municipal federation of community organizations and a People's Defense Front, which took the lead in the massive movement in defense of free education. But in 1969 the faction suffered a double defeat that deeply affected its development.

On the one hand, in June of that year, the free education movement suffered harsh repression. The leaders of the People's Defense Front were arrested, and the Front would never recover its former power (however, shortly after the crackdown, the government did restore free education). The other defeat came within the party. Several top leaders of the Red Faction, among them Guzmán himself, were arrested, along with the Front leadership. While Guzmán spent long months in jail, a fierce internal struggle shook the Maoist PCP. By the beginning of 1970, Guzmán had been expelled from the party, reduced to his Ayacucho stronghold, and weakened even there. It was then that the Red Faction decided to become the Communist Party of Peru — Shining Path. I began teaching at the University of Huamanga in Ayacucho during that year and had the opportunity to observe the development of Sendero firsthand.

At the same time, the military government undertook a series of reforms that began to change the face of the region and the country. The days of the Peru that, at least from Ayacucho, could still be seen as a semifeudal nation similar to China of the 1930s were numbered. Sendero, converted by then into a party, began a quiet race against time. During the first half of the 1970s, many professors and students at the university, who made up the backbone of the new party, devoted themselves to developing a coherent and all-encompassing discourse following the strictest Marxist-Leninist orthodoxy. In that sense, Sendero was moving in the opposite direction from the rest of the Peruvian left who, during the 1970s, left the universities to participate in increasingly frequent social movements.

Ideology and Strategy

Sendero compensated for its weakening impact on society by building increasingly well-organized cadres steeped in ideology. What it lost in influence among the masses, it gained in ideological rigidity and organic cohesiveness, until it became a sort of dwarf star — the kind in which matter gets so compressed it acquires a great specific weight disproportionate to its size. For that reason nobody detected it in 1980; nobody noticed that despite its small size, it had the power to affect decisively the Peruvian political scene of the 1980s. Sendero had become a classic example of a party built from the top down and from its ideology out. It adhered strictly to Stalin's dictums: "The line decides everything"; and, when the line has been worked out and is "correct," "The cadres decide everything." While the rest of the left was concerned with openly influencing labor unions and creating peasant federations or regional fronts, Sendero concentrated its attention on what it called "generated organisms": nuclei that were generally small but ideologically rigid and organically dependent on the party. They operated as factions within those mass grass-roots organizations that Sendero had ever greater difficulty attempting to lead in a democratic fashion — such as the People's Defense Front, the national teacher's union, and other urban unions.

Generated organisms were defined by Sendero as "separate movements, organizations generated by the proletariat on different workfronts."[2] Of course it was not the proletarian masses that made up these movements but Sendero itself, perhaps the party that had done the least work with labor of all the left parties of the 1970s. In Sendero's view this was no confusion; it was the proletariat. The workers themselves had no capacity for initiative; they were simply passive spectators of the vanguard's activities. In the 1980s the generated organisms, transformed from transmission belts into belts of subjection and control, would become the "thousand eyes and thousand ears" of the party, the most frankly terrorist face of its undercover power.[3] And in the isolated countryside where Sendero was strong, these groups would become the basis of the "new state in formation," often displacing or absorbing preexisting grass-roots organizations.

Sendero's decision to pursue the armed struggle was not only the product of a strategic and tactical evaluation. It also involved, in a very important way, an ideological mutation. Sendero launched its adventure at a crucial moment in history for both the Peruvian left and the international Communist movement — in a situation clearly disadvantageous to itself on both fronts. On the national level, it was a time of great activism. During these years, the general strikes of 1977 and 1978, in which Sendero took no part, contributed to a democratic opening in 1980. The left became a mass political force for the first time in Peru's history. On the international level, Mao Zedong died in 1976; the Gang of Four, headed by his widow, was defeated; and the Cultural Revolution, which fed the imagination of a good part of the Peruvian left and continues to inspire Sendero, had come to an end.

Denying those realities, Sendero proposed another scenario. It rejected the leading role of the masses in favor of the leading role of the party; the party decides everything. It rejected the primacy of politics in favor of the primacy of violence; violence is the essence of revolution; war is its principal task. According to Sendero, Peru was still semifeudal and the change of government meant nothing. Fernando Belaúnde Terry, the winner of the 1980 presidential elections, represented "fascist continuism." Faced with the impossibility of stopping time or blocking out the sun with one finger, Sendero chose to become the sun. With Mao Zedong dead and the Gang of Four defeated, Sendero proclaimed itself the beacon of world revolution, its leader the "fourth sword of Marxism," after Marx, Lenin, and Mao.[4]

It was a classic retreat forward. To sustain this alternative scenario required not only an act of supreme political will and enormous organizing ability, but also an ideological rigidity unprecedented in Peruvian political history. To resist the powerful currents sweeping the left nationally and internationally, Sendero turned to a fundamentalism that maximized and lionized violence. Sendero was able to pull this off because it was basically outside the movement, disconnected from the classes that participate in production, from their daily lives and their pragmatic demands.

Explanation: Return to the Past

Several questions remain open. Why did such a group emerge? Was it because its sympathizers had been reduced to a small political-intellectual nucleus in a region of ruined lords and rebellious serfs, a region closed off and abandoned by capitalist development yet achingly desirous of progress? How did Sendero manage to carry forth its scenario relentlessly throughout the 1980s? It is my position that as it matured, Sendero picked up the outdated characteristics of that regional society and of national political life and, in the middle of the generalized crisis of the 1980s, became the active vanguard of social and political "return to the past."

Some consider Sendero to be a messianic or millenarian movement, rooted in Andean Indian culture. But its leadership has always been made up of *mistis* rooted in the Andean seigniorial system.[5] If they incorporated some form of messianic or religious context, it was not due to Indian traditions but on account of what we could call an "excess of reason." They are the last children of the Enlightenment who, two hundred years later and isolated in the Andes, ended up converting science into religion. Given the degree of passion that Shining Path developed and unleashed, it seems strange to define it as a hyperrationalist movement, at least among the leadership. But for the top leaders of Sendero, Pascal's phrase "The heart has its reasons of which reason knows nothing" should be inverted to say "Reason has its passions of which the heart knows nothing."

The founders of Sendero form part of a long tradition of provincial elites who rose up against a system that concentrates everything in the capital, and who embraced *indigenismo* (glorification of Indian customs and traditions) as a reaction against the *hispanismo* (glorification of Hispanic customs and traditions) of the Lima upper classes. Since the 1920s, but especially since midcentury, such elites in many parts of the country have adopted Marxism, most often combining it with a reevaluation of Andean reality that links them to indigenismo. That is not the case with Sendero, whose official documents ignore the ethnic dimension or reject out of hand Andean cultural reevaluation as folklore or bourgeois manipulation.

In that sense, Sendero is the most coldly analytical of the Marxist ventures that arose in Peru during the 1960s and 1970s. Nevertheless, its vision, one that sought to be absolutely scientific, became exceedingly emotional, offering its members a strong quasi-religious identity. One of its most important documents defines communism as:

> the society of "great harmony," the radical and definitive new society toward which 15 billion years of matter in movement — the part of eternal matter of which we know — is necessarily and irrepressibly heading.... A single, irreplaceable new society, without exploited or exploiters, without oppressed or oppressors, without classes, without state, without parties, without democracy, without arms, without wars.[6]

Sendero's epic, then, is a cosmic one. Its leaders are intellectual warriors in the service of a most exact science that regulates the universe like a limitless cosmic ballet. They must put everything in order according to Marxism-Leninism-Maoism, overcoming or destroying whatever resists its ineluctable laws. As it turns out, according to that science Peruvian society is semifeudal. Maybe Sendero's venture would not have had to generate so much violence had it evolved in China of the 1930s, because in that semifeudal society it would not have found, for example, engineers repairing electric towers, agronomists doing rural extension work, anthropologists advising peasant federations, or foreign volunteers developing health programs. The possibility of assassinating those people would not have come up: They did not exist. The degree of violence is as great as it is, among other reasons, because Sendero has to make reality fit an idea — it must not only stop time but turn it back until the page is once again blank, and on it Sendero can then write the script the party has worked out.

Authoritarianism Reformulated

This is not to imply that there is no point of contact between Peru's reality and Sendero's vision of it. If that were the case, SL could not have been able to build up a base of support. Sendero takes up the population's longstanding desire for progress and focuses it through the lens of Marxism- Leninism-Maoism. But at the same time, it carries to an extreme the authoritarianism of the old provincial *misti* elites — against the grain of the principal trend in the country that is aimed, rather, at breaking *misti* power. A fundamental characteristic of Sendero's activity is disregard for grass-roots organizations: peasant communities, labor unions, neighborhood associations. These are all replaced by generated organisms — that is, by the party that decides everything, just as before everything was decided by the *misti* lords and officials.

The best-known example is the armed strikes that have been announced since 1987 in various localities. These are not called by any union or regional front but by the party or its generated organisms. This contrasts with Sendero's attitude regarding national strikes called by the labor movement. Between 1977 and 1988 nine general strikes took place in Peru. Millions of people took part in the July 1977 and May 1978 strikes, the most important mobilizations in contemporary Peruvian history. Sendero's stance varied between absolute indifference and frontal opposition. In January 1988, for the first time, Sendero decided to back the ninth strike, which turned out to be quite unremarkable. Sendero's participation was limited to very minor actions. They burned tires on the Central Highway and disrupted the rally of the General Workers Confederation in the Plaza de Mayo, shouting slogans and setting off dynamite caps. Nonetheless, on the next day, the headline in *El Diario*, the semiofficial party mouthpiece, read "Historic Day for the Peruvian Proletariat." Obviously it was not a historic day because of the magnitude of the strike, but because the party decided to back it, producing a kind of proletarian Pentecost that marked "a new direction for the working class, nourished for the first time by a more elevated experience of struggle."[7]

The point is that if, "except for power, all is illusion," as a favorite Sendero slogan maintains, then the party, conceived as the central instrument for winning that power is the only reality. Except for the party, everything is an illusion: Society, for example, only acquires reality when the party touches it. Gods of a belligerently monotheistic religion, they do not let anyone else onto their Olympus: They must be the only force that brings order to the rural world. But in Peru, unlike China of the 1930s and despite the growing weakness of the state and of civil society amid the current crisis, those spaces where Sendero would like to be a solitary demiurge are relatively well populated with peasant organizations, unions, left parties, the progressive church, non-governmental development organizations, and the like. Sendero lashes out not only at the state but at these other actors, believing that the PCP-Shining Path should be the only one that relates to those masses, so as then, finally, to "educate them in the people's war."[8]

Sendero's leaders take on the role of traditional authoritarian teachers who believe they possess the truth and, therefore, ought to have the absolute power over their students. That is how the major Sendero documents set forth the party-mass relationship: "people's war is a political exploit that by means of overwhelming actions hammers ideas into the minds of men..."[9] Abimael Guzmán himself stated that

> the masses have to be taught through overwhelming acts so that ideas can be pounded into them...the masses in the nation need the leadership of a Communist party; we hope with more revolutionary theory and practice, with more armed actions, with more people's war, with more power, to reach the very heart of the class and the people and really win them over. Why? In order to serve them — that is what we want.[10]

The language itself displays an impressive degree of willingness to use violence against the masses, who the same paragraph says are to be loved and served. This ambiguous relationship is deeply rooted in the Andean seignorial tradition. The mestizos, who make up the backbone of the party, are a group that has always considered Indians to be inferior and, even when they identified with them sentimentally, called for their liberation from servitude and sought their support to confront Lima's westernized creole elite. Sendero's attitude resembles that of certain *indigenista* intellectuals of the past who expressed the authoritarian, tortuous, violent love of the superior for the inferior, whom they sought to redeem or "protect" from the evils of the modern world. Sendero's behavior could also be compared with that of the traditional teacher in his relationship with a student who is good, but somewhat awkward or rebellious, and has to be shown that, as the Spanish proverb puts it, *La letra entra con sangre* (a more explicitly pedagogical version of "Spare the rod, spoil the child").

Deception, Domination, and Education

Why do such conceptions capture the imagination of certain circles of provincial youth? Often in Peru, in order to explain something, one has to go far back into history; in this case, back to the very beginning, to the conquest and the ambush that took place in November 1532 in Cajamarca. The Spaniards, having arrived on the scene, sent an invitation to the Inca emperor, who, curious to meet them, set out for the encounter. He entered the plaza of Cajamarca surrounded by his warriors, but found only a priest who handed him the Bible and said, "This is the word of God." The Inca raised the book to his ear, heard no word, and disappointed, threw the Bible to the ground. The priest then shouted, "Christians, the word of God is in the dirt!" The conquest was justified. The hidden arquebuses could begin their task.

Thus emerged a society based on deception, a deception made possible, in part, by the monopoly that the rulers exercised over knowledge of the Spanish language. From that time on, the conquered peoples fluctuated between resignation and rebellion. Rebellion, in turn, fluctuated between rejection of the West — Andean culture withdrawing into itself — and appropriation of the conquerors' instruments of domination. Both tendencies are present throughout Peruvian history, but in the twentieth century the latter predominates. Among the instruments of domination Andean people seek to appropriate, one stands out: education. To take away from the *mistis* their monopoly on Spanish, on reading and writing, is equivalent to Prometheus' feat of taking fire from the gods.

As the century advanced, the energy with which Andean peoples launched into the conquest of education was exceptional. According to the United Nations figures on access to education in Latin America, Peru moved from fourteenth place in 1960 to fourth place in 1980.[11] In the seventy-odd countries that the UN considers to be at a "middle level of development," the percentage of eighteen- to twenty-five-year-olds currently studying at the secondary level or higher rose from 17 percent in 1960 to 52 percent in 1980. In Peru it jumped from 19 percent to 76 percent. This stands out even more when compared to other vital statistics, such as infant mortality or life expectancy, in which only Bolivia and Haiti are worse off in Latin America than Peru.

But what are people seeking in education? They are of course looking for practical tools: learning to read and write and do basic arithmetic. But in addition, as children of the deceived, they are looking for truth. Several testimonies gathered in Ayacucho in 1969, immediately after the movement on behalf of free education, were highly revealing.[12] A peasant leader, asked about the situation of people from his region, answered, "They need to be instructed, they need someone to give them orientation, they need courses...to see if in that way they can move forward, get out of slavery, free themselves from deception. Otherwise they will continue to be poor and exploited."

Being educated, in short, is the equivalent of gaining freedom from deception. Another leader said about the University of Huamanga: "The university is waking us up, we are learning something new, something objective, which [the powerful] do not like; it doesn't suit them at all because they want us to remain deceived." Opposed to that deception would be the objective truth, to which one would gain access through education. Traditional authority, based not only on its monopoly of the means of production but also on its monopoly and manipulation of knowledge, crumbles when the dominated break up both monopolies.

But even if education has democratizing effects visible on the social level, the same does not necessarily occur on the political or cultural plane. According to the first leader just quoted, "the peasant needs to be instructed, needs someone" — implicitly from the outside — "to give him orientation." The old hierarchical order is translated here into the relationship of teacher (urban, mestizo) to student (peasant, Indian). Mass education can come about, there-fore, without substantially breaking up the authoritarianism of traditional society. The same peasant went on to say "Our highest aspiration is for the progress of rural people; that their collaborators, or rather their guides, orient them toward achieving progress — in my view, by avoiding the vices that peasants have: drinking, coca, cigarettes."

If there is a need for a guide from the outside, there is no reason to be surprised at the appearance of a *caudillo* teacher such as the one who heads Sendero. The moralizing nature of SL and its punishment of adulterers and drinkers also fits the bill. Nor is there anything surprising about the rise in popularity of the most hard-line Marxist-Leninist tendencies in the nation's universities during the 1970s. It was the children of the deceived — young people of Andean origin from the provinces — who entered the university en masse at that time. There they met up with a simplified and accessible version of a theory that defined itself as the only scientific truth and was legitimized through references to the Marxist classics — the true authorities. That science proposed a new but strictly hierarchical order where the students, upon acceding to the party and its truth, could move from the base to the peak of the social pyramid.

Conclusion

Thus, at root the revolution is perceived by Sendero militants as a means of social mobility. One participant told me: "They said, look, it's 1981. By 1985 Ayacucho will be a liberated zone; by 1990 Peru will be an independent country. Wouldn't you like to be a minister? Wouldn't you like to be a military chief? Be something?...In 1985 the revolution is going to triumph, and those of us who have been in the party the longest will be the bosses."[13]

This great need for order and progress in a context that is still traditional points to one of the roots of Shining Path's quasi-religious scientism, according to which "the ideology of the proletariat...is scientific, exact, all-powerful" or, as its official documents say, "all-powerful because it is true."[14] It also points to one of the roots of the personality cult and the hallowing of "Gonzalo Thought" (Guzmán's guerrilla alias is Presidente Gonzalo): The leader-teacher is education incarnate and, therefore, truth incarnate, virtue incarnate. No other group in the Marxist tradition has placed such emphasis on the intellectual status of its leader. On Sendero's posters Guzmán occupies the center, dressed in a suit, wearing glasses, book in hand, surrounded by masses carrying rifles and flags, with the great red sun setting behind him.

The "Andean Maoism" of Shining Path is a hybrid, woven from Maoist authoritarianism and the most authoritarian aspects of Peruvian political tradition. This philosophy resonated in the mountains of Ayacucho, but as Sendero moved into the rest of the nation, it has been obliged to exercise growing violence against a people that dares to go beyond the designs of the party and travel its own road to liberation, refusing to be a blank page and, instead, entering into history with all its complexity — and its ambiguity.

THE CENTER'S MULTIPLE FAILURES[*]

Ton de Wit and Vera Gianotten

In April 1977 we were guests at a party in Ayacucho. All of a sudden people started to sing the Shining Path (SL or Sendero) hymn. Of course we knew that the people present included leading Sendero activists, but the song was not intended as a threat or a serious provocation. The Cultural Revolution of China was still a serious issue, and so the fact that these people were ideological followers of Mao and the Cultural Revolution was nothing special. What was curious about Sendero was its call for an armed struggle; but nobody in those days believed SL was really serious about that, including us.

Before 1980 it was also quite normal to make jokes with Sendero students, asking them why they were studying at the university when, according to their party, the only solution to underdevelopment was a war starting in the countryside and spreading to the cities. SL was considered by everyone to be one of the quainter features of Ayacucho and its university. The national political parties viewed Sendero in much the same fashion. They laughed at Sendero's analyses, that Peruvian society was semifeudal and that the armed struggle was at hand. Other Marxist party militants at the University of San Cristóbal de Huamanga in Ayacucho argued that neither objective conditions

---

[*]Derived in large part from the authors' experiences in Ayacucho between 1977 and 1983 while workng on a rural development program sponsored by the Dutch government.

nor radical popular movements were sufficiently developed. The peasants who invaded some of the large state farms and other cooperative production units recently established by the reformist military government (1968-1980) were seen as new popular movements with restricted goals. Once they obtained land, the peasants demobilized.[15]

The military regime's land reform had definitively removed the landlords' traditional source of power and influence. However, the military government was not willing to give political power to the peasants in the highlands, to the workers of the modern agricultural cooperatives on the coast, or to the industrial workers in the cities. This was the case even though a new government agency created by the military, the National Social Mobilization Support System (SINAMOS), was ostensibly designed to help empower local groups within the cooperatives and other organizations set up by its reforms. Once people tried to claim real power, SINAMOS become an apparatus for control from the center and was strenuously opposed.[16]

Shining Path was working hard in this climate of change and efforts to expand control from the center. Sendero militants argued that agrarian reform did not change the socioeconomic and political structure of the country. In their view, Peru was still a semifeudal society. Antonio Díaz Martínez, then a professor of agricultural economics at the university, Sendero's second-ranked man until his death in the 1986 prison riots, began a study in Cusco in 1980, financed by the Ministry of Nutrition, to prove this thesis. At the university, Sendero professors had encouraged students to write their theses on the power structures of peasant (i.e., Indian) communities in areas potentially appropriate for starting the armed struggle. The analyses of the class structures of these communities were always the same: rural bourgeoisie, rich peasants, middle-income and poor peasants. In 1980 we arrived at a community shortly after Shining Path had visited. According to the peasants, Sendero had explained that the armed struggle was about to start and that they — the peasants — had to invade the private estates. To the peasants, however, this made no sense, as no big landowners lived in or near the community. An old woman asked us: "Does Sendero want us to invade the garden plot of our neighbor?"!

Although control of the university between 1968 and 1975 had been highly useful to Shining Path, once they lost the university elections they did not make any major effort to win back their influence. In the second half of the 1970s,

Sendero concentrated its work in rural areas, particularly through the formal education system. Sendero militants who worked as rural teachers surveyed their communities for their party. They also labored very conscientiously in local schools to raise the class consciousness of their young charges. Accompanied by their teacher with his guitar, we have heard young primary school children singing in Quechua: "The right? no no no; the left? no no no; the armed struggle? yes yes yes!" Few national government authorities paid any serious attention to this work of Sendero even though it constituted SL's main effort at that time. The party leadership received precise and detailed information on the area's geographic and topographic reality, the internal structure of the communities, the aims of the peasants, and, above all, the local power and authority networks whose key figures were to be removed or co-opted once the armed struggle began.

In some communities, Shining Path took power even before 1980. Huancasancos in the remote Ayacucho province of Víctor Fajardo was one example. Its secondary schoolteachers succeeded in forcing out the central government's police forces in 1979. These teachers, University of Huamanga Education Program graduates, were assigned to Huancasancos and other distant places by the military government as punishment for their participation in the teachers' strikes of 1977 and 1978. Once in communities far away from effective political and state control, these teachers worked diligently to fill the power vacuum, and often succeeded in influencing local events. Getting community members sufficiently agitated to force out the police was a highly significant action toward establishing Sendero control in advance of the formal initiation of the armed struggle in April 1980.

From the perspective of Shining Path's leadership, methods of indoctrination were perfectly clear. There was only one course of action to be followed; that of the armed struggle. Political debates with outside parties and groups stopped in 1980 and have not played any major role since then. However, inside Sendero's party structure debates did arise. The first major discussion came about in 1983, when high-ranking party members insisted on the need for political work alongside armed actions. In this case, as well as in others before 1988, when party members stressed the need for political action they were forced out of the party and sometimes even threatened with death.

After years of armed struggle, terror, and "dirty war" in Peru, Shining Path's significance is no longer underestimated, even though the phenomenon is still not well understood. We will now turn to our own explanation for the rise and expansion of Sendero, an explanation that focuses on regional context, sociological mores, the gulf between center and periphery, and the limits of national government.

Regional Context

Ayacucho's poverty provided fertile soil for the growth of Shining Path; it is one of the three poorest departments (states) of Peru.[17] But poverty is not the only factor involved. Another is the longstanding conflict at the grass roots among the hundreds of Indian communities that dominate the area, communities of distinctive backgrounds, heritage, and origins.[18] Most are the product of the defeat of the Chanka Confederation, which had joined the early Wanka, Pokra, and Chanka residents of Ayacucho, at the hands of the expanding Inca empire in the early 1400s. The vanquished groups were transported to other areas by the Incas, and the Ayacucho region was then repopulated by ethnic groups from other parts of the empire. This produced a profound trauma of cultural dislocation that has yet to be resolved, as well as the origin of continuing conflicts between the different communities.[19] Peasants still make reference to territorial disputes that started in those days.

Sociocultural Mores

To defend their cultural identity and their new territory, the various ethnic groups, later organized into communities, closed themselves off from the wider society and started a struggle to define the frontiers of their community vis-à-vis their neighbors. Far from resolving these conflicts, almost three hundred years of Spanish colonial rule, intensified them by arbitrary resettlement of its own as well as by arbitrary distribution of documents relating to landownership. Since independence in 1824, communities have continued to fight over the boundaries of their communal land. In most cases, the disputes concern infertile areas above 4,000 meters or 13,124 feet. These cannot be cultivated but can only be used for grazing on the thin pasture grasses.

So the economic value of the land was not at issue; rather it was the defense of their cultural identities that caused the communities to reopen hostilities continually. These conflicts did contribute over time to the development of strong communal organization within individual communities. Because most peasants of the region saw the neighboring community rather than regional or national power elites as their primary enemy, a wider organization of the peasant population never emerged. For this reason, peasant unions and the traditional political parties have generally been of little importance in the region. Furthermore, the low fertility of the land made the area unattractive to colonial landlords, so no significant agrarian oligarchy ever developed in Ayacucho either. Most of Ayacucho's urban population works in the service sector, followed by trade and small cottage industries. There is no urban industrial proletariat. The few unions are confined to civil servants in the ministries, municipal service workers, university lecturers, and bank employees.

When Shining Path initiated the People's War in 1980, its knowledge of the area and the people enabled it to expand quickly. Sendero forced the local community leaders to resign by threatening their lives; some peasant leaders were killed if they were not willing to quit. Neither the leaders nor the communities themselves received central government protection, political or military, and the communities were further handicapped by their lack of ties to each other. When Sendero started to act against the police, the central government personnel often saw the communities and their leaders as the culprits, since there were some who identified with Sendero. For example, in March 1983 Juan Cisneros, a peasant leader from Pampa Cangallo, a small farming and market community about three hours' drive from the city of Ayacucho, was arrested by police and accused of belonging to Sendero. The police held him for a couple of weeks but set him free after the community protested. A month later he was killed by a Shining Path annihilation squad, which left a note on his body proclaiming "This is what happens to the collaborators of imperialism!" This case illustrates the impossible situation in which many communities of rural Ayacucho found themselves. Communities were attacked and citizens massacred by Sendero, which accused the population of supporting the government. And conversely, the police and armed forced committed similar atrocities, accusing the population of supporting Sendero.

Center-Periphery Gulf

It is certainly clear that Shining Path started the vicious circle of violence, but it is equally clear that neither the central government nor the national political parties responded properly. The first armed action by Sendero took place in 1980; at the end of 1982 a state of emergency was declared in and around Ayacucho and the region was put under military rule. Not until 1985, after Alán García and the American Popular Revolutionary Alliance (APRA) party came to power, did the government make substantial new resources available for social and economic development in Ayacucho. Peru's left, mostly Marxist parties, also had great problems in dealing with the Sendero phenomenon. It was very difficult for left intellectuals and party militants to condemn the movement because of their ideological affinity. They opposed Sendero's means, not its ends, and focused more on military and police excesses than on Sendero atrocities. Sendero and the left parties share a number of political principles, such as Lenin's idea of the vanguard party. However, these parties did not place sufficient emphasis on the future society to which Sendero aspires. When they realize that Sendero's goal is a new society based on terror and repression they will begin to understand something of Sendero's logic, and thus be able to condemn and oppose it.[20] As in the case of the Khmer Rouge of Kampuchea, Peruvian intellectuals and political parties of the left did not want to believe that Sendero committed the reported atrocities.[21] They believed that the government was distorting and manipulating the news, and criticized it repeatedly. They did not ask the peasants what they thought of Sendero.

Peru's centralized polity makes it even more difficult for parties to take seriously anything that is happening outside Lima. Local party activists often find themselves isolated in their efforts to oppose Sendero. Even after over ten years of violence and terror in the provinces, no political party has yet to make any major effort to strengthen its presence in the departments that are suffering most from the conflict. The problem is discussed incessantly in the capital, but local representatives continue to govern with little political or economic support from the center. One of many examples is the movement for peace that some local representatives of left parties undertook with initial success in 1988; it was easily overthrown by Sendero, using threats and murder, because those starting the movement did not get the necessary backing from their compatriots in Lima. Furthermore, news of the mass demonstrations attended by the majority of Ayacucho's inhabitants did not even appear in the Lima newspapers.

Sendero's Attraction

Young people, both rural and urban, often believe that they totally lack social and economic mobility and political influence. In addition, much of the lower-middle-class population of Ayacucho, which actively supported the reopening of the university in 1959, feels the same frustration. A deficient infrastructure, permanent shortage of drinking water, limited production of energy, and inadequate means of communication perpetuate indefinitely the already limited possibilities. One example is that for more than a century Ayacucho's senators and representatives to the national congress have promised to get the central government to invest in a project to bring adequate water to the city and its environs, but they have never succeeded. This and other failures by Lima to respond to Ayacucho's needs have sharpened regionalism and a wariness of outsiders.

The frustration has been strongest among the lower middle class, the same class that in the 1970s provided the bulk of Sendero's recruits, particularly at the university among students, professors, and administrative staff from Ayacucho and its provinces. The university became a center of regionalism as well. Both Sendero's ideology and Ayacucho's strong provincial perspective were increasingly in conflict with those of people from outside the area. Adding to the frustration is the failure of education to provide the expected social mobility. While both adults and young people obtain a certain local status simply by completing their education at the University of Huamanga despite all sorts of hardships and financial problems, they have great difficulty in securing a secure career position and national status. At the university's Education Program, from which most Sendero militants were recruited, the situation can be observed in its extreme form. Many students come from poor peasant families and hope that, once graduated as teachers, they can move beyond the social and economic situation of their parents.

However, the only job that turns out to be available, and badly paid at that, is schoolteacher, often in the very village they came from. Thus they must go back to the same poverty from which they had hoped to escape by means of their university education.[21] It should not be too surprising that this first generation of educated sons and daughters of the peasantry would be both susceptible to recruitment by Sendero and extremely ambivalent about their relationship with this same peasantry they thought they were leaving behind.

Many were especially attracted to Lenin's concept of the vanguard party, which ascribed a leading role to the "intellectuals." The vanguard party

> serves to transmit the socialist theory created by intellectuals to the proletariat, serving as an organizational instrument through which ideological influence over the proletariat could be exerted....With its correct theoretical consciousness it embodies the proletarian consciousness irrespective of what the empirical proletariat may think. The party's interest is automatically the interest of the proletariat and of universal progress. This entitles it to ignore the actual wishes and aspirations of the people it has appointed itself to represent....Here lies the legitimization of the use of violence by the party to achieve these ends, even against the real proletariat, if need be.[23]

After starting armed actions, Sendero was greatly encouraged by the weakness of local administration. Before March 1982, no citizens of the city of Ayacucho had been chosen as victims of armed operations. Sendero carried out few military actions in the town, while the police arbitrarily arrested and even tortured many residents. In this context support for Sendero grew quickly. The movement fired the imagination of the youth and succeeded in recruiting many militants from the town's school population. By 1982 many local citizens had lost all faith in government promises.

The situation was different in rural areas, however. Peasants initially viewed Sendero in a positive light as long as its actions were not aimed at peasant leaders and at the community organization. Once peasants became victims of Sendero terror, passive resistance began. In the second half of 1982 we observed that peasants in some areas that had suffered the most from Sendero were planning violent opposition. This atmosphere of resistance by the peasants was exploited by the armed forces. In January 1983 they began to encourage the peasants to oppose the movement more actively.[24]

This atmosphere of peasant resistance to Sendero did not exist in the city of Ayacucho itself. Here many inhabitants supported SL's selective assassination of citizens because only "bad" people were killed. There also was a general lack of knowledge and interest among the urban population about what was going on in the Ayacucho hinterland. City dwellers tended to have a generally positive view of Sendero based on a number of dramatic actions taken against authorities that embarrassed and even humiliated central government. They preferred to downplay the reported atrocities committed by Sendero against the rural population.

Explanations for the Center's Ineffective Response

When military and police authorities of the central government used repression in retaliation, they had very little success against the Sendero organization. Thus it appears that intelligence services also downplayed the Shining Path phenomenon during the early years of its existence. Until 1982 many Sendero leaders were publicly seen in Ayacucho, and everyone knew who its followers were. In a provincial town like Ayacucho, small talk makes people aware of everything, whether they want to be informed or not. How then could the intelligence services not have been aware, or, if they did have good information, then why were they so unsuccessful and so disrespectful of local citizens' human rights?

Part of the answer may be found in the heterogeneity of Peruvian society and the racism that accompanies it.[25] Racism can be observed in a wide variety of situations. Society is split into three major groups: Caucasian, mestizo, and Indian. There are only a few settings, such as sports, music, and dance, in which they understand each other and communicate. Such a lack of communication based on race is also translated into the educational system, the workplace, and social settings, and it greatly affects social and economic mobility. Caucasians are concentrated in the wealthier parts of Lima and in some provincial capitals; mestizos in lower-class and slum areas; and Indians in the slums and the rural Andes and Amazon. Because of the de facto racial separation by residence and occupation, the groups are only marginally involved with each other and do not have a sense of belonging to the same nation. Thus when Sendero became active in the overwhelmingly Indian Andean communities of rural Ayacucho, the mestizo and Caucasian inhabitants of the cities took little interest; they saw the conflict in terms of Indians confronting other Indians. It was not until Sendero directly attacked intellectuals, leftist politicians, and nongovernmental organizations that most Peruvians began to recognize its tactics. Even though peasants were violently massacred from 1982 onward, such events were downplayed, attributed to the police or armed forces, or simply disregarded.

Ignoring Shining Path was possible, therefore, because of Peru's lack of integration in economic, social, cultural, and political terms, which expresses itself territorially as well. This factor facilitated Sendero's operation, since it knows the Andean countryside far better than any other group or institution in Peruvian society. Only when Shining Path's activities became more violent and more generalized did most Peruvians become interested in the phenomenon. However, no one knew how to explain it. Poverty was advanced as one explanation; others included Indians' lack of education, which made them susceptible to Sendero's appeal, or foreign support and alien ideologies intended to destabilize Peruvian society. There were even analyses published presenting Sendero as a Central Intelligence Agency (CIA) ploy to gain control over the country![26]

From the perspective of Indian peasants, early Shining Path assassinations in their communities were interpreted as removing "bad people" from their midst and were often supported. The assassinations of cattle thieves in different communities in the Ayacucho region in 1981 and 1982, for example, gave a certain legitimacy to Sendero. Andean communities consider stealing cattle to be one of the worst possible crimes. During our investigation of community archives, we found that a community we studied had been trying since 1936 to get government protection from cattle thieves. When their repeated requests evoked no response, the community took matters into its own hands. It declared in 1976 that the community itself would take responsibility for trying and executing any cattle thief it captured and subsequently did so. When Sendero began to administer the same kind of justice to similar undesirables, communities affected immediately accepted its actions.

Similarly, the first assassinations in the city of Ayacucho also found a certain acceptance, because in most cases the victims were alleged to have been involved in cocaine dealing. In those cases where a Shining Path killing caused resentment among the population, Sendero would defend its action by asserting that the person was tied in with drugs or the CIA. In December 1982, for example, when SL killed Ayacucho native Walter Wong, director of the

Ayacucho Art School and Museum, Sendero asserted that he had been in regular direct radio contact with the CIA. Sendero continued with its terror in Ayacucho city for some time without causing any major protest, and the armed forces responded in kind: indiscriminate murder, disappearances, and mass graves, among other unspeakable actions. Even so, many city dwellers pretended for some time that a problem did not exist. This action and response can be understood only in a context where the formal legal system is not functioning and where the government's use of violence is not under democratic, civilian control.

Conclusion

The underlying context for Peru's violence is a weak civil society and a weak state — a society made up of disarticulated groups that are seldom mutually involved and a state unable to process effectively and respond appropriately to the demands of its population. Given this context, state coercion is the mechanism often used to maintain order and putative national unity. Unfortunately, the state has usually viewed a solution to the problem of Shining Path exclusively in military terms. True, without military action, the problem of Sendero cannot be solved; Sendero's organization and activities make a military response an essential part of any definitive resolution. But a key component of any solution must also include creative proposals for building a civil society that gives content to human rights in the broadest sense without differentiation by race.

The results of the 1990 national elections have shown that the Peruvian population is not willing to define social change according to Shining Path's perspective. These elections dramatically demonstrated Sendero's limited political success after ten years of armed struggle. The voters most responsible for the big surprise in the first electoral round, a 25 percent second-place showing for the unknown Alberto Fujimori, were young people living in the slum areas of Lima and in the emergency zones in the countryside. By and large, these are people who for the past five to ten years have tried to survive in a situation of growing social turmoil, economic erosion, political irresponsibility, and militarization. By voting for Fujimori they demonstrated simultaneously both their lack of confidence in established Peruvian institutions and their distrust of any radical alternative. The second-round absolute majority garnered by Fujimori simply reconfirmed these concerns. Even so, comments by intellectuals and political parties after the elections showed once again the lack of a perception of Peru as a nation; once again they tried to explain the outcome as proof of the political underdevelopment of the poor. In their view, poor people were still looking for a myth. Nobody analyzed the results of the elections as a protest by the poor majority who are tired of being neglected and who demand full citizenship, proper incomes, and security and protection from a democratic state and civil society.

Notes

1. Between 1967 and 1981, out-migration from Ayacucho fluctuated between the second and third highest among Peru's departments, with a net annual average migration rate between eight and fourteen per thousand inhabitants. Instituto Nacional de Estadística (INE), *Las migraciones internas en el Perú* (Lima: INE, 1987).

2. "Bases de discusión: El PCP llama a las masas a luchar por el poder: El pensamiento Gonzalo y los trabajadores," *El Diario*, Lima, special supplement, August 1, 1988.

3. Norberto Bobbio, *El futuro de la democracia* (Mexico City: Fondo de Cultura Económica, 1986).

4. "Bases de discusión."

5. *Mistis* are the mestizos who live in middle-size and small towns of the Andes. They traditionally made up part of the local elites who oppressed the indigenous campesinos. They are the equivalent of those who are called *ladinos* in southern Mexico and Guatemala.

6. Partido Comunista del Perú-Sendero Luminoso, "Desarrollar la guerra popular sirviendo a la revolución mundial," mimeo, 1986.

7. *El Diario*, January 28, 29, and 30, 1988.

8. "Bases de discusión."

9. *Ibid.*

10. Luis Arce Borja and Janet Talavera Sánchez, "Presidente Gonzalo rompe el silencio: Entrevista en la clandestinidad," *El Diario*, July 24, 1988. pp. 2-47.

11. Economic Commission on Latin America (ECLA), *Statistical Yearbook for Latin America: 1984* (New York: United Nations, 1985).

12. The testimonies are taken from Aracelio Castillo, "El movimiento popular de junio de 1969, Huanta y Huamanga, Ayacucho," Ph.D. dissertation, University of San Marcos, Lima, 1972.

13. Author's interview.

14. Partido Comunista del Perú-Sendero Luminoso, "Documentos fundamentales del Primer Congreso del Partido Comunista del Perú (Congreso Marxista-Leninista-Maoista, pensamiento Gonzalo)," *El Diario*, January 8, 1988.

15. Diego García Sayán, *Toma de tierras en el Perú* (Lima: DESCO, 1982).

16. Sandra Woy-Hazelton, "Infrastructure of Participation in Peru: SINAMOS," in John A. Booth and Mitchell A. Seligson, eds., *Political Participation in Latin America, Volume I: Citizen and State* (New York: Holmes and Meier, 1978), pp. 189-208.

17. See Vera Gianotten, Ton de Wit, and Hans de Wit, "The Impact of Sendero Luminoso on Regional and National Politics in Peru," in David Slater, ed., *New Social Movements and the State in Latin America* (Amsterdam: CEDLA, 1985), pp. 171-202, for an early interpretation.

18. Indian or peasant communities make up a larger portion of the total land area in Ayacucho than in any other department of Peru. The application of the agrarian reform (1969-1975) provoked a sharp escalation in intercommunity conflict, often based on these age-old grievances, due in part to the resulting change in local power relationships and in part to the extremely limited land available for redistribution. See David Scott Palmer, *"Revolution from Above": Military Government and Popular Participation in Peru, 1968-1972*, Dissertation series #47 (Ithaca, NY: Latin American Studies Program, Cornell University, 1973), pp. 196-199.

19. Carlos Iván Degregori, "Ayacucho, la guerra ha comenzado," *El Diario*, January 13, 1983, pp. 11-12.

20. Partido Comunista del Perú, *Desarrollemos la Guerra de Guerrillas* (Lima: Ediciones Bandera Roja, 1982), and "La entrevista del siglo: Presidente Gonzalo rompe el silencio," *El Diario*, July 24, 1988, pp. 2-47.

21. R. A. Burgler, *The Eyes of the Pineapple: Revolutionary Intellectuals and Terror in Democratic Kampuchea* (Saarbrucken: Breitenback Verlay, 1990).

22. The regional office of the Ministry of Education was in charge of assigning teachers. If you did not have money for bribes, it was virtually impossible to get a job in the city of Ayacucho and you were sent to the countryside instead.

23. Burgler, *Revolutionary Intellectuals*, pp. 185-186.

24. President Fernando Belaúnde Terry (1980-1985) also encouraged the peasants to administer justice. In a public speech in 1982 he said that the peasants who had killed a group of Sendero militants had given the country an example of good citizenship. He applauded them for having taken justice into their own hands.

25. José María Arguedas, *El zorro de arriba y el zorro de abajo* (Lima: Editorial Horizonte, 1983); Alberto Flores Galindo, *Buscando un Inca: Identidad y utopia en los Andes* (Lima: Instituto de Apoyo Agrario, 1987).

26. Andreo Matías, *C.I.A., Sendero Luminoso: Guerra política* (Lima: El Universo Gráfico, 1988).

4

SHINING PATH AND PEASANT RESPONSES IN RURAL AYACUCHO

Billie Jean Isbell

Since Shining Path's declaration of a "prolonged people's war" in 1980, one of the most frequently asked questions has been "Does Shining Path have peasant support?" McClintock's assessment in 1984 was encapsulated in the title of her article: "When Peasants Rebel." In contrast, however, Carlos Iván Degregori cautions against such a generalization.[1] During his address to the 1988 Latin American Studies Association (LASA) meeting in New Orleans, Degregori stated that what is really surprising is that Sendero has not been more successful in receiving peasant support. I am going to address that issue by analyzing the local history of a locality that has been the focus of Shining Path (Sendero or SL) activities since the mid-1970s: the Rio Pampas region of the province of Cangallo in the department of Ayacucho, Peru. This analysis is based on my own research in Chuschi, which began in 1967 in the Rio Pampas and continued until 1975. I returned to Peru in 1986 and conducted interviews with a wide range of people in order to reconstruct a history of the events since 1975. I was able to interview people from the Rio Pampas and other areas of Ayacucho who had fled to Lima to escape the violence that has caused some 120,000 people to flee the countryside. I was unable to travel to

Chuschi, as it was located in the epicenter of the Ayacucho Emergency Zone (EMZ). Nevertheless, a number of interviews in the communities of the Rio Pampas were conducted by Peruvian colleagues and the materials were shared with me.

Chuschi is the capital of a district in the Rio Pampas valley that had a total population in 1975 of about 6,500 inhabitants and is connected by a one-lane dirt road to the provincial capital of Cangallo. The district covers an upper region of the river valley that is narrow and steep, unlike the broader part of the valley near Cangallo, where small haciendas developed. Haciendas did not develop in Chuschi's marginal land with its immense expanse of high puna communal pastures. The closest hacienda (prior to the 1969 agrarian reform) was fifteen kilometers or nine miles away in the province of Huamanga. In addition, the communities in the district of Chuschi did not participate to any great extent in the market economy. I believe that Sendero chose Chuschi for its initial military operations precisely because of this absence of haciendas, which allowed SL to experiment with peasant communities that had strong communal structures, autonomy over their resources, and whose experiences with capitalistic market penetrations were minimal. By initiating their revolution in what they believed to be a region that had escaped many of the semifeudal relationships of the hacienda system, Sendero perhaps hoped to avoid the mistakes made by the guerrillas inspired by the Cuban revolution who failed to gain the support of hacienda peons for their short-lived insurgency in 1965.[2] It is likely that Sendero viewed these communities as already having the communal structures like those it would establish in the New Peru after the revolution.

In the 1970s, other regions experienced rapid commercial expansion in the space left by the exit of the *hacendados* (large landowners) after the military government's agrarian reform (1969-1975). Chuschi, without a landed class, experienced only a minor growth of petty merchants. For example, only five families took advantage of the new commercial opportunities offered by the reforms: a young mestizo couple from Cangallo opened a store; a family that had lived in the village for four generations but who, nevertheless, were considered foreign, farmed commercially and also established a small store; and finally, three migrants, former community members, attempted to change their ethnic and class identities by returning to their village of origin as petty merchants. Notably, however, the migrants' wives retained two significant ethnic markers, traditional dress and monolingualism.

Even though it was a very small change in Chuschi, the emergence of this new rural class of "rich peasants" was signaled in 1969 by Díaz Martínez in *Ayacucho: Hambre y esperanza,* and his prophetic words are echoed in Montoya's 1980 analysis of the military's agrarian reform.[3] Montoya concludes that a new class of petty merchants moved into the space created by the rural changes initiated from the center. Harding has published a fascinating analysis of Díaz Martínez's role in shaping Sendero strategies and ideology.[4] Díaz Martínez, a well-trained agronomist turned revolutionary, concluded that state and international development efforts in Ayacucho during the 1960s had failed. In 1969 he advocated total transformation of Peru's semicolonial and semifeudal structures. According to Harding, Díaz Martínez traveled to China in 1974 and found that many of his proposed programs and reforms (which had been rejected by the Peruvian state in favor of foreign development programs) were being carried out successfully by Mao.[5] Upon his return to Peru in 1977, he wrote *China: La revolución agraria,* which provides the language and ideology for Sendero's declaration of a prolonged peasant war to liberate the semifeudal and semicolonial masses of Peru from bureaucratic capitalism. Díaz Martínez laid the foundation for the pragmatic preparation of the insurgency throughout the mid-1970s by organizing popular schools and setting up structures in the Ayacucho countryside to win the confidence of the peasants.[6]

Initial Peasant Support

The most significant factor leading to initial peasant support was that, at the beginning of Shining Path's insurgency, peasants in Chuschi were in favor not only of the popular schools and the moralization campaigns, but also of Sendero's program of eradication of "public enemies." In Chuschi, the first enemies to be executed (in 1981) were cattle thieves from the village's traditional enemy, the neighboring village of Quispillaqta. The identification of appropriate enemies meant that SL's information network was highly efficient. However, Sendero quickly exceeded the shared definitions of enemies and met with resistance when its cadres attempted to assassinate people whose infractions were deemed minor. With the declaration of the first

EMZ in the Ayacucho area and the beginning of military intervention in 1983, large parts of the Rio Pampas became so opposed to Sendero that Chuschi requested the establishment of a Civil Guard (national police) post.

However, Shining Path's early success must be seen within the historical context of a region of the southern Andes that has experienced centuries of rebellions and insurgencies.[7] Moreover, Andean peasants were essential to the national resistance movement during the War of the Pacific (1879-1883), especially when Chilean troops occupied Peru from 1882 to 1883. According to Mallon, landowners would not join the peasants and instead collaborated with the Chilean forces.[8] The major nationalist peasant movements took place between the Mantaro and Ayacucho valleys. Twenty years of class conflict followed the war. Therefore, the peasants of this region have a long history of nationalism and distrust of the landed class, the church, and the military. Thus, it is no surprise to find that various types of conflict between peasants and landowners, clashes with the military, and battles with the church have become annual representations in village festivals throughout the southern Andes.[9]

Class conflict is kept alive in annual enactments and reinterpretations of history. Each community represents its critical historical conflicts in ritual. For example, in Chuschi during annual celebrations, dancers represent a historical event that is said to have taken place twenty or thirty years ago in which a village priest and Civil Guard captain shot into the market crowd during a drunken birthday party for the priest. The villagers attacked the parish house and captured the priest and members of the Civil Guard. According to oral tradition, they were marched barefoot, with their hands bound behind their backs, 120 kilometers or 75 miles to the departmental capital and turned over to the prefect. The priest and the captain became immortalized as vile but comical characters in a parody that was an integral part of an annual fertility ritual that initiated the agricultural cycle. The villagers of Chuschi immortalized their representation of this historical conflict year after year and thereby created stereotypes of enemies that were later utilized cleverly by Sendero. Another historical conflict that has become a part of ritualized representations of history is the great peasant rebellion over an attempt to impose a tax on salt in 1890 in the Ayacucho provincial capital of Huanta.[10]

In Ayacucho, peasant mobilizations against landowners continued into this century. Peruvian anthropologist and archeologist Luis Lumbreras describes the conditions that existed in Ayacucho in his youth.[11] He states that the peasant takeover of the giant hacienda, Pomacocha, which covered parts of three provinces along the lower Rio Pampas, signaled a hopeful end to the feudal era in Ayacucho. But by the mid 1970s, when Shining Path was forming as a political reality in the University of Huamanga, the end had still not arrived and the times were marked by increasingly belligerent peasant actions. The *hacendados* were gone but the same relations of exploitation were reproduced by the new class of rich peasants, the new state bureaucrats who replaced the old officials, and on ex-haciendas by the administrators of the new state cooperatives.

For example, during the first part of the 1970s as I began my second field work in Chuschi, three major confrontations occurred in the span of three years: (1) with the church, (2) with a retired Civil Guard sergeant whose land bordered on Chuschi's herding lands, and finally (3) with Chuschi migrants who attempted to form a cooperative with encouragement from the National Social Mobilization Support System (SINAMOS) coordinating office in Ayacucho. The *cofradía* holdings of the church were confiscated and the priest was expelled in 1972; the church has not functioned since with a resident priest. In that same year, some two hundred horsemen from Chuschi invaded the retired sergeant's lands and destroyed his crops by driving communal herds onto the fields. The community members claimed that he was a *hacendado* who had been encroaching on their communal herding lands for twenty years. The retired sergeant, on the other hand, claimed that the villagers were greedy capitalists trying to take over his small holding. The rhetoric of the agrarian reform had taken a peculiar turn.

The community leaders demanded that the agrarian reform judge survey their boundaries. He did so with the aid of copies of pages from the *visita* of 1593 that had established the original boundaries of the community. I was asked to videotape the proceedings, which I did in spite of a great deal of initial reluctance from SINAMOS. In 1975 migrants from Lima attempted to establish a cooperative from the confiscated church *cofradía* holdings: 150 head of beef cattle, 1,500 sheep, and 13 of the best and largest corn fields in the area. Resounding opposition from the community prevented its formation. The argument that won the debate in the public assemblies was that if a cooperative was established, the community would lose control over its resources. Time has shown that the Chuschi peasants were correct. The cooperatives established under the agrarian reform left peasant communities at the mercy of state administrators.

Chuschi and the surrounding communities in the district controlled a large territory; during the 1970s, they struggled to retain control over their lands, or fought among themselves over boundaries. Nevertheless, a new class of merchants did appear during this period that took advantage of the new commercial opportunities promoted by governmental development and reform programs. In addition, these merchants were often disproportionately represented among the new array of officials accompanying the agrarian reform. During this period, tensions increased between the Indians and mestizos, part of the process of heightened ethnic and class distinctions as people climbed the social and economic ladder and carved out new identities. As bureaucrats took advantage of their new managerial positions, an upsurge in distrust for state representatives also occurred.[12]

In the 1980s the already severely impoverished department of Ayacucho was hit hard by the most serious national economic crisis in a century. Wages fell, inflation rates spiraled, and 60 percent or more of the nation's industrial capacity was idled. Therefore, the traditional escape route for peasants as urban wage laborers was closed. In addition, peasants suffered a crisis of subsistence in the countryside; potato production in the southern Andes fell by 40 to 50 percent.[13] This crisis followed years of rising peasant expectations in response to the promises of government reforms. Nevertheless, the state continued to be unresponsive.[14]

It was also Ayacucho's misfortune to be a center of the guerrilla war during the 1980s. The villages of the Rio Pampas went through a cycle of abandonment after major violence often involving attacks from both sides, repression resulting in "disappearances," conflicts between villages and organized civil patrols, followed by slow repopulation. These communities and others of the south-central Andes became lands of the aged and the very young, while cities coped with the influx of the eighteen- to twenty-four-year-olds who became part of the so-called informal sector. They were caught in the middle of a protracted war not of their making, as well as in the contradictions of their own historical processes.

Events in the Rio Pampas Valley — 1980-1986

On May 17, 1980, four masked students from the University of Huamanga successfully entered the town hall of the village of Chuschi, seized the ballots being stored for the national elections, and burned them. The students were armed with two nonfunctioning pistols. New ballots were delivered the next day, and the elections proceeded without incident. This was the first public action by Shining Path after years of debate and organizational preparation at the University of Huamanga.[15] In September Sendero representatives returned and demanded that all teachers attend a meeting. This marks the beginning of their moralization and consciousness-raising campaigns in the region. One schoolteacher and one school custodian notified the Civil Guard post in Cangallo. Police arrested four schoolteachers who had not been involved in the burning of the ballots and tortured them. Subsequently, the chief district official publicly whipped the school custodian. Two young men, sons of mestizos, who had extorted money for years from market vendors were also punished. Masked Sendero representatives from Ayacucho returned with loudspeakers and held a public meeting, praising the public sanctioning of informers and thieves.

In August 1981 eight unknown, hooded militants executed two cattle thieves in the plaza of Chuschi. The thieves were from the neighboring village of Quispillaqta. It is significant that the two villages, literally only a stone's throw from one another, were age-old enemies. Battles over land boundaries were legend, and two of the earliest documents that I found concerned land disputes between the two in the latter part of the sixteenth and first years of the seventeenth centuries. Within the memory of the adults of the two communities, bloodshed had resulted from one such boundary dispute in 1959 when three men from Quispillaqta were shot by villagers from Chuschi. The insurgents played not only upon the age-old animosities between the two communities, they chose the archetypical enemy of songs and poetry, the cattle rustler, for their first public executions. Sendero had taken into custody three other well-known thieves, but they were released after being whipped publicly. Then the leaders of the tribunal announced that if anyone suffered theft of cattle, everyone would know who stole them and they promised to return to punish the guilty. Reportedly, support for the executions and public whippings was almost universal. Two months later Sendero returned and held another tribunal, this time aimed at the family. They publicly castigated a man who was living with two women and another who beat his wife. Several women thereafter denounced their husbands to the tribunals for similar offenses.

During the latter half of 1981 and the beginning months of 1982, SL stepped up its efforts in the moralization campaign and followed up by establishing organizational structures. In October 1981 they closed the municipality. The next month SL returned to Chuschi, for the first time without hoods or masks. They held a meeting with all of the schoolteachers and formed the Laborers and Workers Class Movement (MOTC); the various components included an organization for intellectuals (the schoolteachers), two for women, four for peasants, and one for youth. They also established a Popular Committee. All local officials resigned their posts in a general assembly and signed a document to that effect on November 22. To the outside world, however, the village still appeared to be functioning as usual with the officials named by the prefect's office in Ayacucho supposedly presiding.

Then Sendero attempted to impose a structure for communal planting based on local residential neighborhoods. It failed miserably. In hindsight, it is clear that none of the Sendero organizers had participated in the extensive anthropological field work directed from the University of Huamanga in the Rio Pampas in the 1960s and 1970s, nor had they read the numerous dissertations that resulted from that research. One of our major research findings was that the residential neighborhoods (moieties) of Chuschi and other villages in the valley had very little to do with the organization of production. Rather, agricultural labor was organized through a complex network of reciprocity. Therefore, the organizers of the insurgency, in trying to engender peasant support, failed when they tried to impose an idealized view of the moiety system that had no basis in local reality. They were as ill-informed as the military government's agrarian reform planners.

Other Shining Path initiatives were also unsuccessful. SL attempted to mediate the boundary disputes between Chuschi and Quispillaqta, but animosities between the two communities continued. Sendero also attempted to abolish the civil-religious hierarchy, the traditional *varayoq*, but that too failed. Another failure was its effort to close the road and prevent the weekly markets from functioning. One peasant said, "We could not let them close the markets. Where would we get our salt and matches?" A series of minor clashes occurred when Sendero tried to prohibit fiestas and drinking. One of our oral historians recounted that the *terros* (terrorists) ended up dancing in the streets during carnival holding their rifles over their heads. Also notable was Sendero's failure to prohibit the youth from celebrating *Vida Michy*, the adolescent competitive games accompanied by song duels, riddle games, dancing and drinking, which culminate in marathon group sex.[16]

The province of Cangallo was placed under a state of emergency in October of 1981, along with La Mar, Huanta, and Víctor Fajardo. When the state of emergency was lifted from the district of Totos in the province of Cangallo in December, twenty insurgents, a few of them in uniform, attacked the police post with machine guns and revolvers.[17] According to numerous interviews, Sendero gained control over at least nine villages in the Rio Pampas region by the end of 1981: Tambo, Paras, Totos, San José de Secce, Vilcas Huaman, Chuschi, Quispillaqta, Cancha Cancha, and Pomabamba. However, few actions in the Rio Pampas valley were reported in the news, either Sendero operations or early police excesses.

One of the events that did get reported was the attack on Chuschi and Cancha Cancha on July 1, 1982. Ten masked militants armed with machine guns blew up the post office in Cancha Cancha and captured the governor of Chuschi, Bernadino Chipana, whom SL considered a police informer. They paraded him through the streets naked and took him to the plaza with the intent of executing him. They turned to the villagers for support and received a resounding "No, don't kill him."[18] This cry became common throughout the valley as opposition to SL grew in other parts of Ayacucho.[19]

Only a couple of actions led by Shining Path were recalled by villagers as having massive support. According to various versions that we collected throughout the Rio Pampas, some two thousand people invaded the University of Huamanga's agricultural experimental station, Allpachaca, with two hundred oxen and plows and planted the fields communally in August 1982. People claimed that the fields were never harvested because the military arrived in full force and prevented them from returning. Nevertheless, the Allpachaca invasion and communal planting of the fields have taken a place in the mytho-history of the short period of support given to SL activities.

The other action by SL that is fondly retold as an example of successful rebellion involves the redistribution of wealth. Some time during the latter part of 1982, Sendero brought two hundred head of sheep that had been "liberated" from neighboring Huancasancos and distributed them to the communities in the Rio Pampas. Evidently, the plan was to produce meat for the People's Army. These events culminated in a celebration during which SL slaughtered six bulls and distributed two pieces of meat to every man, woman, and child. SL announced that it had established the New State of Peru, which would develop so that *campesinos* would be self-sufficient. During the festivities, we were told that the insurgents brought casks of red wine from the coast and distributed two glasses to everyone. Sendero more than likely has different versions of these two events that form part of its own mytho-history, but for local communities, with their tendency to incorporate such events into their ritual activities, we can expect the great invasion of Allpachaca and the redistribution of wealth from the coast to appear in dance, in song, as well as in ritual and narrative forms.

After the failed attempt to assassinate the governor of the district, another major event occurred in early December 1982, when Sendero organized a celebration in the village of Cancha Cancha to commemorate the birth of the Popular Army. People did not, however, recount the story with much relish. According to our interviews, five prisoners were put on trial: two from Cancha Cancha and three from Chuschi. They were petty bureaucrats who had abused the powers of their offices. One of them was the municipal mayor of Chuschi with whom I had major confrontations in 1975.[20] He accused me of being a CIA agent, and I accused him of stealing village funds. When I inquired why such a corrupt man had been named mayor, I was told by departmental officials that he had been put into office so that he could be caught and jailed. But, of course, he was never jailed or tried, so when Sendero arrived and drove him and the other mestizos out of the district, the action received enormous support.

We were told that all of the surrounding communities took part in the celebration of the birth of the Popular Army: "Ten blocks of marchers arrived; each Laborers' and Workers' Class Movement (MOTC) group with its flag, shouting — 'Long live the armed struggle! Guerrilla War!'" The celebration was short-lived, however; the Popular Army never took part in armed conflict. About December 20, 1982, combined forces from the army, the Peruvian Investigatory Police (PIP), and the Civil Guard arrived by trucks at the village of Chuschi, located at the end of the road. Those who had participated in

Sendero activities fled to the hills, leaving behind women, children and older men. The retreat had been well planned, with homemade grenades providing cover for the dispersing Sendero militants. The armed forces did not pursue the guerrillas; rather they took four elderly peasant men into custody and blew one of them up with one of SL's hand grenades in the plaza of Chuschi. Shortly after the confrontation, the leaders of the guerrilla movement returned and attempted to organize a victory celebration. Their efforts were rejected and again they retreated into the hills.

During the climax of the violence between Sendero and the armed forces in 1982, Sendero killed two Protestants in Chuschi while the church was holding a twenty-four-hour prayer vigil for peace. The pastor of that church was interviewed. He allowed that even when the faithful were attacked by Sendero, they were steadfast in their faith. He was convinced that only their prayers were keeping the region peaceful. In numerous interviews, Protestants interpreted the violent events they had experienced as signaling the coming of the apocalypse and the reign of Jesus Christ, followed by a new utopian age. When asked directly if the violence they had experienced was an act of purification that would enable them to join the new utopian world, the pastor emphatically answered yes, they were now purified and were waiting for the coming of Christ.

In February 1983 the community of Chuschi flew white flags from the municipal building and requested that a military defense post be established. A Civil Guard (now National Police) post was set up and has become a permanent part of the political structure of the region. The armed forces also organized civil patrol groups in early 1983. Chuschi complied with these orders, but Cancha Cancha refused, declaring that Sendero would attack those communities that had civil defense patrols. This has proven to be the case in other regions. The military forces arrived in helicopters and combed the region for guerrillas.

In the Rio Pampas valley, the village of Quispillaqta has been the hardest hit by military repression. By the end of 1984, seventy-seven people from that community had been "disappeared" during night raids. Official documentation exists for fifty-three of these, who have become "officially disappeared," while the others remain undeclared. Many family members interviewed expressed great anxiety over being "disappeared" themselves if they approached the authorities and pressed the case of their loved ones. In Chuschi, six people lost their lives during this period, including three evangelists and one storekeeper who were assassinated by SL and the old man who was blown up by the military. In the nearby village of Pomabamba, the military killed three people during the first year of its occupation. Nevertheless, Pomabamba refused to form the required civil patrols. By 1984 most of the villages of the district had been partially or almost completely abandoned; however, by January 1986, repopulation of the region was beginning.

The great difference in the levels of repression experienced by Quispillaqta and Chuschi, traditional enemies for at least four centuries, illustrates how local conflicts are played out in the context of the current national violence. The two villages increased their differences along religious lines during the 1970s when Quispillaqta converted almost en masse to a Protestant sect, the Brothers and Sisters of God. Chuschi, on the other hand, remained Catholic through the 1970s even though the priest was expelled and the *cofradía* holdings were confiscated. By the time Sendero began its activities in 1980, a Protestant church had also been established in Chuschi, much smaller and with a separate pastor. The two communities had a Catholic church as well, but no resident priest. Even as rapid change brought Protestantism into the region, the two villages chose to remain distinct. When the pastor of the sect in Chuschi was asked about the increase of Protestantism in the Rio Pampas during the 1980s, he gave an account of its growth since 1982. Chuschi, he said, grew from only a handful to over two hundred members and Quispillaqta, with its separate church and pastor, had more than doubled its membership. When asked about why the military had "disappeared" so many people in Quispillaqta, he said that everyone knew that they supported Sendero. The people of Chuschi had no choice but to tell the military commanders. When asked if the Protestants in Quispillaqta supported Sendero, he said, "No, Sendero kills us Protestants." The contradiction of declaring that Quispillaqta also had a large number of converts but at the same time supported Sendero did not occur to him. What seems clear is that the age-old feud between Chuschi and Quispillaqta took on new dimensions during the years of repression and disappearances. By the end of 1982, when the combined military forces went into the region, Chuschi, Quispillaqta, and other communities in the Rio Pampas valley withdrew their support even though this put them at grave risk for Sendero attacks. Notably, this period corresponds to the upsurge of Protestantism described by the pastor of Chuschi.

It is not difficult to imagine that Chuschi's civil patrols might have helped the *Sinchis* (specialized anti-terrorist police) attack Chuschi's traditional enemies in nighttime raids. This has occurred in other parts of Ayacucho; when a family member is carried off by masked attackers, the burden of proof rests with the family. They cannot bring charges unless they know the name of the assailants. This kind of a "legal fig leaf" means that animosity of all sorts can be played out under the cloak of generalized violence. Whatever happened, the descriptions I gathered from wives and mothers of the "disappeared" from Quispillaqta leave no doubt that the attacks were by *Sinchi* forces and not by Sendero. Moreover, in 1986 there were orders for the capture of suspected Sendero militants in the district that had not been carried out. A young captain whom we interviewed in Chuschi said he refused to carry out the orders that had arrived from his superiors. Instead he turned the documents over to a Peruvian senator who was a member of the human rights commission, saying: "These people are not terrorists. It is now your obligation to protect them. I am leaving soon; the next officer might carry out the orders and arrest them." Sadly there are no guarantees under the law and those who, by whatever means, are named on such a list cannot be protected.

Initial Support Turned Sour

The communities of the district of Chuschi supported Sendero for the first two years because SL's short-term goals corresponded with their own: first, get rid of enemies (in most cases the *mistis* who seemed to be gaining power), then set up better schools, and finally, comply with SL's demands at gunpoint to organize committees to govern without corruption. To the traditional authorities, Sendero's New Democracy of Peru probably meant that, after their enemies were eliminated, they would be free of the abusive bureaucrats sent by ministry officials in Ayacucho. Moreover, the traditional authorities more than likely expected to exercise their power within the consensus framework common in the villages in the past. During the first year of Sendero's actions, it did rid the district of thieves, abusive bureaucrats, state agents of change, and the new rich peasants. Education, the avenue to a better life, seemed greatly improved. The great march to Allpachaca and the accompanying communal planting signified a unification of communities under a common productive goal; the glorified redistribution of wealth meant a different sort of "New Peru" to the peasants, though not what SL had in mind.

However, when Sendero then moved to form committees for women, youth, peasants, and intellectuals, a societal reorganization that did not fit political or kinship structures central either to economic production or reproduction of society, peasants began to realize that they were not participants in the revolution. Whether they were aware or not of how SL viewed the peasant masses is unclear. But once peasants began to realize that the committees imposed by Sendero gave them less voice in deciding their own destiny than the governing structures imposed by the departmental and state bureaucracies, they began to retreat from SL's programs. That realization became clear with the formation of the People's Army in Cancha Cancha; it had neither arms nor plans of action, and its main purpose seemed to be to serve as a delaying force for any military advance to enable SL to escape. The end of the brief period of support came when Sendero fled over the hills and left the peasants to face repression by the armed forces, including massacres of entire villages, random disappearances, and a return of semifeudal practices. For example, in 1983 and 1984 peasants were required to supply meat, firewood, eggs, chickens, and even render maid and valet service to military personnel.[21]

As Sendero attempted to gain control over the district of Chuschi, it struggled to transform villages into its New Democracy of Peru, born out of a romanticized combination of Inca past and lessons learned from the Chinese revolution. However, as Degregori correctly argues, SL leaders became the new *mistis*, the new mestizos and lords.[22] Shining Path had simply transformed the power structure with itself at the top and with the peasant masses, whom it considers in need of leadership and instruction, at the bottom. Villages were admonished not to participate in the capitalistic market but to be autonomous. Whole populations had to attend obligatory meetings. Not only were peasants marched to Cancha Cancha to form the People's Army, they were expected to provision the army as well. Sendero also failed in its attempts to install puritanical codes of morality, which seem to have been fashioned after the Chinese experience. It also failed to outlaw fiestas or to restructure communities and their bases for economic production. When its efforts to shut down all commerce failed, it resorted to searching trucks for informers and assassinating them.

A nurse who had worked in Quispillaqta before the violence began described how that community was once organized and progressive. She states that the youth have left or have been "disappeared"; the community is fearful of Sendero, on the one hand, yet on the other hand people are obliged to participate in the military's civil patrols. The only solution, she says, is to flee. The peasants are between "the sword and the wall." Any kind of health or development work in the area is difficult if not impossible, she recounts, because the armed forces suspect her and her colleagues of being Sendero sympathizers. On the other hand, if by chance they did succeed in any development efforts, SL would target them for assassination.[23]

One of Sendero's major mistakes in provincial Ayacucho was to consider the peasants as an undifferentiated mass with no will of their own. SL viewed them as clay that could be molded in the service of the revolution. The preceding examples illustrate the complexities of local histories as they interact with major political and social forces. Sendero's ideology of a future without distinctions — no differentiation of class or wealth, no government (except SL hegemony) — must have been an unfathomable mystery to Andean people, who move in a world filled with distinctions. For outsiders, the world of Andean peasants often appears static and unchanging, but the reality they create through social relations is never static or completed but rather tactile and ongoing. Therefore, SL's conceptualization of utopia is an impossibility for Andean people, who take pleasure in and survive by keeping their world in motion. They are experts in the game of social mobility.

If we use this perspective to answer the question at the beginning of this chapter — "Why hasn't Sendero been more successful?" — we can now appreciate that SL both misunderstood the peasants of Ayacucho and underestimated them. Sendero imposed an ideological agenda on people who move between categories SL considers fixed: rural peasants and urban laborers, capitalism and semifeudalism. Many peasants have opted to participate in the market economy while keeping their reciprocal exchanges and their civil-religious hierarchy, the *varayoq*, who are traditional community officials, usually illiterate Quechua-speaking elders. Others have managed to maintain rituals and traditions while migrating to cities within and even beyond Peru.

Some peasants can form alliances with former large landowners, prefer private property over cooperatives, and generally adhere to a vision of the future that confounds rigid classificatory schemes. These communities are not made up of homogenous masses, but rather of individuals who pursue their self interest extremely well even as they meet their community responsibilities. The political life in any Andean region is fraught with conflicts, tensions, and intrigues. Clearly, by rejecting Sendero's attempt to reproduce the semifeudal conditions of power that it professed to destroy, the peasants of the region have demonstrated far greater political awareness and sophistication than SL realized or can deal with.

In spite of Sendero's opposition to development projects, the villagers of the district of Chuschi, in meetings with their elected representatives in 1986, requested aid from the state for the same things they had been asking for fifteen years earlier: health centers, schools, potable water, and irrigation canals. They also requested government guarantees for their personal safety in order to resume a semblance of normal life in their communities. But they continue to live under a double threat from the military and from SL and still have no personal safety guarantees. It is therefore even more surprising that these communities, abandoned during the height of repression from 1983 to 1985, were being repopulated in 1986. As a consequence of the dislocation caused by years of violence and flight to the urban centers, the *varayoq* were replaced by literate young bilingual men who have learned important political lessons from the war and from their enforced urban experiences. In the 1990s the state will have to negotiate with a new kind of peasant in the Rio Pampas area. Similarly, SL will have to deal with leaders with greater political vision and experience than those it attempted to displace in the early 1980s.

The New *Ñaqas* and Other Things Out of Place

Numerous interviews indicate that instead of becoming the revolutionary vanguard in the communities, Shining Path has been perceived, because of its violence in Ayacucho, as a new form of *ñaqa*, the supernatural being that robs body fat to build churches, to make bells, and, more recently in Andean mythology, to pay the enormous foreign debt.[24] In many versions of Sendero's atrocities, it was equated with a *ñaqa* who cuts the flesh of victims to feed the Sendero armies. SL members have become flesh-eating beings feeding off a population with no more fat to give. These new *ñaqas* are believed to be especially common near the frontier with the lowland tropical forest in the province of San Miguel, where SL's training camps are said to be located across the Apurímac River. One community leader from that region said:

> We are more afraid of Sendero than we are of the army or of the police. Let me tell you something that happened. I have a friend who is a health worker. He works in the medical post of Lechemayoq, the seventh annex of San Pedro. In a meeting of the five communities there which he attended, they told about one thousand Sendero militants who entered the region and killed the young and old. They carried off flesh; that is to say, they cut off the flesh with knives and carried it off in sacks. They left behind only bones and skeletons.[25]

These village authorities from the province of San Miguel see themselves trapped between flesh-eating *ñaqas*, and "foreigners" who know no fear, who are more savage than Peruvians. They cannot imagine that their own countrymen could act so brutally. These are the new figures of power and control — fearless foreigners and flesh-eating supernatural beings from the "other side." These figures of power are out of place — not from one's own place and time.

In a general assembly with community leaders from several villages in the district of Ayna, also in the province of San Miguel, members of a government human rights commission asked for the names of people killed. As nineteen names were called out for one hamlet, the investigators asked whether the victims had been killed by Sendero or the military. The village authority replied:

> When the whole district of Santa Rosa was combed in 1982 or 1983 . . . the rumors that were going around were that they were foreign troops. They weren't afraid of anything. Not anything. That was the time when they killed the peasant leaders, the school teachers, and many, many other people who were blamed for bringing guerrilla ideas. As many as twenty to thirty people were killed every day.

Another community authority interjected: "But most of them are foreign, right? They don't speak Quechua. They're from the other side." The investigator asked: "What did these foreigners look like?" The first speaker replied: "They were more ruthless; they dressed in a different style;...[they were] more...savage; they demonstrated that they were not Peruvians."[26]

In such situations, even ethnic identity becomes dangerous. The "foreigners" and the *ñaqas* prey on Andean peasants, recognizable by dress and language, and sometimes even disguise themselves as peasants. In Ayacucho, when the interviews were conducted in 1986, Shining Path was commonly referred to by Quechua-speakers as *puriqkuna*, the people who walk or travel; that is to say, people who travel from village to village without belonging to any one place. They belong to no community at all and, like the "foreigners" who massacre whole villages, they too are from "the other side." This characterization contrasts with the term used to refer to members of one's own community, *llaqtamasi*, or village-mates. This perception of Sendero as being "out of place" helps explain why its members came to be perceived as flesh-eating *ñaqas*.

The Coming of a New Age

For many of the Andean people interviewed, the cataclysmic violence of the 1980s announces a *Pachacutic*, a transformational world turn, a new age, an escape from the current epoch of power and the beginning of a new one. For many in the Rio Pampas, the recent violence signals the end of the world, the apocalypse, and the coming of Jesus Christ. For example, the Protestant pastor in Chuschi declared that "we are living in an antibiblical time." He went on to explain that such an age signals the coming of "Our Lord Jesus Christ." "The time is near," he proclaimed. Others looked to the coming of a new age with hope for radical secular change such as better education and health facilities and more economic opportunities. It is clear that the youth of these communities have a different vision of the future than the view held by their parents. In hindsight, when Protestantism began to increase in Quispillaqta and Chuschi in the 1970s, the sense of time and the future were already undergoing radical transformation. Sendero arrived on the scene as these changes were underway. The worldview that had prevailed in the recent past is one in which peasants faced the past, not the future. The past was expected to repeat itself in a cyclical fashion, while the future remained behind one, approaching, but not in view.[27]

In many ways, the future is in the hands of the youth who survived the violence of the 1980s. Sendero counts on the youth becoming radicalized. But in its attempts to shape a new utopia through violence, Sendero went too far.

It went beyond killing known enemies and killed village authorities. It promised a better world where "truth without deceit is supreme." But Sendero did not bring the promised truth; rather, it replaced the old power with its own authoritarianism. Sendero did not expect that people in so many of the communities in the Rio Pampas would consider themselves citizens of the Peruvian nation even after the worst years of violence and repression. Many communities, such as Chuschi, chose the state over Sendero. When citizens requested that the police post be established and dutifully complied with military orders to organize civil defense patrols, the "new age" they were choosing anticipates that the state would better respond to their needs for education, for health, and for better economic opportunities than Sendero.

Other villages realized that they have some power over their own future. Pomabamba, for example, demanded that all of their fifteen teachers be replaced both in 1985 and in 1986. They hope for integration into the nation without losing local control over the resources that will help them achieve that goal, of which education may be the most important. However, the danger of continued repression still hovers over these villages in spite of their declared loyalty to the nation and threatens the fragile alliance between Andean communities and the state. These communities, without civil rights or access to the law, are acting in faith that their concerns will be heard and profess their loyalty on these terms. State forces, nevertheless, continue to be suspicious that peasants continue to be supporters of Shining Path.

In the case of Chuschi, the dramatic increase in Protestantism is founded on a new truth with a different sense of time that culminates in a hoped-for utopia under the word of Jesus Christ. In many cases, that hoped-for utopia includes migration outside of one's community of origin, even out of Peru. The world is suddenly future-oriented, not only for Protestants and migrants but also for those who have returned from urban centers to their communities of origin to become authorities. These new leaders are not only literate with greater political experience, they are also less passive than their elders were in negotiating with the state. If regionalization proceeds as planned, these new leaders will be in a position to act with greater autonomy and political acumen. It may appear contradictory that these new political actors have assumed positions in the traditional civil-religious hierarchy. But the civil-religious hierarchy has seen several transformations in the past, and this is but one of many that will more than likely continue into the future.

The interpretation of history and time promoted by conversion to Protestantism or to Sendero, for that matter, differs radically from the traditional views that shaped history in the Rio Pampas prior to the violence of the 1980s. Major historical events before 1980 were generally verified in local and even personal terms. Among many of the citizens interviewed, especially those in communities pinned down the hardest between the "wall and the blade," a collective history has not yet developed whereby a chronology of events is recounted and compared across valleys or regions. People fled or retreated to the safety of their immediate family groups and waited for a new age or new epoch of power to begin. This appears to have been especially true in the province of La Mar.[28]

For those who converted to Protestantism, a different sense of time, oriented to the future, was acquired. Both Protestantism and "Senderoism" encourage a linear path to utopia, but Sendero's path is the inevitable march of revolution that moves toward a utopian society to be born out of the embers of their purifying fire. Its utopia is a motionless world without differentiation of any kind — no class, no hierarchy, no state. Protestantism as practiced in the Andes may also share a similar notion of an undifferentiated utopia. However, the "new age of power" ushered forth by Sendero in the Rio Pampas reproduced the semifeudal relations of the previous age. Ironically, SL eliminated old enemies only to become the new *mistis* as it tried to effect a world turn, or *Pachacutic*, so that it could assume the position of dominance and power. As Protestantism spreads, will similar relations of power and combination be reproduced? What kind of "new age" will the next ten years bring? Even though the definition of such a *Pachacutic* is not agreed upon, everyone awaits its arrival.

Notes

1. Carlos Iván Degregori's book, *Ayacucho 1969-1979, El surgimiento de Sendero Luminoso* (Lima: Instituto de Estudios Peruanos, 1990), summarizes his two earlier publications (1985 and 1986) and provides a history of the movement in Ayacucho. Also of importance is his *Que difícil es ser Diós: Ideología y violencia política en Sendero Luminoso* (Lima: El Zorro de Abajo Ediciones, 1989). Another important study of SL is Gustavo Gorriti, *Sendero: Historia de la guerra milenaria en el Perú*, vol. I (Lima: Apoyo, 1990). Lewis Taylor gives one of the first analyses of Sendero's organization and structure in "Maoism in the Andes: Sendero Luminoso and the Contemporary Guerrilla Movement in Peru," Working Paper 2, Centre for Latin American Studies (Liverpool: University of Liverpool, 1983). Henri Favre, "Sentier Lumineux et Horizons Obscurs," *Problèmes D'Amérique Latine* 72, 2e trimestre, 1984, pp. 3-27, also published in Spanish as "Perú: Sendero Luminoso y horizontes oscuros," *Quehacer* (Lima) 31, 1984, pp. 25-34, observes that Sendero's support in Huancavelica comes from what he calls the depeasantized youth. David Scott Palmer, "Rebellion in Rural Peru: The Origins and Evolution of Sendero Luminoso," *Comparative Politics*, 18:2, 1986, pp. 127-146, argues that Sendero plays upon the pattern of periodic organization of the periphery against central authority, except that in this case, Sendero's goal is to destroy the center. Alberto Flores Galindo and Nelson Manrique, *Violencia y campesinado* (Lima: Instituto de Apoyo Agrario, 1986), have collected some of the best critical essays on violence in Peru. Colin J. Harding, "The Rise of Sendero Luminoso," in Rory Miller, ed., *Region and Class in Modern Peru* (Liverpool: University of Liverpool, Institute of Latin American Studies Monograph, 1984), 14, pp. 179-207, is an excellent summary in English. I also recommend his more recent article analyzing the role of Antonio Díaz Martínez in shaping Sendero ideology: "Antonio Díaz Martínez and the Ideology of Sendero Luminoso," *Bulletin of Latin American Research*, 7:1, 1988, pp. 179-207. The most comprehensive summaries of reported violence in Peru are those published monthly by DESCO (Centro de Estudios y Promoción de Desarrollo), in Lima, Peru.

2. See Héctor Béjar, *Las guerrillas de 1965: Balance y perspectiva* (Lima: Ediciones PEISA, 1973).

3. Rodrigo Montoya, *Capitalismo y neo-capitalismo en el Perú* (Lima: Mosca Azul, 1980); Lino Quintanilla, *Andahuaylas: La lucha por la tierra: Testimonio de un militante* (Lima: Mosca Azul, 1981). Quintanilla is a former agronomist turned organizer who describes his experiences leading the land invasion movement in Andahuaylas. Rodrigo Sánchez, *Tomas de tierras y conciencia política campesina* (Lima: Instituto de Estudios Peruanos, 1981), provides an analysis of the same phenomenon.

4. Harding, "Rise of Sendero."

5. Ibid., p. 70.

6. Ibid., p. 71.

7. Steve J. Stern, *Peru's Indian Peoples and the Challenge of Spanish Conquest: Huamanga to 1640* (Madison: University of Wisconsin Press, 1982), and *Resistance, Rebellion, and Consciousness in the Andean Peasant World, 18th to 20th Centuries* (Madison: University of Wisconsin Press, 1987). Florencia E. Mallon, "Nationalist and Antistate Coalitions in the War of the Pacific: Junín and Cajamarca, 1879-1902," in Stern,

Resistance, Rebellion, and Consciousness, pp. 232-280, and *The Defense of Community in Peru's Central Highlands: Peasant Struggle and Capitalist Transition, 1880-1940* (Princeton, NJ: Princeton University Press, 1987).

8. Mallon, "Nationalist and Antistate Coalitions," p. 232.

9. Of special interest is Deborah Poole's analysis of the rituals in Cuzco that recount the War of the Pacific. Her title is very appropriate, "The Choreography of History in Andean Dance," unpublished manuscript, n.d. In his article about the massacre of eight journalists in Ayacucho, Mario Vargas Llosa puzzles over why an old Quechua-speaking woman danced around him during his investigation in Uchuraccay. I think it is possible that she was "dancing the foreigner away," as Andean peasants have been doing for centuries. See "Inquest in the Andes," *New York Times Magazine*, July 31, 1983, pp. 18-23ff.

10. See Patrick Husson, "Guerre Indienne et Revolte Paysanne Dans la Province de Huanta (Peru)," Theses Université, Paris IV, Sorbonne, 1983.

11. In an interview with Raúl González, "De como Lumbreras entiende al Perú de Sendero," *Quehacer*, 42, 1986, pp. 34-43.

12. Orin Starn, "Missing the Revolution: Anthropologists and the War in Peru," *Cultural Anthropology*, 6:1, 1990, pp. 63-91. He rightly criticizes the anthropology of the 1960s and 1970s as "andeanism." However, Starn cites selectively from the working paper version of this chapter to argue that "many Chuschinos and other Andean peasants proved ready to embrace the concept of revolution," (p. 80) even though my early draft clearly states the opposite. While Starn selectively quotes from the paper, he leaves out the relevant fact, which I discuss at length, that Chuschinos requested that a police post be established in the community. They did not embrace the concept of revolution; rather, they initially supported Sendero in killing old enemies, then withdrew their support when SL tried to impose new structures.

13. Cynthia McClintock, "Why Peru's Alán García Is a Man on the Move," *LASA Forum*, 16:4, Winter 1986, pp. 9-12.

14. Palmer, "Rebellion in Rural Peru."

15. For details see Degregori, *Ayacucho, 1969-1979.*

16. Billie Jean Isbell and Fredy Roncalla, "The Ontogenesis of Metaphor: Riddle Games Among Quechua Speakers Seen as Cognitive Discovery Procedures," *Journal of Latin American Lore*, 3:1, 1977, pp. 19-49.

17. DESCO, *Violencia política en el Perú 1980-1988* (Lima: DESCO, 1989), p. 75.

18. Ibid., p. 83.

19. Carlos Iván Degregori, "A Dwarf Star," *NACLA Report on the Americas*, 24:4, December 1990-January 1991, p. 14.

20. Billie Jean Isbell, *To Defend Ourselves*, 2nd Edition (Prospect Heights, IL: Waveland Press, 1985), pp. 228-237.

21. See the accounts published in *Ideología, Revista de Ciéncias Sociales* 10 (Huamanga, Ayacucho: Instituto de Estudios Regionales José María Arguedas, 1987). I am not going to recount the stories of rape, massacre, and exploitation that were described to us nor the accounts in the publication cited above. The *Sinchis* and the navy are described as especially abusive. We interviewed Civil Guard policemen from the coast who felt that even old women and small children were Sendero militants. "You never know," one young man said, "Sendero has been preparing, preparing for years."

22. See Degregori, *Que difícil es ser Diós*.

23. Ibid., p. 28.

24. Juan Ansión, *Pishtacos de verdugos a sacaojos* (Lima: Tarea, Asociación de Publicaciones Educativas, 1989). In this edited collection of new versions of *ñaqa* and *pishtaco* tales, several recount how the *pishtacos* now work for the military who have been sent by President García to rob body fat to send it to creditors to pay the foreign debt.

25. Interview by the author in Ayacucho in 1986.

26. Ibid.

27. Catherine J. Allen has discussed the concepts of time of an Andean community in the Cuzco region in *The Hold Life Has* (Washington, D.C.: Smithsonian Press, 1988).

28. I discuss these topics more fully in "The Texts and Contexts of Terror in Peru," Columbia University Research Conference, Violence and Democracy in Colombia and Peru (New York: Columbia University and New York University National Resource Center Consortium, December 1988).

5

PEASANT RESPONSES TO SHINING PATH IN ANDAHUAYLAS*

Ronald H. Berg

Shining Path (SL or Sendero) presents us with a disturbing paradox. It is a sectarian, extremist organization, operating in the context of a relatively open, diverse, and democratic political system, yet it has phenomenal staying power.

Sendero holds to a strict Maoism, emphasizing obedience to the party line and devotion to the dictates of its leader, Abimael Guzmán Reynoso, also known as Presidente Gonzalo. Its writings emphasize a protracted guerrilla

*The author would like to thank the following organizations for supporting field work in Peru: the Doherty Fellowship Committee, the Organization of American States, and the Rackham School of Graduate Studies, University of Michigan (1981-1982); also the Kellogg Institute for International Studies, University of Notre Dame, and Sigma Xi (1985). Thanks are also due to Billie Jean Isbell, Carlos Monge, David Scott Palmer, and Steve Stein, who commented on earlier drafts of this paper.

This chapter is based in part on an earlier article, Ronald H. Berg, "Sendero Luminoso and the Peasantry of Andahuaylas," *Journal of Inter-American Studies and World Affairs*, 28, Winter 1986-1987, pp. 164-196.

war, virtually as an end in itself, and the rejection of any types of reform.[1] This has led to the actions that have been well described in the literature, including the mutilation and murder of informers, the destruction of agricultural cooperatives and rural development programs, and the prevention of peasants from selling their produce on the market. The movement can be compared in some ways to the Khmer Rouge of Cambodia.[2]

A Maoist strategy is combined with the radical *indigenismo* of José Carlos Mariátegui, a Peruvian Communist theoretician of the 1920s. Mariátegui called for an agrarian communism based on the indigenous peasant community, a goal that was utopian even in the 1920s and that now, after massive urbanization, is all the more remote. Sendero remains sectarian, inward-looking, and isolated from developments in other countries.[3]

The growth of Sendero is particularly remarkable considering the overwhelming military force directed against it. A major consequence of this has been the brutalization of the civilian population of the emergency zones (EMZs). The army and police have surpassed the guerrillas in violence against civilians. Kidnapping and murder of political prisoners, massacres of whole villages, and the systematic torture of prisoners are well documented, and the number of political killings reached record levels in 1989 and 1990.[4]

Any explanation of Shining Path needs to address its apparent success and popularity in the core area around Ayacucho, one of the poorest and most underdeveloped areas of Peru. Several hypotheses have been suggested. McClintock explains the growth of Sendero there in terms of a subsistence crisis, a radical decline in standards of living. She explains this was caused largely by government policies favoring multinational corporations, the military, and urban consumers at the expense of the highland peasantry. Palmer adds another dimension of the crisis affecting the region: the failure of government reform. Aspirations were raised by development projects and agrarian reform measures, but these hopes were dashed in the 1970s. Favre and Degregori give a local perspective on these problems. Support for Sendero arises among a marginal, "de-peasantized" stratum, no longer able to support itself by agriculture but unable to find work in the cities.[5]

Taken together, these articles provide a global understanding of the economic and social forces giving rise to Shining Path. However, their explanations are relatively thin, relying on one or two social factors. They assume that increasing poverty and economic insecurity lead to revolutionary sentiment — yet rural poverty, even on the level of a subsistence crisis, is not inevitably followed by an insurrection. Little indication is given of the relation between guerrillas and peasants or the peasants' perceptions of the guerrillas.

This chapter provides a local-level perspective on Shining Path acquired through field work in a peasant community involved in the war. Field work took place from August 1981 to November 1982 in the province of Andahuaylas, department of Apurímac. A follow-up visit took place in June to July 1985.

Field work centered in Pacucha, a community of fewer than two thousand inhabitants. Even so, Pacucha is a relatively large and diverse community and is a district capital. In 1981 the district of Pacucha had 10,139 inhabitants living in small, dispersed hamlets (the census counted sixty-two distinct settlements). It was one of twenty-one districts in the province of Andahuaylas, whose total population was 145,066.[6]

Pacucha remains a peasant village in that the main economic activity is household agriculture for home consumption, but few households rely entirely on subsistence agriculture. This is supplemented by wage labor, craft production, and labor migration. The community is stratified; a small group of peasant-entrepreneurs engages in a combination of commercial agriculture and storekeeping. The past forty years have seen an increase in labor migration, occupational multiplicity, and greater reliance on a monetary economy. In sum, Pacucha is relatively large and complex, and it reflects the complexity of contemporary Andean society.

The perspective from Andahuaylas shows how Sendero has been able to play on social conflicts, in particular the conflict over landownership in the aftermath of an agrarian reform program. The land issue is central to an understanding of Sendero's tactics and its popular support. All the same, the guerrillas have not been able to sustain a high level of active participation. Sendero exploits popular resentment against merchants, cooperatives, and the state, but it has not succeeded in rallying the peasants under the banner of Mao. Why this is the case is discussed below.

Andahuaylas: Historical Background

Andahuaylas is a highland province within the department of Apurímac, bordering on the department of Ayacucho. Apurímac is one of the most economically underdeveloped departments in Peru, together with Ayacucho and Huancavelica, the other two core areas that formed the crucible of Shining Path. The economy is predominantly agricultural, and a large majority of the inhabitants are Quechua-speaking peasants.

The bulk of the population of Andahuaylas is concentrated in valleys in the central and northern part of the province, north of the main highway that runs from east to west.[7] Here sugarcane has been grown since the colonial period and cattle have been raised for sale in regional markets and in Lima. In addition, potatoes and cereals (maize, barley, wheat) are grown for the market. From the colonial period through the midtwentieth century, the production and sale of these crops were controlled by large estates, or haciendas. These haciendas relied on a body of "unfree" laborers. Thus in spite of some attempts to rationalize production and to purchase machinery, these were not purely capitalist operations.[8]

The basic dichotomy in the rural areas was between haciendas and small-holding peasants. A minority of the rural population lived on hacienda land, renting plots in exchange for heavy, unpaid or poorly paid labor duties. At the same time, even the peasants of the supposedly free communities were tied to the haciendas in a number of ways. Both free and hacienda-dwelling peasants owned less than enough land for subsistence and had to work on the haciendas to survive. Each household would send laborers to work as shepherds, cultivators, or house servants. In return, the households earned the right to farm or to herd their flocks on hacienda land. The legal and extralegal mechanisms varied, but the system was essentially one of feudal rents.

The peasants of Andahuaylas still remember bitterly the exploitation of this system. Wages were sometimes promised but rarely paid. Laborers worked for one to two weeks per month, twelve hours a day. Worst of all, in the period from 1880 to 1930, the haciendas had been able to expropriate large areas of community land, depriving peasants of an independent livelihood.[9] The large landowners (*hacendados*) relied on coercion and violence to seize land and control labor, and in conflicts they were supported by local politicians and the police. In rural areas, the word of the *hacendado* was law, and peasants still relate incidents of the landowners raping women and murdering rebellious peasants without fear of sanction.

The hacienda system went into decline for a variety of reasons beginning in the 1930s. In the 1940s the owners of the haciendas began to sell out, dividing up their lands into parcels and selling them to the better-off peasants or to townspeople. In the same period, peasant rebellions against the *hacendados* accelerated the process of decline.

Rebellions usually took the form of localized protests and petitions to the authorities to achieve legal recognition of peasant communities and their right to land. This legal action was combined with nonviolent occupation of hacienda land by hacienda serfs and by community peasants. By the 1960s these land seizures had become more organized and more violent as the peasant organizations grew larger and more sophisticated and the *hacendados* grew more desperate to defend the land their ancestors had usurped from the communities.

The haciendas were dealt a serious blow in 1969, when the military regime of General Juan Velasco Alvarado (1968-1975) introduced a sweeping new agrarian reform decree expropriating the large estates in Peru. Valesco hoped to modernized Peruvian agriculture by expropriating the haciendas and forming large state-controlled agricultural cooperatives. However, Andahuaylas was not a high-priority area for the agrarian reform's application, so several years passed after the decree without any substantive change in land tenure. The *hacendados*, believing that expropriation was imminent, took advantage of the hiatus to dismantle their estates, taking away and selling most of their movable property, including livestock and machinery. The peasants of the communities and the haciendas grew increasingly frustrated with this impasse, feeling that they had been deceived and cheated of their right to possession.

As late as 1972, the census data revealed that a few large estates controlled the bulk of the land while thousands of peasants possessed tiny plots insufficient for subsistence. Only 5 percent of the agricultural units held 66 percent of the land, while at the other end of the scale 59 percent of the units were of less than one hectare and included less than 10 percent of the total area.[10] However, most of the haciendas had ceased to function as productive units.

The situation in the late 1960s and early 1970s was one of conflict and uncertainty; a majority of the haciendas were involved in litigation or other conflict and their legal status was unclear. Apurímac ranked highest of any department in the percentage of peasant communities involved in boundary disputes with haciendas or with other communities.[11] Hacienda peasants, absentee landowners, and the neighboring communities fought over the fragments of the haciendas. A 1970 survey of the Andahuaylas haciendas showed that only one, Toxama, was being transformed into a cooperative.[12]

Into this situation stepped three radical student organizers belonging to the Revolutionary Vanguard (VR) party. Two of the students were originally from Andahuaylas while the third, Julio César Mezzich, was from Lima.[13] They began organizing in 1970, and by 1974 they had achieved a network of peasant organizations throughout the province. After a massive show of force in the main plaza of Andahuaylas, during which fifteen thousand peasants demonstrated for land and against the official agrarian reform, the peasants seized all of the remaining sixty-eight haciendas in the province in a few months, from July through October 1974. These land invasions were carried out in spite of opposition from both *hacendados* and police.

Military repression followed on the heels of these actions. The occupations were carried out with little or no bloodshed — deaths were the exception as absentee owners were in no position to resist. However, the threat of military reprisal was strong. As one observer wrote, "In September 1974, Andahuaylas appeared like a war zone because of the presence of the police and the reinforcement of a battalion of infantry quartered in the provincial capital."[14] The peasant leaders were arrested and the majority of ex-haciendas seized by the state, whereupon they were converted into state-organized agricultural cooperatives.

The formation of the cooperatives, then, was an act of "reform" instituted by the state in an effort to block radical, grass-roots expropriation of the haciendas. From the beginning, the cooperatives ran into difficulties due to a lack of capital and administrative experience and to poor coordination of the cooperative program. The following years saw a rapid deterioration as the cooperatives' funds were wasted or embezzled by the administrators and the workers were apathetic and poorly organized. The workers, for their part, blamed the leadership for the problems of the cooperatives.

Another problem facing the cooperatives was the continuing conflict with the neighboring peasant communities. The cooperatives began to take on the traditional role of the haciendas, leasing land to "nonassociates" in exchange for labor and hiring nonassociates at low wages. Thus the peasants living in neighboring communities came to resent the cooperatives bitterly.

At the same time, in the 1970s, there was a resurgence of other forms of economic activity in Andahuaylas. The demise of the haciendas left a commercial vacuum, which was filled by numerous petty entrepreneurs buying grain and selling manufactured goods. In addition, a substantial amount of economic support flowed into the province in the form of loans to commercial agriculture from the Inter-American Development Bank and the Peruvian government, and this contributed to a boom in the production of potatoes and grain for the market.

This boom had serious social costs. The majority of the peasants remained land-poor. Their attempts at seizing the haciendas had been repulsed by force. Now they saw a small number of middle-class and rich peasants prospering, obtaining bank loans to buy fertilizer, seed, and pesticides and to hire labor for commercial agriculture, and opening stores. For example, in Pacucha the number of stores increased from only four in 1970 to around thirty in 1981. In Argama a handful of landowners controlled all commercial agriculture, receiving thousands of dollars in bank loans and producing potatoes on a major scale. The resentment against these rising entrepreneurs was intensified by the fact that many were migrants from other parts of Peru or were returnees who had accumulated capital on the coast or in the jungle. The excesses of these entrepreneurs were constant topics of conversation among the peasants of the area in 1981-1982. For example, one prominent entrepreneur made his way to political office by rigging elections and then used his office to force some older peasants to sell or lease their land to him, under the threat of bringing costly legal suits against them. Other entrepreneurs were accused of acquiring community land for their own use, selling manufactured goods at inflated prices, and manufacturing cocaine paste.

Protests and rebellions were driven underground in Andahuaylas in the 1970s, but they continued. The left-wing press in Lima reported continued repression and jailing of area political leaders. The conflict sharpened in 1980 with the advent of Red Fatherland (PR), a radical faction that attracted a small following and was responsible for a few bombings, but this movement was quickly crushed and its leaders arrested.

This was the situation, then, in 1981. The *hacendados* were gone, but in their place were cooperatives that were plagued by problems of poor administration. The peasants resented both the cooperatives and the state: the first for depriving them of what they viewed as their historic right to land; the second, in addition to its collaboration with the first, for its longstanding association with an exploitive elite. At the same time, social tensions were being aggravated by increasingly polarized differences in wealth. All attempts at peaceful organizing were squelched and revolutionary activity driven underground. It is not surprising that Shining Path found this to be fertile ground.

Guerrilla War, 1981-1982

Shining Path's military campaign in Andahuaylas began only eighteen months after the start of the war in Ayacucho. Andahuaylas was a natural target for Sendero; the province is adjacent to Ayacucho and has many affinities with Ayacucho linguistically and culturally. Travel between the capital cities takes a day by bus and only three to five days by foot following trails over the mountains.

The first major Sendero action in Andahuaylas, in December 1981, was the destruction of the machinery at the Toxama cooperative, north of the provincial capital. Soon afterward, in March 1982, Andahuaylas was put under a state of emergency, which gave the police the right to arrest and detain suspects for any reason and suspended most other civil liberties. A curfew was imposed for the entire province. Civil Guard units in the countryside were reinforced and patrolled at night. Counterinsurgency units arrived in the provincial capital and boasted that they had arrived to "fight the terrorists."

These actions proved ineffective. The town police garrisons were helpless to enforce the curfew or to watch over a network of mountain trails after dark. The town of Andahuaylas, with its banks and government buildings and houses of the wealthy, was guarded by hundreds of police, but the countryside saw little police activity. In contrast, the guerrillas were active, assassinating several public figures, including a judge who lived in a village near Pincos and who had been involved in the agrarian reform. Death threats were slipped under the doors of merchants in the villages at night; even some of the major merchants in the provincial capital received threats. These took the form of simple warnings on slips of paper, signed "PCP" (Communist Party of Peru), the name Shining Path customarily uses. In some cases the threats were more elaborate, warning the merchant to leave the area but not to sell off his stock or holdings since these would be distributed "to the people."

In early April 1982 an incident in Pacucha brought home the superior tactics and intelligence of the guerrillas. A detachment of about thirty Civil Guards drove from Andahuaylas to Pacucha, left four men there to guard the village, and then set off to the north to search out a Sendero detachment. That night a group of guerrillas slipped past the police, attacked the garrison in Pacucha, and escaped. The guerrillas moved along paths to the main plaza, fronted by the government building where the police were quartered. Dynamite charges were set off inside metal cans, blowing out the windows of the police bus and government building. Then the guerrillas opened fire, but the police, demoralized by the noise, did not even return fire. The gunfire ended when the guerrillas retreated.

This action revealed some classic military errors on the part of the police, such a dividing their forces and failing to post sentries. It also revealed the superior tactics of Sendero, whose small, mobile bands could outmaneuver the police. As a result of this and other incidents, the morale of the Civil Guards was shaken. They withdrew from their village posts in a large populated area north of the provincial capital and the main highway.

So began a new stage of the conflict of Andahuaylas. Garrisons were reinforced in major towns along the highway. In the town of Andahuaylas itself, guards with submachine guns stood on every street corner; plain-clothes security officers of the Investigatory Police (PIP) were a common sight, and heavy equipment was flown in from Lima. Reportedly, the new PIP forces used increasingly brutal measures to interrogate suspects, including immersion in the filthy Chumbao River that flows through the central valley.

Meanwhile, in the countryside, the guerrillas reinforced their position, bringing in new bands from Ayacucho via mountainous trails along the edge of the jungle or remote valleys. These lines of transportation were not accessible to wheeled vehicles even in the dry season (May through October), and they lay beyond the reach of patrols from the police garrisons. From this semicircle along the northern edge of the province, the guerrillas began to attack almost simultaneously at a number of points, sometimes hitting several targets in the same night. In July they attacked the cooperatives of Pincos and Toxama, destroying a truck and threatening to kill anyone who attempted to dismantle the cooperatives. In August they assassinated a number of people who had previously received death threats, including alleged informers and former leaders of the cooperatives who had been accused of corruption.

After April 1982 the guerrillas essentially operated with a free rein. They traveled in bands of six or seven, wearing masks, normally by night but sometimes by day as well. These bands could attack a target and disappear well before the police arrive. The movement of the guerrillas was said to be facilitated by a network of safe houses, sleeping spots, and sources of supply. The guerrillas also received food, although opinions varied as to whether this was given by sympathizers or by people frightened into assisting. There was certainly a great deal of anxiety about the latter possibility, particularly after some alleged informers were shot. It was possible to piece together a picture of the guerrillas as a core group of young people from Ayacucho (speaking Quechua with an Ayacucho accent), but able to utilize contacts and even to recruit some followers.

Sendero targeted the cooperatives in particular. Since 1974, and in spite of their problems, the cooperatives at Toxama and Pincos had managed to stay in operation. By August 1982 both of these were destroyed, their produce distributed among nearby peasants or appropriated by Sendero. At Pincos, sugarcane was planted but never harvested — it rotted in the fields, was taken by neighbors, or was set afire.

Other attacks in the dry season were directed against state agencies associated with the cooperative movement or with commercial agriculture. A Dutch-Peruvian development agency, the Microregion Development Project (PRODERM), had been providing low-interest loans and technical assistance to cooperatives and to groups of low-income agriculturists in support of the agrarian reform. On July 25, this agency's office in Andahuaylas was hit by a dynamite blast and subsequently closed down. Faced with the growing threat from Sendero, most commercial farmers decided not to plant in the coming season, fearing that their harvests might be confiscated.

July and August also saw attacks on the region's infrastructure. Dynamite charges damaged electric power installations, telephone and telegraph stations, and the regional airport, used for military transport. Rumors circulated that Sendero planned to encircle and then assault the provincial capital itself. In response, the police concentrated on defending the capital while Sendero controlled most of rural Andahuaylas.

The absence of formal government in the rural areas was striking. All authorities at the district level and below, including the justices of the peace, resigned their posts.[15] No legal cases could be heard or decided; disputes were settled between families or not at all. The authorities did not intervene in regulating the community irrigation systems for September planting. Nonetheless, the planting went smoothly and there was little violence or robbery. In general, people were able to settle disputes peacefully, neighbors allocated water using traditional irrigation rights, and even trade and commerce continued. The peasant communities resorted to autonomous rule in which central government representatives were not needed.

Increasingly Shining Path intervened in village affairs during this period. In Andarapa, the guerrillas had a public forum in a school in which the teachers, who had asked students' families to contribute money for school improvements, were forced to justify this charge. In another incident the guerrillas entered Kaquiabamba, redistributed the cattle of wealthier landowners, broke into stores and gave away goods, and accused a judge of informing to the police. They beat him but let him live after asking for a verdict from the assembled public. Then in early November, the guerrillas entered Pacucha, dragged three merchants out of their beds, and shot them. Their stores were sacked and their goods distributed or taken. Meanwhile other attackers destroyed the small electric plant and robbed the medical post, a government facility that had provided medical care for a nominal charge. The leaders of this last attack were unknown Sendero militants, but the mass of the assailants, estimated at fifty people, were residents of a nearby village. Two of the three victims in Pacucha had left-wing credentials of a sort. One, although wealthy in local terms, had been a member of the Moscow-line Communist Party. He was an admirer of General Velasco and Ché Guevara, and he had hoped to send his children to study in the Soviet Union — or the United States. Another of the murdered men had been a leader of the land invasions of 1974. However, all three were merchants and were unpopular, primarily because of their wealth and their perceived exploitation of the peasants.

By this time, pressure was increasing on the central government to respond more effectively. In December 1982 the military entered the fight when the province of Andahuaylas was declared part of the EMZ, which also included provinces in Ayacucho and, later, Huancavelica. Reports of atrocities against civilians began to increase, but now committed primarily by the military and not Shining Path. The pattern continued of Sendero waiting for the military to grow careless and then attacking in quick raids. When I returned in 1985, I was able to follow the course of this new, more brutal stage of the counterinsurgency campaign.

The War Continues, 1983-1985

After 1982 the cooperatives ceased to exist as functioning units. The land of cooperatives such as Laguna had been distributed to its members as part of the Fernando Belaúnde Terry government (1980-1985) modification of the military's agrarian reform, so that now the cooperatives were no more than collections of small-holders. The larger commercial farmers, in contrast, had cut back or stopped production, so the income from commercial agriculture dropped considerably.

In Pacucha there were two striking changes from 1982 to 1985. First, there was now a permanent garrison of thirty Civil Guards in the community. Second, there were remarkably few young adults. In 1982 young people in their late teens and early twenties, including many returned Lima migrants, had been a conspicuous part of village life, but now they were absent. In part this phenomenon can be explained by the economic depression of the 1980s; the level of unemployment and underemployment reached unprecedented levels of nearly 60 percent.[16] The agricultural wage fell from U.S. $1.20 per day in 1982 to U.S. $0.50 in 1985. One result was that young migrants in Lima could no longer afford to travel to Pacucha and remained in the city.

It became evident, however, that the major reason for the absence of young people was that they had been killed, jailed, or driven away by the police (or had joined Sendero) in the previous three years. In 1983 to 1984 a detachment of approximately one hundred counterinsurgency forces, including the specialized anti-terrorist *Sinchis* of the Civil Guard, were sent in to occupy the district of Pacucha. This force's main activity consisted of rounding up, arresting, and interrogating suspected guerrillas; the primary targets were young men who were returned migrants. Those against whom there was evidence of "subversion" were beaten or tortured and taken away to jail in Lima. In one case the evidence consisted of a red flag, which turned out to be cloth owned by a boy's mother, a seamstress. Electric shock was now used in

Andahuaylas police stations against political prisoners. From the district of Pacucha alone, informants claimed that between forty and fifty young people were taken away and had not returned. At one site in the district, according to a reliable informant, a number of accused guerrillas from the area were shot and buried secretly one night.

In 1985 there was less police activity in Andahuaylas and the situation was relatively stable. However, in other parts of the province another Peruvian police unit, the Republican Guard, continued to harass suspected individuals and communities. One such community was Tancayllo (west of the provincial capital), the adopted home of Lino Quintanilla, one of the leaders of the land invasions of 1974. Written testimony from Tancayllo, signed by fifty residents, describes the kind of intimidation used by the police in June 1985. Police beat peasants indiscriminately, including old people and children, and threatened to massacre the entire village. In one incident, they beat and robbed store owners, beat a man with rifle butts in the main square, and raped two women. These events are consistent with the pattern of police violence against peasants throughout the EMZs.

Most charges against detainees are weak and will not hold up in court, in part because of the nature of the evidence, which consists of suspicion of sympathy with the guerrillas or with left-wing ideas in general, rather than violent acts. For example, in June 1985 it was reported that twenty-nine people from Andahuaylas who had been accused of "subversive activities and assaults with dynamite" were being released from prison where they had been held for four years with all charges dropped for lack of evidence.[17]

The police were unsuccessful in their efforts to identify or capture Sendero militants. Rather, many suspects were rounded up in hopes of capturing a few active guerrillas. A central problem was a lack of intelligence about guerrilla operations in rural areas, largely because the population neither trusted nor cooperated with the police. The balance of military power shifted during 1983 to 1985, but this was due as much to fundamental weaknesses of Shining Path — small number, lack of arms, and lack of active support — as to the massive force deployed by the military.

The Peasant Response to Shining Path

The guerrillas had access to food and supplies, they could evade the government forces, and they were remarkably precise in their targeting of unpopular individuals and institutions. Clearly, Sendero had established an underground network in Andahuaylas. This fact tends to confirm reports that other radical organizations based in Andahuaylas merged with Sendero in 1982. Julio César Mezzich, one of the organizers of the 1974 land occupations and a former leader of VR, is now believed to be a regional commander of Sendero.[18]

What is less clear is how much active support there is for the movement in Andahuaylas. It is important to distinguish here among active support, passive support, and sympathy. Sympathy means a general or specific agreement with the actions or philosophy of the guerrillas. Passive support refers to a willingness to tolerate the presence of the guerrillas and a disinclination to take any action against them, including informing to the police. Active support refers to acts of commission.

The evidence from Andahuaylas suggests that the peasants have a great deal of sympathy for the actions of Shining Path, and this leads to widespread passive support but not a great deal of active support. Active support is limited to attacks on unpopular individuals, usually between villages with historical reasons for mutual antagonism. Sendero has not mobilized a "people's army" in any sense of the term.

When Sendero first emerged in Andahuaylas in 1981, peasants were unclear about the guerrillas' aims. Discussing this, people often remarked simply, "We do not know what the terrorists want." After political assassinations began in 1982, opinions began to be more strongly felt and more polarized. On the one hand, there was considerable approval of "killing the rich." On the other hand, there was some question about whether the choice of targets was always just. As a number of people stated, "I have nothing against their killing the rich, but I don't like it when they kill peasants."

Generally, discussion about the guerrillas in 1982 did not concern the question of redistributing land, much less any broader Maoist program. It was rare, in fact, for people to discuss Communist principles, and when people discussed communism they generally opposed it, fearing that Sendero might want to expropriate private land to form collectives. Rather, what people focused on in daily conversation and what they generally approved was revenge against "the rich."

The resentment was particularly strong against some of the wealthier peasants who were assassinated. As one person remarked, the men killed in the attack on Pacucha in 1982 deserved what they got because they were rich, had two or three houses, and had acquired their wealth through unfair exchange (e.g., buying grain at a low price and selling high). They received bank loans, which gave them plenty of cash for buying materials and hiring laborers when others had nothing. In addition, the men who died pretended to be unable to speak Quechua, holding themselves aloof from the community.

Sympathy for the guerrillas, then, was based on notions of economic justice in Andahuaylas communities where the core value is reciprocity and there is resentment against those who accumulate wealth, particularly if they do not remain involved in relations of reciprocity. The peasant household economy relies on mutual assistance between households, particularly for agricultural production. Economic relationships are strongly conditioned by sets of social obligations; all relations between people are defined and maintained by exchanges of labor and goods.

Some terms used by villagers in evaluating the morality of Shining Path are comprehensible only in light of these notions of reciprocity. The entrepreneurs who were killed are perceived as having cut themselves off from others socially. They are selfish egotists who only look out for themselves. They refuse to speak Quechua — that is, they reject the cultural heritage of the community, including reciprocity. They act like *mistis* (Quechua for *mestizo*), adopting the culture of the towns. In short, they are no longer peasants and thus they are beyond the moral economy of the community.

Importantly, the Spanish word for peasant, *campesino*, as it is used here contains both class and ethnic connotations. When asked to explain the term, people described a person who is "poor, like us," that is, like us of the communities. Yet there is a clear ethnic dimension as well, since the "rich" also live in the towns, do not speak Quechua, practice standard Catholicism, and dominate the peasants. When people debated the morality of killing a person, the discussion centered around whether or not or to what extent he or she was a *campesino/campesina*.

Another source of sympathy and support was the guerrillas' targeting of the cooperatives. Very few people in Pacucha opposed the bombings and other attacks on the cooperatives. What people discussed was the history of the exploitation by the cooperatives and their leaders. Tales were told of the cooperative leaders eating in good restaurants and otherwise living beyond their apparent income, of entire shipments of grain being unaccounted for, and of the associates being left with virtually nothing. In addition, there was resentment because the cooperatives retained the areas of land formerly held by the haciendas. Overall then, sympathizers believed that the guerrillas were fighting for economic justice.

There was also great resentment and fear of the police who, from the peasant point of view, acted more cruelly and arbitrarily than the guerrillas. When the guerrillas struck, it was against people whose "crimes" were well known or against specific targets such as cooperatives. On the other hand, the police arrested and interrogated blindly, the numbers of "disappeared" increased rapidly, and those whose relatives were taken away were left with great bitterness. Aggravating the situation even more was an underlying conflict between Quechua-speaking peasants of the highlands and the police who, due to class and ethnic bias, looked down on Quechua speakers and poor agriculturists.

By 1985, then, sympathy for the guerrillas was stronger than ever. One indication of this is the changing terminology used by peasants when referring to members of Shining Path. In 1982 they were known as "terrorists" (*terroristas, terros, terukuna*) or sometimes, sarcastically, as *los universitarios*. In 1985, in contrast, they were often called "comrades" or "buddies" (*compañeros*). To be sure, opinions about Sendero were often ambiguous and equivocal, an expression of admiration for Sendero mixed with anger over the brutal murder of neighbors, or a fear of both the police and the guerrillas. Increasingly peasants felt trapped between two hostile forces. Yet some degree of sympathy for Sendero could be found over a broad range of people, including men and women, old and young people, and monolingual Quechua speakers as well as bilingual speakers of Spanish and returned urban migrants. The only group among which there was no sympathy for the guerrillas was that of the merchants and store owners who were clearly threatened by the movement from the outset.

Another group, although on balance no more sympathetic to the guerrillas than any other group, expressed the reasons for its sympathy on a different basis. This group was the young adults, in their late teens and early twenties, particularly those with formal education and migratory experience. These young people described their approval of the guerrillas' actions in more nationalistic and nation-oriented terms than expressed by older peasants. One informant, for example, said that the guerrillas were fighting against foreigners, including the United States, England, and Russia, and that the guerrillas were seeking to regain the ancient territory of the people of this region. Others sympathized with Sendero because it opposed inflation and supported full recognition of the provinces. Before the movement emerged, it was remarked, no one in Lima paid any attention to places like Andahuaylas. Still others admired the guerrillas simply for their courage in taking on the military. There is nothing very communistic about these sentiments, even though some of the people who expressed them support legal, left-wing parties such as the United Left (IU) coalition.

It was this group, however, which bore the brunt of the repression. This is because of a view that it is this type of young person who is most likely to be radical and to support Shining Path. This does not mean that a majority of this group supports Sendero. Like their parents' generation, the young adults of Pacucha resent the state and aspire to holding plots of land as a guarantee of basic subsistence. They also have broader goals due to more education and greater exposure to other parts of the country. Returned migrants from Lima describe their experiences with political parties, labor unions, and better working conditions. These experiences were central to their political development by making them more aware of alternatives to the hacienda system of domination.

It is misleading to view these young people as alienated from their peasant origins, which is an important aspect of their political education and their economic orientation. Teodor Shanin notes that one needs to view peasant migrants in terms of their places of origin, not as political actors without a past.[19] Shining Path expresses the frustration that many of them feel about the continuing neglect of the highlands at the expense of the coast and Lima. Thus, there is sympathy for the movement among young adults, but this reflects neither revolutionary sentiment nor active support. The indiscriminate targeting of this group on the basis of presumed left-wing sympathies is both unjustified and tragic.

Comparisons with Other Regions

The core areas of Sendero organizing encompass the poorest areas of the Peruvian highlands, including Ayacucho, Huancavelica, Apurímac, and Puno.

While these regions are diverse, certain patterns seen in Andahuaylas are also visible elsewhere, illustrating both the sources of SL's appeal and some obstacles to its success. Common themes include economic pressures on the peasantry, frustration with the obstructed agrarian reform, and the remote and exploitive heritage of the state. The course of the war has been similar, as Sendero attacks unpopular institutions and individuals, and the police or military respond with massive, indiscriminate force.

A major factor that differentiates these areas is the presence or absence of an effective political opposition or alternative to Shining Path. Where present, grass-roots political organizations have represented a major obstacle to Sendero's growth. In Puno, in particular, Sendero's greatest rival is not the state but moderate, left-wing organizations, including political parties and religious-based organizations, which provide an alternative vehicle for political protest and reform. This presents a sharp contrast to the political vacuum found in Andahuaylas in the 1980s. Thus, although SL has been able to achieve some success in Puno, it has had a greater challenge on the local level and its support has eroded quickly in some areas.[20]

In all areas, Sendero has consistently emphasized land redistribution, obviously in an attempt to appeal to the small-holding peasants and rural laborers. This focus on inequality in land tenure is apparent in the early writings of some people who later became Sendero leaders, such as the economic anthropologist Antonio Díaz Martinez, who described the stark contrast between land-poor communities and wealthy haciendas in the Pampas River Valley of Ayacucho.[21] The emphasis on land is also seen in the constant reference to the work of José Carlos Mariátegui (1895-1930), whose entire program was based on the need for the return of land to the so-called indigenous communities. Among Sendero's first actions in Ayacucho, as early as 1971, was the driving out of representatives of the official agrarian reform agency.[22] Recent Sendero writings describe "the land problem: *the motive force of the class struggle in the countryside.*"[23]

This issue continually reappears in various accounts of Sendero organizing. In the Tayacuja region of Huancavelica, there is a history of organizing by peasants against haciendas, particularly since 1973. The Tayacuja Peasant Organization was drawn into conflict with the official agrarian reform bureaucracy over the disposal of hacienda land, and this erupted into land seizures and government reprisals from 1976 through 1980. Thus when

Shining Path entered this region in 1982, it was able to exploit similar issues of land redistribution and anticooperative sentiment to those of Andahuaylas.[24]

In Puno, Sendero focused on the longstanding resentment against the haciendas and the failure of earlier agrarian reforms. Although the hacienda system was destroyed, the social relations between landowners and peasants continued along the lines originally established by the haciendas. Sendero entered the area as early as 1982 and began recruiting university students. Its first actions were bombings followed by assaults on a large, state-run cooperative in Azángaro. This met with some degree of popular support, judging from Sendero's ability to gather followers for these assaults (although afterward when questioned by police, people claimed that they had been forced to participate). The attacks on large landholdings have continued; in 1986 Sendero occupied and sacked sixteen cooperatives and haciendas. Other terrorist actions of mutilation and murder focused on the leaders of agricultural cooperatives. In response, the government of Alan García Pérez (1985-1990) attempted to carry out a land redistribution program of its own in order to head off Sendero's appeal to the peasantry.[25]

In Ayacucho as well, the land issue has been important as an organizing tool. A key example is Sendero's apparently senseless sacking of a university research station, followed by attempts to organize a collective on the university-owned lands. Although widely condemned, this action was obviously designed to appeal to land-hungry peasants. Shining Path attempted to justify the attack based on the need for land redistribution as well as a tactic of sabotaging the production of food for the market.[26]

Clearly the land issue is not the only explanation for the growth of Sendero, particularly since the movement has been able to develop in such diverse areas of Peru. The surprising flexibility of the movement is seen in its ability to organize factory workers in Lima and coca-growing peasants in the Huallaga Valley. All the same, Sendero's strongest support still comes from areas of the south-central Peruvian Andes, and this is where the issues of land, ethnicity, and economic pressure are most relevant.

Conclusion

Our case study of Andahuaylas has focused on the specific economic and social processes in the region, particularly since the agrarian reform beginning in 1969. The state thwarted a radical, grass-roots movement for land reform and imposed its own bureaucratic cooperative structure. The cooperatives lacked accountability and functioned in many respects as the haciendas had. Because their very creation ended the possibility of large-scale land redistribution, the cooperatives became foci of resentment by the peasants.

During this same period, the economy became increasingly polarized and social tensions mounted. An entrepreneurial class filled the commercial vacuum left by the departure of the landlords, and these entrepreneurs prospered with the help of loans for commercial agriculture. At the same time, the downturn of the Peruvian economy led to depressed wages and unemployment for the rest of the population.

The emergence of Shining Path should not be seen simply as a reflection of poverty but rather in terms of these specific circumstances. Sendero has been adroit at taking advantage of this situation, recruiting a core of devoted followers, organizing over a period of years, and attacking the objects of popular resentment — upwardly mobile peasants and state-sponsored cooperatives.

The specific character of this peasant economy conditions the form of the rebellion. A majority of households depend on wage labor, both locally and in the cities, and the increasing dependence on wage labor makes peasants especially vulnerable to economic fluctuations. At the same time, Andahuaylas remains a region of small-holding peasants whose desire for land is intense. As peasant-workers, the agriculturalists of Andahuaylas rely on wages for a portion of their income, but they retain landholdings as a source of economic security. They also depend on forms of economic reciprocity as a central element in the agricultural economy. Peasant economy and society still are central to an understanding of Shining Path's growth in these areas.

Many peasants sympathize with Sendero because the movement reflects their longstanding aspirations for local control and for ownership of plots of land. The movement attacks elements in rural society that are perceived as unjust and as in conflict with these fundamental goals. In this sense, support for SL fits a pattern of peasant rebellions against haciendas and the state since the end of the nineteenth century. For Sendero sets itself up as a moral authority and as a voice for peasants' grievances, playing upon cultural principles including notions of folk justice and opposition to *mistis.* Although many of

Sendero's active supporters are young, mobile people with urban experience, their aspirations and values are shaped by their peasant background.

In spite of its ability to attract sympathy and support among parts of the peasantry, it is highly unlikely that Sendero will be able to capture state power or even to control large areas of the Andes for long periods of time. Sendero's secretive cell organization leads to effective small-scale guerrilla harassing operations, but not to the mobilization of mass support. Its ideology is foreign to the peasants and at odds with many of their fundamental beliefs. It remains a highly destructive organization, offering the illusion of the resurrection of the Andean community but the reality of short-lived revenge against some of the objects of popular resentment.

Notes

1. See especially, "Develop the People's War to Serve World Revolution," Revolutionary Communist Party, *A World to Win*, March 8, 1987, pp. 4-13, 77-88.

2. These actions are described in Carlos Iván Degregori, *Sendero Luminoso, lucha armada y utopia autoritaria* (Lima: Instituto de Estudios Peruanos, 1986); and in Lewis Taylor, *Maoism in the Andes: Sendero Luminoso and the Contemporary Guerrilla Movement in Peru,* Working Paper No. 2, (University of Liverpool, Centre for Latin American Studies, 1983).

3. Sendero writings adopt Mariátegui's outdated terms as the "semi-feudal foundations of the state." See Sendero Luminoso, "Develop Guerrilla Warfare." Pamphlet, originally published March 1982, translated by the Revolutionary Communist Party, n.d., p. 6.

4. Instituto de Defensa Legal, *Peru 1989, En la espiral de violencia* (Lima: Instituto de Defensa Legal, 1990); Inter-Church Committee on Human Rights in Latin American, *1989 Annual Report on the Human Rights Situation in Peru* (Toronto, Canada, January 1990); Amnesty International, *Caught Between Two Fires* (New York: Amnesty International, November 1989).

5. Cynthia McClintock, "Why Peasants Rebel: The Case of Peru's Sendero Luminoso," *World Politics*, 37, October 1984, pp. 48-84; David Scott Palmer, "Rebellion in Rural Peru: The Origins and Evolution of Sendero Luminoso," *Comparative Politics*, 18:2, January 1986, pp. 127-146; Carlos Iván DeGregori, *Sendero Luminoso: Los hondos y mortales desencuentros* (Lima: Instituto de Estudios Peruanos, 1985); Henri Favre, "Perou: Sentier Lumineaux et Horizons Obscurs," *Problèmes D'Amérique Latine*, 72, 2e trimestre 1984, pp. 3-27.

6. Peru, *Censos Nacionales, VIII de Población, III de Vivienda, 12 de julio de 1981, Resultados Definitivos*, vol. A, tomo I, II, Departamento de Apurímac (Lima: Instituto Nacional de Estadística, 1984).

7. In 1983 the new province of Chincheros was created out of portions of northwestern Andahuaylas, including the districts of Chincheros, Ongoy, and Ocobamba, among others.

8. Rodrigo Montoya, *Capitalismo y neo-capitalismo en el Perú* (Lima: Mosca Azul, 1980).

9. On the hacienda system's expansion and decline, see Ronald H. Berg, "The Effects of Return Migration on a Highland Peruvian Community," Ph.D. diss., University of Michigan, 1984; Abdón Palomino, "Movimiento campesina de 1974 y reforma agraria en Andahuaylas," *Allpanchis*, 11/12, 1978, pp. 187-211; Lino Quintanilla, *Andahuaylas: la lucha por la tierra* (Lima: Mosca Azul, 1981); and Rodrigo Sánchez, *Toma de tierras y conciencia política campesina; Las lecciones de Andahuaylas* (Lima: Instituto de Estudios Peruanos, 1981).

10. Peru, *Censo nacional agropecuario, II: Departamento de Apurímac (1972)* (Lima: Ministerio de Agricultura, 1975).

11. David Scott Palmer, *"Revolution from Above": Military Government and Popular Participation in Peru, 1968-1972*, Dissertation Series #47, Latin American Studies Program, Cornell University, 1973, Table 13, p. 198.

12. Peru, *Estudio socio-económico de la provincia de Andahuaylas* (Lima: Ministerio de Agricultura, Dirección de Comunidades, 1970), pp. 63-67.

13. Sánchez, *Toma de tierras*, pp. 85-86.

14. Palomino, "Movimiento campesino," 208.

15. The local justices of the peace (*Juezes de Paz*) arbitrate civil and some criminal cases on an informal basis. They, along with other district or local authorities, including governor (*gobernador*), mayor (*alcalde*) and president of the community (*presidents de comunidad*), all left their posts. This fits a pattern of intimidation seen nationwide in Peru.

16. Cynthia McClintock, "Why Peru's Alan García Is a Man on the Move," *LASA Forum*, 16:4, Winter 1986, pp. 9-12.

17. *La República*, Lima, June 10, 1985, p. 17.

18. Palmer, "Rebellion in Rural Peru," p. 140. See also "El Sendero de Mezzich," *Caretas*, 752, June 13, 1983, pp. 22-23, 64.

19. Teodor Shanin, "The Peasants Are Coming: Migrants Who Labour, Peasants Who Travel, and Marxists Who Write," *Race and Class*, 19, Winter 1978, pp. 277-288.

20. On Puno, see Raúl González, "Puno: El corredor senderista," *Quehacer*, 39, February-March, 1986, pp. 49-58.

21. Antonio Díaz Martínez, "Ayacucho y las comunidades del hambre," *América Indígena*, 30, April 1970, pp. 307-320.

22. Palmer, "Rebellion in Rural Peru," p. 136.

23. Sendero Luminoso, "Develop the People's War," p. 84. Emphasis added.

24. José María Salcedo, "The Price of Peace: A Report from the Emergency Zone," *NACLA Report on the Americas*, 20:3, June 1986, pp. 37-42.

25. *The Andean Report*, July 31, 1986, pp. 2-3. For other accounts of Shining Path in Puno, see González, "Puno: El Corredor Senderista," and Instituto de Defensa Legal (IDL), *Perú 1989: En la espiral de violencia* (Lima: IDL, 1990), pp. 33-55.

26. Degregori, *Sendero Luminoso, lucha armada*, p. 11.

6

GUERRILLAS AND COCA IN THE UPPER HUALLAGA VALLEY[*]

José E. Gonzales

Until 1937 the Upper Huallaga Valley (UHV), spreading along the banks of the Huallaga River in the departments of Huánuco and San Martín, was accessible only by long boat journeys and jungle paths. Only in 1937 did a one-lane highway reach the upper reaches of the Huallaga River, at what as to become the settlement of Tingo María. The settlers brought their traditions with them. Among them was the *chaccheo*, or coca leaf chewing, which farm workers in particular found useful to reduce sensations of thirst, hunger, and fatigue.

Today, over 25,000 people live in Tingo María, and the original one-lane highway has become the city's principal avenue. Outside of a half-dozen paved

[*]Part of this chapter is based on the author's "Perú: Sendero Luminoso en el valle de la coca," in Diego García Sayán, ed., *Coca, cocaína, narcotráfico: Laberinto en los Andes* (Lima: Comisión Andina de Juristas, 1989), pp. 207-222.

streets, however, all of the city's thoroughfares are still of dirt and only the main square displays a few substantial buildings. Were it not for a large number of bank offices and a very active and visible commercial trade, little would indicate that the city is one of Peru's most prosperous. The regular transit of trucks with soldiers, large numbers of policemen with automatic weapons patrolling the streets, and camouflaged helicopters whirring past at treetop level are evidence of dangers that are not immediately apparent.

Between 1970 and 1980 coca plantings increased at least sixfold in the area around Tingo María, to over six thousand hectares (one hectare equals two and one-half acres). The ease of growing the coca plants in the area (three crops a year using little or no fertilizer) and the quality of the production (the varieties produced in the area, *erotoxilon* and *novogratense*, contain the highest levels of alkaloid) sparked the interest of Peruvian and Colombian traffickers. The rapid increase in demand for cocaine in the United States led them to appreciate the possibilities for increased production in the Upper Huallaga valley.

By 1987 official figures listed the annual production of coca leaf as 28,560 metric tons,[1] while agronomists responsible for compiling this data stated in interviews with the author that the actual figure was 80,000 metric tons. The same year, government officials in the UHV maintained that about 95 percent of the local economy was based on the illegal activities of drug trafficking or coca production; the balance, from such legal enterprises as a coffee and cacao cooperatives, a tea plantation, a sawmill, a palm oil plantation, and a brick factory.[2] The volume of coca production not only led to rapid increases in coca paste trafficking but also created the necessary conditions for the appearance of Shining Path guerrillas in the valley.

The Maoist Guerrillas

Shining Path began its political work in the UHV in 1980.[3] Several militants arrived in Puerto Pizana and Aucayacu at that time and settled as coca growers. Two years later the buildup of the organization began with the help of several members who came from Tarapoto.[4]

The central government discovered the first signs of Sendero's presence in the area during an antidrug operation organized in 1984 by a specialized 500-man police force, the Mobile Rural Patrol Unit (UMOPAR), in a joint effort with the U.S. Drug Enforcement Administration (DEA). Originally designed as an exclusively antidrug operation,[5] it turned into an antisubversive campaign when policemen found evidence of the existence of Sendero People's Schools in small hamlets and coca paste laboratories on the banks of the Huallaga River and detained several members of the organization. Shortly afterward, the mayor of Tingo María, Tito Jaime, who also happened to be a *cocalero* and the major organizer of the coca growers as well, was murdered. While initial reports pointed to drug traffickers as the killers, in light of Shining Path's strategy it could just as easily have been a Sendero assassination to eliminate the head of an established organization that could represent the coca growers.

Shining Path has rarely claimed responsibility for its actions. In this case, however, several clues linked the murder to it. Jaime had founded the Defense and Development Front of Leoncio Prado Province, an organization that represented regional interests clearly linked to coca, and one that Sendero subsequently tried to topple and use for its own purposes. Jaime's assassination also served as a warning for any other individual with leadership ambitions. The murder also reflected one of the constants in the Sendero strategy, opposition to any legal organization that could defy its supremacy. The subsequent systematic assassinations of local authorities in the area and in other parts of the country attest to this.

These incidents forced the government to place the area under a state of emergency starting in July 1984, with a political-military command that concentrated on repressing the guerrillas rather than on antidrug operations. Army General Julio Carbajal D'Angelo, placed in charge of the emergency zone (EMZ), did not consider drug trafficking to be the real problem for the area or for the country. He also claimed that involving the military in the fight against drugs could subject his officers and men to the temptations of easy money and corrupt his forces. Carbajal maintained that the coca business was actually beneficial for the country; it gave work to thousands of peasants and generated substantial foreign currency. During his six months in the post, Carbajal was quite successful. By dropping platoons of soldiers along the valley floor and patrolling escape routes through the mountains and along the roads, the army was able to disperse the guerrillas' columns within three months. At the same time, General Carbajal kept UMOPAR from executing antidrug operations, a move that gave him the support of both the local peasant growers and the traffickers.

Thus free from police action, a new coca boom permitted an increase both in crop production and in other kinds of violence. With Shining Path and UMOPAR out of the UHV, the leading drug lords were left to exercise authority over local traffickers. Carbajal and the officers under his command then applied a strategy in which many active in drug production and trafficking were used as sources for intelligence information and as local armed groups against the guerrillas.[6] However, the drug lords took advantage of the temporary power vacuum to begin a terror campaign in the UHV that thoroughly frightened the population. They also began paying lower prices for the coca leaf in order to increase profits. Most of the violence was perpetrated against bodyguards and other employees of the *patrones*, or coca lords. Tales of such coca lords as Catalino Escalante, "the Vampire," are still passed around in the UHV heartland of Uchiza and Tocache. Escalante, as a youth of twenty, killed a local journalist in the main square of Tocache after he published a story referring to Escalante as a drug trafficker. Escalante also frequently terrorized opponents by beheading his victims and throwing their bodies into the Huallaga.

The police also contributed to the problem. In collusion with local traffickers, some policemen based in the UHV did nothing about the trafficking and actually participated in the extortion of the coca growers. These abuses of the population by the traffickers on the one hand and the police on the other generated the opening that allowed the Sendero guerrillas to regroup and begin again the process of reestablishing their influence in the valley. They were aided by the actions of President Alán García Pérez (1985-1990), who lifted the state of emergency and ordered a new wave of antidrug operations that continued until 1987. The police resumed coca crop eradications and the interdiction of drug trafficking, and in the process revived repression of the local population.

Shining Path then took advantage of what its own documents refer to as "power vacuums" and "internal contradictions." Between April and May 1986, Shining Path held the fourth plenary session of its Central Committee. There, the guerrilla leaders defined the "Topping of the Great Leap with a Golden Seal,"[7] the beginning of a "New Great Plan" in January 1987, and the organization of its first congress. The plan included the Upper Huallaga Valley as one of the main areas of concentration. At that time, from 60,000 to 300,000 families[8] grew coca leaf in the Upper Huallaga; it was precisely those people, trapped between the rule of the traffickers and the corruption of the police, that Sendero addressed. The guerrillas, seeking a social base to expand its movement in the UHV, designed a strategy based on an alliance with the peasants and a *modus vivendi* with the coca lords. By then it was clear that the military's 1984-1985 strategy of provoking a split between the coca producers and traffickers, on the one hand, and the guerrillas, on the other, had failed.

In early 1987 Sendero guerrillas launched open attacks against police stations and organized the first of several armed strikes.[9] By August guerrillas and peasants demonstrated that they could completely control the valley if they wished. They blew up two bridges and destroyed the highway through the UHV by digging ditches across it every hundred yards (273 in all between Tingo María and Nuevo Progreso!). This stopped traffic completel y for three days, from commercial vehicles and private cars to police and military patrols. The government responded by placing the area once again under a state of emergency. It also organized a police operation that, under the guise of an antidrug effort, attempted to dismantle the guerrillas through repression and intimidation. The operation failed; its principal result was to increase the animosity of the local population against the police once again.

As 1987 drew to a close, circumstances continued to favor Sendero's UHV strategy. Cooperation in antidrug efforts between the Peruvian police and the DEA was increasing with the presence of U.S. advisors and instructors and with the use of U.S. helicopters. Coca crop eradication, once done by hand by Control and Reduction of Coca Crops (CORAH) workers transported overland, began to be carried out by crews carried to the sites by helicopters piloted by American crews with gasoline-powered weed cutters to cut down the coca bushes.[10] The apparent success of the new antidrug strategy in the UHV, highly publicized by the government, gave Sendero new opportunities. During 1988 the guerrillas' actions increased both in number and in levels of violence. A second armed strike, complete with rebel ambushes, blew up six bridges and killed over fifty police and soldiers. It represented the most dramatic evidence of growing Sendero power against the government in the region. With the slogan "Against genocide and eradication," suggesting how much the crop eradication program had alienated UHV residents, the guerrillas began to control entire towns, including Uchiza and Tocache, the largest in the valley after Tingo María. In those communities, the guerrilla organized the inhabitants for various activities, including teams to keep the town cleaned up; everyone participated, including bank officials! Sendero soon concluded that it had done well; it noted in July 1988 that the valley was a key arena for the "vigorous development of the popular war," "open work with the masses," and the "peasants war."[11]

With the growing immobility of the police and the continuing passivity of local authorities, Shining Path continued to consolidate its authority and dispersed "revolutionary justice" throughout more and more of the valley. Sendero "law," as described by a foreign priest who lives in the UHV, is one with "hyper-Christian" morals except for the death penalty as a punishment for transgressions.[12] This "law" has two parts: cardinal rules and commandments. The three cardinal rules are: (1) Obey orders; (2) Take from the masses neither a single needle nor a piece of string; (3) Turn over everything which is captured. The eight commandments are: (1) Speak courteously; (2) Pay an honest price for everything purchased; (3) Return everything borrowed; (4) Give compensation for anything broken or destroyed; (5) Do not hit or injure people; (6) Do not take farm produce; (7) Do not abuse women; (8) Do not mistreat prisoners.

These guidelines gave many peasants an order they had previously lacked.[13] To apply its rules, Sendero formed Popular Committees, elected in every community and made up of a delegate and a subdelegate. The guerrillas also established Popular Bases, party organs consisting of a political, a military, and a logistical officer. The committees supervised community activities, from celebration of weddings, to supervision of local production, to control of sexual mores (prohibiting infidelity, prostitution, and homosexuality), and even determining on which days drinking would be permitted. The bases applied penalties, organized Popular Schools and political rallies, enlisted youth in the guerrillas' Popular Army, gave military instruction, provided economic and military support to Shining Path's party structure, and controlled military operations. Rules were enforced with iron-handed discipline: There were no second chances, with offenses punishable by either exile or summary execution. The popular army had, according to local and official sources, main, local, and base forces, with about three thousand armed fighters in the Main Force and about the same number in the others.[14] In this manner, Shining Path gave the UHV population a simple, functional order and ended their previously unsettled and precarious situation.

By late 1988 Shining Path completely controlled the valley road. Every passing vehicle paid a fee at the Sendero "toll booth," a rope put across the highway. Driving along the road, one could see extensive party graffiti on every available wall, which made clear that the guerrillas were throughout the area. At the entrance to towns such as Paraíso and Tocache, Sendero manned the control posts armed with submachine guns. Every outsider who arrived was required to show identification documents and to explain the purpose of the visit. The guerrillas decided how long the visitor could stay (sometimes less than an hour) and assigned someone to accompany the individual on foot or by motorcycle. During the visits, a "guest" could note a certain tension in the towns along with a certain tranquility among the populace not seen before Shining Path's arrival. In one valley town, La Morada, a founder commented:

> The *compañeros* behave well, they are well mannered and treat people courteously. They helped us get rid of the homosexuals, prostitutes, and criminals that used to gather around here. They told them to leave; those that didn't showed up dead in the road. No town official was about to intervene. In addition they organize weekly meetings; they call the people together and we listen to lessons on politics. They taught us that we had been exploited and that now the party will support us. The best thing, though, is that now the police don't abuse us like they used to and nobody steals a thing. You can leave your car in the middle of the road unlocked for several days, go back and actually find it completely intact.[15]

In order to control the area, Sendero did not use the brutal methods it had been known to practice elsewhere. The support it received in the UHV was based more on SL proselytizing of selected individuals than on its efforts to gain the ideological allegiance of the masses. This made it strong but also fragile. Its support among the general population was based more on local concern for protecting and expanding coca crop and coca paste production than on the political cause of orthodox Maoism that Shining Path offered. Other potential problems the rebels had to face included corruption among Sendero militants and the possibility of a rebellion from the local coca lords.

None of these challenges turned out to be the direct cause of Shining Path's second defeat in the valley. The unheralded arrival of an army officer, hitherto unnoticed by everyone, including the government, posed an obstacle for Sendero that it could not surmount and that may well have set back its plans by several years.

The General and His Weapons

During much of 1989, the guerrillas were able to continue to consolidate their control of the UHV, with the significant if unwitting help of the programs in the area against drug production and trafficking. A new base of operations for crop eradication and interdiction was constructed on the banks of the Huallaga River near the small town of Santa Lucía.[16] In March an herbicide spray test on sixteen hectares of coca crops with Tebuthieron, manufactured by Eli Lilly and known commercially as Spike, also played into Shining Path's hands. Coca growers and traffickers were profoundly disturbed by this new threat to their livelihood. The Spike issue also was a major factor in provoking one of the worst defeats the government suffered in the valley. This was the massive Sendero attack on the Uchiza police post in which ten police and two civilians died.

The attack of March 27 continued throughout the night. Shortly after dawn on the twenty-eighth, guerrillas seized the post. The surviving policemen surrendered; while those of the lower ranks were pardoned, all the officers were executed in the main plaza. The guerrillas then raised their red flag with the hammer and sickle on the town flagpole. The guerrillas, supported by the local populace and the traffickers, not only defeated the police but also forced the resignation of Armando Villanueva, Minister of the Interior and head of the National Police.

Villanueva, one of the most respected leaders of President García's American Popular Revolutionary Alliance (APRA) party, had recently been appointed to the position, in part because of his reputation as a hard-liner on the issue of Sendero. His reputation did not help him, however, in handling the guerrillas and the problems of his ministry. The APRA leader faced an economic budget crisis, a general lack of discipline among the police, and an incomplete understanding of the guerrilla phenomenon and its strength in the UHV. His resignation was provoked in part by the publication of the transcript of radio communication he maintained with the policemen of Uchiza who pleaded in vain for help and support for almost ten hours. Villanueva tried to get some air support but was not able to convince either the DEA at Santa Lucía or his own Peruvian Air Force to fly reinforcements to the area. Both responded that their helicopters were not equipped to fight at night and remained, like the minister, listening to the desperate pleas of the policemen throughout the battle.[17]

Villanueva's resignation was also related to the responses of the local population after the attack. In several television and press interviews, the inhabitants of Uchiza talked openly of their support of the *compañeros* and of how the policemen deserved the punishment they had received because of their regular abuse of the citizenry.[18] These statements revealed the high levels of support the guerrillas enjoyed, the total lack of coordination between the police and the military, and the utter incompetence of the government in managing the situation.

Contributing to the problem was the work of the CORAH crop eradication crews supported by U.S. funds and helicopters, which eliminated 5,130 hectares of coca plants in 1988. This effort intensified peasant hostility to the government and gave Shining Path the additional political support it wanted to further legitimate its attacks. In addition, the eradication effort was insufficient to reduce coca cultivation or production. The amount of coca paste leaving the UHV actually increased during this period, as did the total amount of land under coca cultivation. Shining Path used the opportunity to increase its harassment of the CORAH crews and the police and to channel peasant resentment into support for the Sendero guerrillas. The risk posed to the individuals and equipment performing the eradication efforts of the Peruvian and U.S. governments was sufficiently great to result in the withdrawal of the crews and the suspension of all DEA eradication, interdiction, and logistical efforts in the UHV between February and September 1989. In this context, the García government declared a state of emergency in the UHV area that included San Martín, Ucayali and Huánuco.[19] This meant that the military became the administrative directors of this increasingly conflict-ridden region rather than civilian authorities with the support of the police. Lima's concern, in other words, shifted from the drug war to the guerrilla war.

Peruvian Army Brigadier General Alberto Arciniega assumed control over this emergency zone (EMZ) in April 1989, and from his first day on the job laid forth a different view of how military strategy should be conducted in the area. He gathered Uchiza's citizens in their main plaza and ordered that the Sendero colors be struck immediately. In response to the citizens' concern that the *compañeros* would carry out reprisals, Arciniega responded, "if the Peruvian colors don't fly in your plaza, I'm the one who's going to kill you; not with knives, but with helicopters that will destroy the entire town....But if you raise Peru's flag, you can count on my protection and support."[20] With that initial stance, Arciniega demonstrated his authority over the area in the name of the central government and began the change in official policy that substantially shifted the equilibrium of forces in the UHV.

With the full support of the government and his superiors, Arciniega opened up two fronts in his fight against the guerrillas. Four days after his arrival, he began an intense patrol activity, directly engaging any Sendero column in his path. A day after his visit to Uchiza, he prevented the reestablishment of the police post, thereby demonstrating his objection to official abuse. He also made clear from the outset that his efforts would focus on subversion rather than on drug trafficking, which gained him immediate popular support.

The policemen arrived by truck. They told Arciniega they wanted to stay at the military base, a large house donated to the military by its owner, because the old post had been destroyed and was unusable. Arciniega, wary of their presence because of the townspeople's distrust, told them this was impossible. When the police commander began to argue, the unexpected happened: Hundreds of Uchiza's inhabitants spontaneously organized a meeting in front of the military base. Their representatives told Arciniega they wanted the policemen to leave. After a brief conversation with the group's leaders, Arciniega faced the police commander and told him, "You may stay, but not at my base. You must find another place." That afternoon the police contingent returned to Tingo María by helicopter![21]

Despite what many analysts predicted, Arciniega did not behave in the normal Peruvian military manner of being concerned more with armed repression than on building political support. He seemed to realize from the beginning that the insurgent problem could be solved definitively only by gaining coca producer backing. The general found one of his major sources of support in a peasant organization that was then only a few months old. The Upper Huallaga Agrarian Cooperative had been founded in December 1988 by Mario Escudero, an ex-policeman and the son of settlers who had spent two years organizing the coca growers; by Justo Silva, the principal of one of the two local schools; and by half a dozen coca growers who filled the cooperative's other administrative positions. Fed up with police abuse and corruption, the risks of coca cultivation, and Sendero's political agenda, forty-two of the one-hundred-odd coca-producing communities of the UHV that formed part of the organization presented the possibilities of crop substitution as the best way out of the coca problem in their valley. They found a willing listener in Arciniega.

As their leader, Mario Escudero, said:

> Coca brought money, but it also brought abuse, corruption and insecurity. Later it involved politics, like the *compañeros* who said they cared about us, but, I think, cared more about their cause. Given these problems, I decided to go to every community and talk with my countrymen to convince them that together we would be stronger. Substitution of new crops for coca rather than coca eradication would make Uchiza a better place for us and our children to live. It took two full years of convincing before we could put together the cooperative.[22]

General Arciniega seemed to understand the logic of this message. He noted that it was necessary to fight the Maoist guerrillas:

> but not in just any manner. It is necessary to consider that any rebel group seeks to gain the people's support, and in the Huallaga Valley these are primarily cultivators of coca and are repressed. How can we win their support? By taking them out of their present precarious situation, that's how. The *cocalero* peasants were harassed by the police and by any other official organization that happened by because they were considered to be criminals. CORAH harassed them by eradicating their crops, the police by considering that they were engaged in criminal activities...We are talking about 80 percent of the population! What we do then is to change the situation to keep the coca grower, the group which Sendero supports in order to accomplish its goals, from being subject to harassment. If we can persuade the people to join us, the war is won.[23]

The question of legitimization

By applying this perspective, Arciniega displaced the guerrillas. He became the referee who dealt directly with conflicts among growers, traffickers, and the police and gradually made it possible to build up support among the population. The growers, now forced to choose between support for an outlaw organization or support for the military, did not think twice before throwing their lot in with Arciniega. They perceived that they had no other alternative. Arciniega's strategy was so successful that, after a bombing by army helicopters against La Morada ordered for continued support for Shining Path, the village's inhabitants blamed the guerrillas for a lack of protection and for their weakness against the superior firepower of the military.[24]

Popular support for Arciniega was a direct result of the large number of missions carried out by his men. After gathering the necessary intelligence, the military regularly struck the guerrillas in successive waves. A desperate attempt by Shining Path to recover its image of strength and to restore its declining support in the UHV occurred with the launching of a major offensive against the army in the area. According to official reports, in late June 1989, just before dawn, about one thousand guerrillas tried to attack the military base at Madre Mía. During the attack, Sendero, due to a mistake in its battle plans, ended up firing at each other in the darkness. At least fifty guerrillas died, with the army reporting only seven casualties.

7 month

During Arciniega's seven-month command, the army claims to have carried out 320 aerial support operations, had 44 clashes with Sendero columns and inflicted, according to the general himself, 1,100 casualties among the guerrillas. Apart from official military reports, however, we have no way of knowing either if the numbers are correct or if all those killed belonged to Shining Path. Hazardous geography and physical danger impeded investigations by human rights organizations that could have clarified suspicions of illegal executions. In fact, it appears that the number of cases of "disappearances" increased during Arciniega's command, with some fifty reported in the UHV during 1989. Early in September 1989, policemen and DEA agents based at Santa Lucía reported finding twenty bodies floating in the Huallaga River. Belated reports claimed that the executions were committed by army men to elicit confessions from suspected guerrillas and to terrorize potential followers in the local population.[25]

It appears that Arciniega based his strategy on aggressive military action without particular regard for potential human rights implications, on promises of short-term crop substitution, and on his charismatic personality. He seems to have been extremely successful in restoring the legitimacy of the government's presence in the UHV. By way of illustration, in his last public appearance, General Arciniega was greeted by some thirty thousand peasants who gathered in Uchiza to celebrate Armed Forces Day and cheer his assertion that the fight was against Shining Path, not the growing of coca. This enthusiasm would soon dissipate with Arciniega's reassignment to Lima and his replacement by successive unventuresome, even passive military officers.

However, Arciniega's approach was controversial and obviously was not greeted enthusiastically by all the official parties in the area. In late September 1989 Melvyn Levitsky, Assistant Secretary for International Narcotics Matters, Department of State, stated before the Permanent Subcommittee on Investigations of the U.S. Senate that there were ties between Arciniega and local drug traffickers in the UHV. "Reports have ranged from taking payoffs from the traffickers so that the military could go after Sendero, to letting drug flights in, to other kinds of collusions," Levitsky said.[26] Arciniega vehemently denied the allegation and became embroiled in a journalistic confrontation with the American official. These accusations had originated among some Peruvian police officials, still smarting from the perceived affronts to which the general had subjected their institution. But in fact Arciniega did have to depend on the local population for material support for his military in addition to his strategy of winning their hearts and minds from Sendero. With the growing economic crisis in Peru (the 1989 inflation rate reached 2,700 percent), Arciniega asked the valley's residents for support with food, transportation, and gasoline for his troops. Yet most of the resources available in the UHV came from the coca trade. So even if Arciniega was correct in his claim that the coca grower was not a trafficker, in some ways he had to ignore the traffickers since they were the only source of demand for the coca growers' product. Thus he proved more vulnerable when attacked by those ostensibly on his side than by Shining Path itself.

The fact that Arciniega's strategy was based on his personal involvement and ability and not on an institutional approach to the problem became clear with the change of command. Arciniega's successor was more than cautious when assuming a post that, because of its complexity and risks, could do irremediable harm to any military career. Army General Luis Chacón seemed aware of that fact and preferred to keep himself apart from his predecessor's activist approach and on the fringe of the problems. However, circumstances conspired to enmesh him in the very situations he had hoped to avoid. In March 1990 Chacón discharged two army captains and two lieutenants when links were discovered between them and local traffickers. The officers were accused by the police, with a videotape offered as proof. In the videotape, filmed from a DEA helicopter, a section of the highway through the Huallaga was shown to be blocked by two military trucks while a plane was being loaded with sacks of coca paste. The men protecting the operations were the four army officers.

Initially Chacón's action was seen as a suitable punishment and a warning against corruption in the military. However, a military-appointed panel gathered evidence linking Chacón himself with the drug traffickers. The panel also found indications of at least one other similar incident as well as the presence of several coca paste laboratories in the vicinity of military bases within the general's command. While Chacón denied any tie, the panel forced him to resign his post in the UHV only two months after assuming it.

His successor, General Mario Britto, was even more cautious. He avoided even visiting the valley for several months. According to the peasants, Britto remained at a base outside the Upper Huallaga Valley away from the problems and the risks. "We are very disappointed, because we thought we had governmental and military support, but now we are thinking it was only Arciniega who understood us and had the courage to live among us," said coca grower Justo Silva.[27] Britto's caution did not serve him well. In mid-October 1990 guerrillas ambushed his convoy near Tarapoto and severely wounded him; his jeep driver and two bystanders were killed. The attack occurred after heavy fighting in the area had claimed the lives of over 160 army soldiers, peasants, and Shining Path guerrillas.[28]

The Arciniega-Chacón-Britto case is one of many that could be cited to illustrate the formidable challenges the government of Peru faces in trying to pursue the guerrilla war to a definitive resolution in its favor. This example illustrates how the lack of a coherent strategy within the military institution itself undermined the quite dramatic progress achieved by an individual military commander by virtue of his own initiative. As a result, an excellent opportunity to change the situation in the UHV in favor of the government was lost.

The Drug War

Within a few weeks after the announcement of the Andean Strategy by President George Bush in September 1989, the Santa Lucía base in the Upper Huallaga became fully operational.[29] But now the drug enforcement activities launched from it emphasized interdiction rather than crop eradication. This change in approach appeared to be related to the danger involved for the eradication crews and to the continued expansion in hectarage under coca cultivation in spite of substantial previous eradication efforts. It could also have the effect, however, of redirecting the drug war toward targets less likely to enrage the growers, thereby making them less susceptible to the appeals of Shining Path.

This new combined DEA-Peruvian police forces approach joined massive efforts by the Colombian government against their own drug lords after the August 1989 assassination of leading presidential candidate Luis Carlos Galán to reduce substantially drug flights from the UHV to Colombia.[30] The result was a large coca production surplus in the valley and a dramatic drop in price, from two dollars to thirty cents per kilo of coca leaf between mid-1989 and mid-1990, a fall to well below the cost of production.[31] For the first time it became realistic to consider crop substitution seriously.

The decline of prices has had a mixed effect on the power of Shining Path in the UHV. In its eagerness to regain the leverage lost in 1989, Sendero began to put pressure on local traffickers to pay better prices for the coca leaf in order to regain standing with the growers. Beginning in April 1990 the guerrillas tried to get better prices by concentrating the supervision of coca leaf dealing in its own local committees and bases. The controlled prices, which affected the half-dozen *traqueteros* who paid a lower price than the one considered fair by the guerrillas, were received in two different ways by the producers. Some claim that this made the guerrillas an obstruction to the market. As an engineer said who had worked in the area for seven years and who owns a couple of coca hectares himself: "The guerrillas act as an obstacle to a free coca market. By forcing prices up in the UHV Sendero forces the Colombian buyers to go to better markets, such as the Lower Huallaga or Bolivia. There coca prices increase; here, they decrease."[32] Yet others vehemently defend the guerrillas' position of pushing for better prices.

Alarmed both by the fall in coca prices and by a fungus spreading among the coca crops in the valley, members of the cooperative increased their verbal attacks on the DEA. They claimed that the fungus was caused by herbicides even though it is actually caused by a local blight that spreads more rapidly when only a single crop is grown. About the same time, a sister organization to the cooperative, the Defense Front Against Coca Eradication in the Upper Huallaga, took a more militant stance. One of its members maintained that "We need help in the valley right away. We are tired of promises and fancy projects. We want a way out of the situation, and we want it now. If not, we are going to fight with our best weapon: coca, which we can use to flood not only the U.S., but all of Europe as well."[33] Another local grower in the Uchiza area put it somewhat differently:

> We really want to move out of coca production because we know that it is harmful and because of all the problems it causes us. We are harassed and persecuted because we grow coca, and we are victims of corruption and abuse as well. But if we can't count on help from our own government or from foreign aid, then our only recourse may be to get Sendero's support.[34]

Shining Path took advantage of such hostile reactions to carry out attacks in Tocache and Aucayacu and to harass police posts. As one Interior Ministry official noted, "With growing peasant discontent, Sendero could recover as a major force in the valley, especially when the local growers continue not to receive the economic assistance that Arciniega promised."[35]

Conclusion

The significance of the drug trade in Peru is intimately related to the resources it generates in an increasingly impoverished society going through its worst economic crisis in the history of the Republic. There are no reliable figures on how widespread coca cultivation is — figures range from 150,000 to 300,000 illegal hectares of coca production, with a general consensus of around 200,000. However, Peru has become the world's largest producer of coca for cocaine — about 65 percent of the total. This production generates about $1.2 billion in foreign exchange per year — about half of legal exports.[36] Estimates on employment generated directly and indirectly by coca production fall in the 300,000-to-400,000 range, or over 5 percent of the work force in a country with 50 to 60 percent underemployment in recent years. Thus massive antidrug operations carried out by coordinated U.S. and Peruvian efforts in the UHV, where most of Peru's coca for export is now grown, adversely affect political and economic situations at both local and national levels.

The link between peasants and guerrillas in the UHV is primarily based on the farmers' economic needs and Shining Path's political needs. What strategy should be pursued to break that link? For the army, the highest priority is to stop Shining Path; for the police and the DEA, it is to halt coca paste exports. If the guerrillas are the primary target, as they were in 1984 and 1989, then drug trafficking will flourish and the peasants will support the government. If the main target is drug trafficking, then many peasants will look for help among the guerrillas.

One approach that could work is to make stopping Sendero and stopping drug trafficking both highest priority objectives.[37] If drug trafficking is hit strongly and constantly, the price of the coca leaf will decrease and crop substitution becomes viable. If the guerrillas are pursued aggressively but appropriately, in terms of human rights issues, they cannot continue to build ties to the UHV peasantry; this opens up political space for democratic parties and organizations. Success of this strategy depends ultimately on substantial increases in resources, on consistency of application over several years, and on imaginative leadership at the contact points between central government and the local population that inspires confidence and trust based on appropriate action. The Alberto Fujimori government (1990-1995) has proposed actions along these lines, but they will be extremely difficult to fund, much less apply quickly and effectively, given Peru's multiple problems.

In the meantime, it is quite likely that Shining Path will continue to see the valley as its major target of opportunity. For Sendero, the UHV represents a major component of its political strategy and the principal source of its economic resources. Estimates of Shining Path's annual revenue range from $20 million to $100 million a year. It comes primarily from "revolutionary taxes" and control of scores of clandestine air strips used to transport coca paste to Colombia for manufacturing cocaine. As an SL leader noted, "It is very expensive to maintain a party that extends throughout the country.

Contributions [taxes] are always assigned to the organization and not to individuals."[38] While maintaining its subsistence and self-sufficiency philosophy for its own Long March, Shining Path did not overlook the opportunity provided by the UHV bonanza. With money from the Huallaga, the guerrillas are able to have a better organization, more support facilities, and improved hideouts. Paradoxically, the ultimate source of Sendero finances are the estimated 6 million cocaine users in the United States. A further irony is that Peru's present foreign exchange lifeline is to exactly the same source.

In political terms, Sendero found in the UHV the power and support it had been looking for elsewhere since 1980. The guerrillas know that Peru's continuing crisis works to their advantage. As long as the country needs the coca dollars, as long as there are coca crops, SL believes there will be corruption, repression, and discontent. Shining Path's worst enemy, besides a truly effective government response, is an organized local population. Thus the guerrillas must fight rival popular organizations, which they attempt to do with verbal attacks — "Their leaders lie and the only way to stop oppression is through the barrel of a gun" — and physical attacks as well, such as brutally assassinating key elected authorities.[39]

The future of Shining Path depends on the failure and collapse of the present system, so its people are doing whatever they can to bring that about. Those who believed Sendero had been defeated in the valley in 1984 underestimated the organization's capacity to mingle with the local population, establish an underground organization, and build a strategy for action for use at an opportune future moment, as in 1988 and 1989. This suggests that as long as the core group of Sendero holds together, thanks to its ideological orthodoxy, among other things, the organization will retain the capacity to act. Actions include recruitment of Peruvians, such as the UHV peasants, who become disaffected with the continuing deficiencies of their own government and its officials and see no other alternative.

Notes

1. Ministero de Agricultura, *Informe Anual* (Lima: Ministerio de Agricultura, December 1987).
2. "Los Intis de la Coca," *Peru Económico*, September 1987.
3. For a detailed explanation of Sendero's plans, ideology, first years of armed struggle, and early government reaction see: Gustavo Gorriti, *Sendero; Historia de la guerra milenaria en el Perú*, vol. I (Lima: Apoyo, 1990).
4. Raúl González, "Coca y subversión en el Alto Huallaga," *Quehacer*, 48, September-October 1987, p. 66.
5. Operation "Bronco" was the fourth massive antidrug effort in the area. It was preceded by Operation "Cerrojo" (1976), "Verde Mar 1" (1979), and "Verde Mar 2" (1980), and was followed by Operation "Condor" in seven phases (1985-1989) and "Snowcap" (1988-1990).
6. This relationship eventually became formal. In late 1984 one of the Carusso brothers, a well-known family of traffickers formerly based in the Monzón region, was detained by the police. Among his documents an army intelligence identification card was found. This case and other information related to links between Carbajal and local traffickers forced the general and thirty-two of his officers to face trial for corruption in military courts in 1987. Apparently, the general and his men accepted money from the traffickers, thus falling into the corruption Carbajal said he wanted to avoid. The trial sentence was never disclosed.
7. The "Golden Seal" was carried out with the help of García's government. On June 19, 1986, about three hundred inmates accused of terrorist actions were killed in cold blood by the police and the military in the Lima prisons of El Frontón and Lurigancho after a failed mutiny organized by prisoners.
8. Cynthia McClintock, "The War On Drugs: The Peruvian Case," *Journal of Interamerican Studies and World Affairs*, 30:2-3, Summer/Fall 1988, p. 128.
9. On May 31, 1987, six policemen and four civilians died during an attack against the police post of Uchiza, the first military action carried out by Shining Path in the UHV. It marked the opening of the new front.
10. This was because the overland approach claimed the lives of thirty-two workers murdered by traffickers or guerrillas between 1983 and 1987.
11. Luis Arce Borja y Janet Talavera Sánchez, "Reportaje del Siglo: El presidente Gonzalo rompe el silencio," *El Diario*, July 24, 1988, pp. 2-47.
12. Interview by the author, August 1989.
13. Lucas Cachay, former president of the San Martín Defense Front, claimed, "What the growers want is protection and money. The traffickers kept telling them that the coca price was down because of overproduction. They know it is not true, but they had no one to protect them. That's what Sendero gives them: protection....Besides, in the area, as long as there is a lot of money, there is alcohol, laziness, and violence....Sendero put an end to all that and made everybody work. It also closed all the discos, the whorehouses, killed the homosexuals, and expelled the prostitutes." González, "Coca y subversión," p. 70.
14. Various analysts saw in this strategy the possibility of a new Sendero approach. In the interview with *El Diario*, Guzmán indicates that the "Popular War" must go through

three stages: the "Defense Strategy" (guerrilla warfare), the "Strategic Balance" (the fight for positions or combat fronts), and the "Offensive Strategy" (general insurgency ending with the cities being taken over). According to the interview, Sendero was ready to begin the second stage. There were those who thought that the first combat front of this second stage as the Upper Huallaga, due to its advantageous terrain and the potential for peasant support.

15. Interview by the author in La Morada in August 1989.

16. The Santa Lucía base is considered to be the logistical center of the antidrug effort in the region and was built between December 1988 and September 1989 for $3 million. Capable of lodging three hundred men, it has the longest landing strip in the UHV (1,500 meters), nine helicopters, a mine field, watchtowers, and several barracks.

17. Off-the-record versions claimed that American embassy officials did not want to be involved in an antiguerrilla clash and that the Peruvian Air Force could not fly its only helicopter due to a dead battery.

18. In an interview conducted in the area a few days after the attack, a local informant told the author that the reason the guerrillas attacked the post was because the policemen broke an agreement with a local band of traffickers. "The policemen were receiving money from a 'firm' so it could do business in the area, but they seized some drugs and asked for more money. Then the traffickers asked the *compañeros* for help and they carried out the attack. Besides, the people were fed up with the abuse of the police chief," he said.

19. An emergency zone (EMZ) is one in which certain constitutional rights, such as freedom of assembly and movement, residence inviolability, and detention with a court order, are temporarily suspended for sixty days, a period that may be, and often is, extended. According to the 1980 Peruvian Constitution, the zones under a state of emergency are placed under the political-military control of the armed forces. Late 1990 EMZs in Peru account for almost half of the national territory and about 70 percent of the population (including Lima).

20. Interviews by the author in Uchiza in 1989 and later confirmed in Lima by U.S. embassy officials.

21. Interview of an army officer by the author at the base in Uchiza in 1989 and later confirmed by Interior Ministry officials.

22. Interview with the author in Lima in February 1990.

23. Raúl González, "Las armas de un general," *Quehacer*, 62, December 1989-January 1990, pp. 38-43.

24. Version told the author by an engineer who works in the area, later confirmed by the police. The hamlet was attacked with rockets and destroyed while its inhabitants were working in the coca fields, so there were no casualties or injuries.

25. This version was obtained by the author in the valley and was confirmed by U.S. embassy officials and members of the army who served under Arciniega in 1989.

26. Melvyn Levitsky, *Hearings Before the Permanent Subcommittee on Investigation of the Committee on Governmental Affairs of the United States Senate.* 101 Cong., 1st sess., September 26-29 (Washington: USGPO, 1989), p. 170.

27. Interview conducted by the author in Uchiza in July 1990.

28. James Brooke, "Peru's Leader Proposes a Market to Fight Coca," *New York Times,* October 28, 1990, p. 9.

29. The base was officially inaugurated on January 19, 1990 in a ceremony attended by Peru's Minister of the Interior Augustín Mantilla and U.S. Ambassador Anthony Quainton.

30. The number of flights between the UHV and Colombia declined from between fifty and sixty per week in July 1989 to five or less by February 1990, according to U.S. embassy sources.

31. See Iban de Rementería, "La sustitución de cultivos como perspectiva," in Diego García Sayán, ed., *Coca, cocaina, narcotráfico: Laberinto en los Andes* (Lima: Comisión Andina de Juristas, 1989), p. 377.

32. Interview by the author in Uchiza in June 1990.

33. Ibid.

34. Ibid.

35. Interview by the author in Lima in July 1990.

36. McClintock, "War on Drugs," p. 129.

37. As presented in José Gonzales, "Peru: Sendero Luminoso en el valle de la coca," *Coca, cocaína, narcotráfico*, pp. 207-222.

38. Interview by the author in Peru in February 1989.

39. As of October 1989, eight mayors had been killed by the guerrillas in the UHV and fifty others had resigned, leaving up to 90 percent of the population without local authorities. Voting turnout in the valley for the November 1989 municipal elections was only about 30 percent.

7

SHINING PATH'S URBAN
STRATEGY: ATE VITARTE

Michael L. Smith

In Abimael Guzmán Reynoso's interview in mid-1988, the head of Shining Path (SL or Sendero) said that the party that he calls the Communist Party of Peru had to prepare for an urban insurrection that would cap off his epoch-ending revolution. "Our process of the people's war has led us to the apogee; consequently, we have to prepare the insurrection which becomes, in synthesis, the seizure of the cities," he said.[1]

These words seemed idle boasting from an insurgent organization that had toed the line of Maoist orthodoxy, inspiring to that point a rural insurgency in remote reaches of the Andes. Its distinguishing urban characteristic had seemed to be terrorism. Some of the most informed analysts saw Guzmán's statement as confirmation that Sendero was recognizing the adverse impact of its rural bias and switching to an urban orientation. This shift seemed to indicate to them a weakening of Sendero's rural backing.[2]

However, such ideological second-guessing obscured a more significant point in the interview. Guzmán's remarks confirmed what internal Senderista documents had been addressing for nearly eight years: The party had to broaden its foothold in urban areas as an integral part of armed insurrection if it expected to take power. Methodically and diligently, Guzmán and his war staff had been laying out a battle plan that required political foresight, detailed preparation, and tactical discipline. In the next two years, Sendero acted aggressively to implement its multifront campaign.

Rather than discuss Sendero's urban strategy in the abstract, this chapter centers its analysis on the district of Ate Vitarte, in the eastern cone of metropolitan Lima.[3] The district has played a unique, symbolic role in Lima's popular movement. Sendero has singled out the district as an urban beachhead in its military strategy and as a window of opportunity within Peru's sociopolitical development. Because of its unique characteristics, Ate Vitarte epitomizes Peru's troubled process of modernization, industrialization, and urbanization during the second half of the twentieth century.

Strategic Importance

Ate Vitarte forms part of Lima's traditional industrial corridor. The manufacturing axis stretches from the port of Callao through the old city core up the Rimac River to where the valley narrows under the steep, barren slopes of the Andes. The central railway and highway run parallel to the river. This corridor contains three quarters of Lima's fixed assets and gross production (Lima, in turn, holds 70 percent of Peru's manufacturing capacity). Between 1963 and 1982, the eastern zone was the most dynamic in the generation of new manufacturing plants. By 1982, the area's industries produced 17.3 percent of Lima's gross production. However, this installed plant was becoming obsolete and less productive because Peruvian and foreign capitalists were unwilling to reinvest.[4]

In 1961, there were 45,000 inhabitants in Ate Vitarte. The industrialization and urbanization processes over the next two decades produced profound changes. In 1986, the district had 181,000 inhabitants. During the 1970s, its growth rate of 10.2 percent per year was three times the overall average for metropolitan Lima. This urbanization process stemmed from the incorporation of workers seeking residence near their place of employment.[5] Unions set up housing cooperatives, frequently drawing on their employers' indemnity funds. Neighborhood associations often organized themselves around places of origin, mainly the Central Highlands, from Cerro de Pasco to Ayacucho. In contrast to other neighborhoods in Lima, squatter settlements within Ate Vitarte did not begin until the 1980s.

The district has clear strategic value in military and economic terms. It is the chokepoint for Lima's water and electrical supplies. Its hydroelectric and thermal plants provide about 60 percent of Lima's power. Transmission lines from the Mantaro hydroelectric complex in the Central Andes pass along the valley ridges and supply the remaining power needs.[6] Crucial materials, such as minerals, metals, and foodstuffs, flow along its transport links.

Ate Vitarte has a geographically immediate relationship with the countryside. The river valley had haciendas and small garden plots until the early 1970s, when urbanization ate into farmland. Small landholdings, requiring day labor, continue along the banks of the Rimac River, and the Jicamarca peasant community (once the pre-Columbian owners of Lima) still exists. Ate Vitarte has natural contacts with the Santa Eulalia Valley to the north and the Lurín Valley to the south. These penetration valleys into the highlands (sierra) provide guerrillas with alternate routes to the Central Sierra as well as accessible training ground for recruits. Ate Vitarte, therefore, is a superb setting for shifting between urban and rural modes of guerrilla operations. The mining centers in the mountains above Lima provide dynamite and tempting targets for extortion.

Political Terrain

In the 1960s, the legal recognition of unions and affiliation doubled and then doubled again during the next decade.[7] The Central Highway, as a major center of industrialization, was a magnet for a new type of union and political organizers. Starting in 1970, young Marxist activists and professors from San Marcos, Catholic, and other Lima universities spent six years organizing on the Central Highway. Although organizers aimed primarily at textile and metallurgical unions, they also meshed with community work because most workers lived in nearby neighborhoods. Cadres drew on the political tactics then in vogue — the classic Leninist interpretation of class struggle, a frontal assault on power, and the inevitability of armed revolution. At the forefront were the Communist Party of Peru-Red Fatherland (PCP-PR) and Revolutionary Vanguard (VR), both strongly influenced by Maoist thinking. They succeeded in recruiting and forming a generation of union leaders.

This new vanguard soon entered politics. It acted on two central ideas: a homogenous leadership and control of a territory (the Central Highway). This approach meant joining the struggles of industrial branches into a single working-class movement and pairing it with community demands. Unions became the most important social and political force in the district. In 1974, the radicals founded the Coordinating Committee for the Unification of the Working Class Union movement (CCUSC), operating out of the nearby national teachers' college (La Cantuta), near Chaclacayo. The Central Highway had its own affiliate branch, the Committee for Struggle, the only one organized on a territorial basis. The district movement mobilized up to ten thousand people in a single march. Workers enlisted community support during strikes, even battling riot police and scabs for control of the streets.

The high water mark of labor militancy came with the July 1977 general strike. It forced the military government (1968-1980) to begin handing back power to civilians. However, the strike action resulted in the sacking of five thousand seasoned labor leaders nationwide, decapitating the union movement and wiping out a large share of fifteen years' political work. Recession and the liberal shift in economic policy took an additional toll of union leadership and rank and file. Management removed troublesome union leaders through administrative procedures or blackballing and cut back on their stable work force. Between 1976 and 1981, Lima's manufacturing plants shrank from an average of thirty-four workers to twenty-three workers.[8] Although some leaders remained active, thanks to support from their parties, community organizations, or sheer perseverance, others drifted back into private life. Though not perceived at the time, this reversal marked a prolonged, gradual decline in the labor movement along the Central Highway. This weakening also sapped the strength of the popular movement in the district.

Already meticulously laying out a blueprint for insurgency, Guzmán spent his last four years of public activity at La Cantuta. As an eyewitness to the events on the Central Highway, he probably took them into account in mapping out future strategy for Lima. Sendero was never a main player in the Lima unions or emerging political movement. It did not join the Central Highway radicals in their plotting and organizing. It concentrated on pushing its own class-based Workers and Laborers Movement (MOTC), an ideologically pure "generated organization" similar to those the party had forged in Ayacucho.

Although the MOTC did not control unions, it was tenacious in supporting strikes. It supplied a ten-man team to aid strike committees, setting up a soup kitchen, supplying food and material, and mobilizing people. At one point, it had three teams active on the Central Highway. It used the occasions to preach its message of the people's war just over the horizon.

In the later half of the 1970s, Sendero probed among the radical Marxist factions for loose cells and militants. It picked up those disgruntled with the parties that were participating in the elections for Constituent Assembly (1978), Congress, and local governments (1980). One of the convert groups, Red Star, a university-based Maoist faction, moved a large group of its cadres to El Agustino, at the eastern end of the Central Highway, in 1980. A characteristic of these early Sendero activists was that many of them had a university education. They had gone out to the plant floor to work in political organization and ended up staying there. Sendero also picked up at least ten stray Maoist-block cadres to add to its existing organization on the Central Highway.

Laying the Groundwork

During the opening six years of armed struggle (1980-1986), Sendero seemed to limit itself to using Lima as an echo chamber for its agit-prop activities and sabotage ("propaganda through action"). It was extremely difficult to piece together a rational pattern or judge its strength from random bombings and blackouts. At first glance, Lima seemed tough terrain for Sendero. The central government and its concentrated security forces outgunned Sendero's Molotov cocktails and sticks of dynamite hurled by Andean slingshots.[9] SL's clandestine cell network was outmanned both by the ruling parties and by the mainstream left-wing parties, grouped in the United Left (IU) coalition, which endorsed an agenda for social and political change but through the democratic process. Sendero's symbolic acts, such as hanging dogs from lampposts or graffiti against revisionists in China, seemed inadequate, even pathetic, to a more sophisticated political forum. Compared to the undernourished, isolated social institutions in Ayacucho, Lima threw up a much denser, interconnected social bulwark against the Sendero onslaught.

Yet these first impressions belied other factors. The PCP-SL's Lima Metropolitan Bureau was not an orphaned branch in the party apparatus. Early party documents show that the Metropolitan Committee was on equal footing with the Principal Regional Committee in Ayacucho. It had to carry out the full range of subversive activities (agitation, mobilization, sabotage, assaults, confiscations, and skirmishes) during the opening phase, accenting the more aggressive ones. Weaker regional committees could limit their actions to agitation, mobilization, and sabotage.[10]

In January 1981, the Central Committee gave the Metropolitan Committee special instructions for urban operations: It was to set up "action committees" organized territorially to carry out bombings, arson, and painting slogans on walls. "Special squads" that answered directly to the Metropolitan Committee were responsible for sophisticated actions (sabotage and assassinations). Urban organizations had to carry out "concrete labors of support for the guerrilla force," such as propaganda and recruiting forces for rural units. The Metropolitan Committee also had to concentrate on intelligence-gathering, a logical assignment since Ayacucho members would soon find it hard to infiltrate state bureaucracy and police-military units.

The Central Committee also gave the Metropolitan Committee two additional tasks: protection of the party apparatus and leaders (Guzmán and other members of the leadership) and carrying out sanctions against traitors and dissidents. After Guzmán's captures in 1969 and 1979, the party was ready to invest huge amounts of resources to safeguard its war staff.[11]

The "three legs" of Sendero's urban work were people's schools, "generated organizations," and metropolitan coordination.[12] The party divided Lima into territorial turfs with clear centralized chains of command but operational freedom. Lima has six zones under the charge of the Metropolitan Regional Committee: North (Comas, Independencia, Puente Piedra), South (Villa María del Triunfo, Villa El Salvador, Pachacamac), West (Callao), Central (urban core of Lima), East (El Agustino, San Juan de Lurigancho, Ate Vitarte), and Chosica. Each zone is, in turn, divided into sectors, subsectors, and cells, each with its political and military cadres.

Sendero's early armed activities often seemed more a nuisance than a threat. The first action in Lima took place on June 16, 1980, when a group of two hundred young men and women attacked the town hall of San Martín de Porras district with Molotov cocktails.[13] The first major military action, an attack on the Ñaña police station in July 1982, took place on the Central Highway, confirming both the political and military importance of the district in Sendero's scheme. The attack against the Bayer acrylic fiber plant in May 1983, punctuated by a citywide blackout, showed that Sendero had moved on to more spectacular strikes.

The Central Committee, however, was already looking several steps ahead to the day when its organization would have to move on to more ambitious goals. It decided to start up the Revolutionary People's Defense Movement (MRDP) in early 1983. This movement is the umbrella organization for a welter of urban "generated organisms" intended in due course to meet up with the countryside equivalents and give birth to the People's Republic of the New Democracy. In the countryside, the Revolutionary People's Defense Front (FRDP), with its Popular Committees, should prevail. The crucial difference is that the party cannot openly exercise political power or create a guerrilla army in urban areas.[14]

Forced Migrants

In December 1982, the elected civilian government of Fernando Belaúnde Terry (1980-1985) ordered the armed forces to enter into action in Ayacucho and declared the region an emergency zone (EMZ). The military's indiscriminate repression against the Ayacucho peasants had another repercussion that would ease Sendero's expansion in Lima. Thousands of Ayacucho peasants fled from the region. In 1985, the Peace Commission estimated there were fifty thousand forced migrants, mainly settled in Lima, Ica, and Huancayo.[15]

The Central Highway was a logical first refuge for these displaced persons. They arrived in the midst of a major economic crisis. Lima was no longer the promised land of job opportunities for unskilled laborers, educational possibilities for children, and abundant open spaces for shantytowns that it had been up to the 1970s. The new flood of refugees swamped the informal social network of provincial Ayacucho migrants' clubs and associations.

The reasons for fleeing the Ayacucho EMZ were diverse. Young people fled from the harassment of security forces who tabbed them as suspected guerrillas. Families fled to keep their teenagers from Sendero's clutches. Others escaped from the economic disruption brought on by guerrilla warfare, counterinsurgency, natural disasters, and dislocated markets. These varied motivations could be incriminating. Once in Lima, carrying a voting identification card with Ayacucho marked as birthplace was a guarantee of two weeks in the security police's prisons and even torture. Police units staked out bus depots to follow passengers coming from the Central Sierra. "Displaced persons faced a double marginality, as migrants and as natives of Ayacucho," says Isabel Coral, who worked with these migrants.[16] In the end, the Ayacucho community in Lima developed the stratagem of simply not asking compromising questions of newcomers. The solidarity of place of origin and shared misfortunes took precedence over political allegiance.

During this period, Sendero began to make house calls on forced migrants along the Central Highway. First, a visitor from their hometown or a relative would make small requests — to allow an overnight visit or keep a package safe. Progressively, these demands increased. Sendero played off personal histories of its People's War to attract support and recruits. Caught between the suspicions of security police and Sendero pressure, between the hardships of survival and the uprooting from their homeland, forced migrants faced unique conditions.

Jurgen Golte and Norma Adams wrote about migrant communities in Lima: "It is impossible to understand the fortunes of migrants in Lima without understanding the local society from which they come and the links which the newcomers establish among themselves in the process of insertion into urban society."[17] From 1980 onward, political violence and repression were constants for EMZ residents and conditioned their insertion into Lima. We do not want to fall into the simplistic reasoning prevalent among police and the public that all Ayacuchans become Sendero activists. The fact remains that in 1985, Lima surpassed Ayacucho as the region with the most subversive activity, with a doubling of incidents over the year before.[18]

Toward an Urban Insurrection

The mutinies in the prisons of El Frontón, Lurigancho, and Callao in June 1986 were the "Gold Seal on the Great Leap" in the 1982-1986 war plan. At the cost of nearly three hundred lives, the mutiny showed the party leadership that Shining Path had reached a critical mass in Lima and nationally and could up the ante. The parallels with Sendero's early Ayacucho offensive and the March 1982 prison break there are striking. Both marked escalations in Sendero's activities. Both were followed shortly afterward with major SL documents being made available to a few diligent researchers.[19] The massacre also showed how counterinsurgency intelligence of both the police and the armed forces completely misinterpreted Sendero's urban presence. They thought that inmates were the brains behind the city network, and perhaps the national apparatus as well, so that by snuffing out the imprisoned militants, they would end the threat. They could not have been more mistaken.

A series of factors contributed to Sendero's conclusion that conditions for social upheaval and a guerrilla insurgency were favorable. The 1983-1985 economic crisis, natural catastrophes, and government mismanagement hit hard at the urban populace. In Ate Vitarte, six of the one hundred largest manufacturing companies went bankrupt in the first half of the decade. A whole generation of workers had been without the benefits of unionization and steady employment because of management's tactic of using temporary contracts (three to twelve months) to avoid hiring permanent staff. The period also increased a trend toward microenterprises and the informal sector.[20]

The 1983 entrance of the armed forces into the fray showed that Sendero was not a radical's weekend fling or the hair-brained adventure of a fanaticized faction. It drove home the message that an insurgent group could challenge Lima authority. This lesson increased Sendero's appeal to radicalized fringe groups and also encouraged other groups to take up arms. The Tupac Amaru Revolutionary Movement (MRTA) took a more conventional approach, striking the romantic pose of Latin American guerrillas. This new rival for insurgent leadership provoked a duel with Sendero, both in Ate Vitarte and in the rest of the country. The East Zone is precisely where Sendero's Central Committee found, in mid-1986, dangerous signs of collaboration because both groups in the district shared a common heritage in unions and neighborhoods. That same year, SL's national leadership declared the Metropolitan Committee in reorganization because of dangerous deviations toward MRTA.[21] The district cells of both parties share a common political past in the 1970s hothouse of radicalism. Even years earlier, in 1975, Guzmán had purged the Lima branch in his preparation to temper the party for armed struggle.[22] To safeguard the party's revolutionary resolve, he institutionalized a series of internal controls that periodically flushed out the "debris" of the perennial struggle between militarists and moderates within the party.

Political dynamics also shifted the balance. Contradictions and internal dynamics were pulling IU apart even when it was positioning itself to run a strong campaign in the 1990 general elections. Despite rhetoric calling for popular participation, the Marxist-Leninist practices of the leadership clashed with the grass-roots democracy of the rank and file. An outgrowth of union and party militancy in Ate Vitarte was three consecutive terms for IU in the district municipal government. However, the administration of Mayor Franklin Acosta was marred by corruption, patronage, and personal ambition. Overruling rank-and-file opposition, IU's national leadership imposed his reelection twice, in 1983 and 1986, because of the quota system for candidacies among the affiliated parties. In the 1989 elections, IU's support slipped to a die-hard 20 percent, losing to the new conservative grouping, Democratic Front (FREDEMO). Acosta had thwarted the development of political competition, leaving grass-roots organizations dispersed, fragmented, and lacking in central direction.

This weakening of local organizations and the divorce from national organizations opened a breach in Ate Vitarte's defenses. In addition, the populist tactics of President Alan García Pérez (1985-1990) and his American Popular Revolutionary Alliance (APRA) chipped away further. In 1988, Sendero went headhunting. It had a list of one hundred leaders who had played a key role in the history of the community but who lost their bearings due to the erosion of the left's organizing capacity. Other potential recruits had been burned out or corrupted by years of struggle. As with Ayacucho migrants, Sendero cadres started by asking for minor assistance and gradually increased their requests. The house-by-house visits also drove home the message that the party knew where they lived and could take reprisals should they oppose Sendero.

Huaycán, Laboratory for Havoc

In 1984, the left-wing Lima municipal government under Mayor Alfonso Barrantes of IU organized a movement of homeless families along the Central Highway. The program tried to meet a pent-up demand for cheap housing that the traditional cooperative schemes could no longer satisfy. The organizers wanted to repeat the experience of planned land seizures such as Villa El Salvador, correcting its flaws in grass-roots organizations and urban planning.

The first census after the seizure showed a population of 22,000 people in Huaycán in 1985; by 1990, it had grown to 70,000. The Barrantes administration's term (1984-1986) was insufficient to deliver on its promises, leaving the settlement adrift. The next Lima municipal administration of APRA (1987-1989) used the project for small patronage appointments and then abandoned the program. Despite these drawbacks, Huaycán consolidated its basic infrastructure almost twice as fast as other spontaneous land seizures and avoided pitfalls common in shantytowns.[23]

The squatters' settlement provided a test tube for another kind of experimentation. Sendero concentrated militants in Huaycán, pulling veteran cadres out of El Agustino, for instance. Sendero also brought in student recruits and converts for periods of training, indoctrination, and rehearsals of political activities. One estimate put Sendero's strength at one hundred activists in the community at its high point. Police and army sweeps targeted Huaycán as a "red zone," especially during the curfew period in Lima between February 1986 and July 1988.

Instead of a blow-by-blow account, we wish to highlight three factors that Sendero exploited in its shantytown penetration: the conflict around and within local communities as an opening for insurgents, a grass-roots tradition of democratic tolerance toward radicals, and the impact of armed force.

First, urban settlements seethe with the constant turbulence of conflicts, both inside and outside the community. The struggle to get legal recognition and public services (light, water, sewage, transport, and education) means that community organizations have to employ an arsenal of pressures, from marches to bribes, to get government action. Other internal conflicts, such as petty corruption, favoritism, and leadership struggles, turn the poor against each other. Residents frequently take out their resentment and frustration on families and neighbors rather than on outside foes.[24] Competition for scarce resources, services, and prime lots in Huaycán frequently divided block and zone organizations. Sendero made strong inroads among late arrivals who scraped for a level patch of land on the upper slopes. Their battle cry was "land for those who live in Huaycán" and against the "weekend tourists," that is, the nonresident builders and cooperatives that participated in the earlier phases.

Second, democracy at the grass-roots is extremely tolerant. In popular assemblies and organizations, participants often range from populists to anarchists. Excluding or expelling radicals from organizations is like cutting off grass-roots organizations' right arm. Radicals provide the muscle and energy to mount communal efforts, meetings, fund-raising events, and protest marches. In communities where most family heads and spouses struggle to survive and feel insecure because of their poor education, it is natural that the most outspoken and active residents rise to time-consuming leadership roles.

Sendero was adroit in exploiting this characteristic. It kept a low profile while building up a pool of intelligence on its adversaries. In the communal election assembly in 1988, Sendero cadres acted openly, no longer hiding behind their role as delegates. They presented their own candidate list for the community board in alliance with other radicals. As a result, IU won the election by only a slim margin, 120 votes to 100. Sendero managed to veto IU's original candidate list because of petty corruption on past community boards. In the end, Sendero showed that it had more political skills at the local level than it was given credit for. Grass-roots leaders had to take Sendero into account in all their actions and plans, whether they liked it or not.

Finally, Sendero's political sway in Huaycán highlights a little-mentioned feature of shantytowns, the political and social weight of those who possess physical force. There is a double face to shantytowns, the official representation open to the outside world and a darker one that governs internal affairs. Street thugs, criminals, and those able to buy influence can exercise power in the community and thwart democratic mechanisms. SL has an additional advantage; it has armed force and is prepared to use it.[25]

Sendero's armed presence in Huaycán undercut a community organizational effort at a crucial time. In September 1987, a twenty-strong Sendero armed unit showed up at a communal assembly called to decide whether to change its status to a "self-managed community" modeled after Villa El Salvador, frequently cited as an example of how to fight off Sendero penetration. The decision was postponed for six months. Other armed tactics included the assassination of an APRA leader on the community board, organized pillaging of nearby farmland, and infiltration of community marches, with deaths and injuries resulting from clashes with the police. Other demonstrations of Sendero's power did not have to draw blood, as with Sendero's midnight marches and guerrilla unit training sessions in the streets of the settlement.[26]

After 1988, Sendero shifted its veteran cadres out of Huaycán to more recent land seizures, especially around the old core of Ate Vitarte. By this time, there were thirty-three shantytowns in the district that had sprung up from these land seizures, compared to none in the 1970s.

"Proletariat of the World, Unite!"

Despite the presence of this phrase at the top of every Sendero document, the party seemed to have little to offer trade union rank and file. In his 1988 interview, Guzmán acknowledged that his party had not made strong inroads among the proletariat: "The majority of our militants are peasants....and a limitation we have is the insufficient number of workers."[27]

However, we should not apply the same criteria for judging Sendero's success as for other political organizations. SL does not aim to win over and conserve organizations; it wants combatants willing to sacrifice themselves on the pyre of the revolution. Guzmán thought there was a short jump from strike picket to urban guerrilla. "They feel and advance the strikes as a main form of struggle in the economic field...but in the actual circumstances they have to be irrevocably linked to the conquest of power. Let us join the struggle for [economic] demands with the people's war for the conquest of power."[28]

Once again, Sendero showed that it had closely observed the events of the radical 1970s and applied this knowledge to its approach in the 1980s. Four unions formed the core of the labor movement on the Central Highway: Manufacturas Nylon, Atlas Copco, Bata Rimac, and Cromotex. In the late 1980s, Sendero managed to gain a foothold in three of them. The fourth, Cromotex, eventually fell to MRTA.[29] In April 1988, Sendero also revived the name of the Committee for Struggle for its own union coordinator on the Central Highway, snatching a banner easily identified by the local population. At its height, seventeen unions attended Sendero coordinating meetings. Union leaders say, however, that many participants had no sympathies for SL. Some went out of curiosity and others to argue against Sendero's tactics.

Sendero tries to generate "gestures of struggle," heroic events that would serve as banners for their cause. At the Peruvian Packaging Company (COPE) in Santa Anita on the Central Highway, Sendero had a small but active cell. The chairman of the executive committee of the Committee for Struggle was Serapio Espinoza, general secretary of COPE workers' union. Under Sendero leadership, the union shunned its labor lawyers and advisors. It imposed its line through coercive measures on the majority. For instance, a SL hit squad gunned down the COPE labor relations manager in March 1987 (Sendero zeroes in on labor relations managers, especially during strikes). On April 11, 1988, a group of workers seized the COPE installations. They claimed that the company was decapitalizing the firm, siphoning off goods to sell on the black market with the aim of bankrupting the company and then setting up another firm. Out of 350 workers and employees, only 46 participated (43 blue collar and 3 white collar). At one point, the strikers threatened to blow up the plant's propane gas tank. Sendero's kamikaze tactics appeared to bring few tangible results. After a fifty-seven-day factory seizure, the police dislodged the strikers without taking a life. The sacking of thirteen workers beheaded the union and temporarily discredited the MOTC movement.[30] However, those workers had little other option than to continue with their Sendero militancy.

Sendero's union strategy in the late 1980s relied on drawing out the work stoppage, sometimes up to one hundred days. It did not negotiate at the peak leverage point for the best settlement. It pushed strikes for the sake of the conflict. Although Sendero almost always had a minority position in the union leadership, it had an effective veto in strike assemblies because it could accuse more flexible leaders of selling out the union and the working class to management. Sendero frequently led strike committees so other workers did not lose their jobs as suspected agitators or terrorists. Sendero also made it hard for workers to reject help; they contributed consistently to the soup kitchen and organized barbecues to raise strike funds.

Sendero's strike platform called for initiatives such as reducing work shifts to a maximum of eight hours a day, less for women and children, and imposing weekly or daily "renewable work contracts." In effect, Sendero wanted to put plant floors on permanent strike standing. Sendero aimed initially at winning over disillusioned prestigious leaders and following among the rank and file. Later, Sendero became less selective, picking up young workers who did not have to worry about family responsibilities.

The reaction of the rank and file was fear and a feeling of being overrun by Sendero. Other parties' work had slackened in unions. Radical groups supported the armed struggle rhetorically, which played into the hands of Sendero and confused the rank and file. A union leader says that for many workers,

Sendero was not the principal enemy; capitalism and management were. Sendero activists were merely militants who have made mistakes. Finally, taking an aggressive stand against Sendero did not get pay raises or guarantees of a steady job.

Sendero also used intimidation, with outsiders brought in to reinforce the SL line. Armed force was never far away. Between January and May 1989, Sendero assassinated more than fifty-one union leaders nationwide. Most were mineworkers in the Central Sierra.[31] In October 1989, Sendero killed Enrique Castillo, a prominent textile union leader among the factories on the Central Highway.

Education and Culture

Sendero has always paid close attention to education and culture. Its use of education goes through public schools, people's schools, and preuniversity academies, drawing on its presence in La Cantuta teachers' college, San Marcos, and other universities. Sendero controlled the two national teachers' union (SUTEP) public school locals on the Central Highway. In just the last year of the García administration, Sendero placed one hundred teachers in the isolated schools of Central Highway shantytowns. Less noticed was intensive work among cultural clubs; folk dance, musical, and theater groups; and barrio and resident organizations. An effective instrument in transmitting Sendero's message has been its use of theater.[32]

The newspaper *El Diario* was a key element in Sendero's urban strategy.[33] SL gained control of the paper in 1987. In 1988, the paper published the preliminary discussion documents for Sendero's first National Congress and what it said was an exclusive interview with Abimael Guzmán himself. *El Diario* was practically the only Lima daily that reported on labor disputes. The use of *El Diario* signaled a change in SL methods. In this new phase, SL was aiming at an urban, educated audience. It needed to multiply its outreach. The party could no longer meet demand for documents with handwritten or, at best, mimeographed copies. It was also appealing to a potential support that had not participated in the crucial formative period (1975-1985), predominantly in Ayacucho. *El Diario* permitted the party to distribute key party documents rapidly to lay out Sendero's positions during the intensely active political period leading up to the 1990 general elections.

Military

After surveying Sendero's activities on the urban front, it may be redundant to talk about Sendero's military presence. Military strategy is its linchpin, around which all else revolves. Indeed, the link between recruits and Sendero flows through its military apparatus: "The Party's work with the masses is carried out through the Army."[34]

Two military tactics figure prominently in Sendero's urban strategy and deserve discussion. Sendero maintained hit squads in Lima. The attacks, requiring elaborate surveillance and careful planning, concentrated on navy officers and APRA politicians. The hit squads were directly responsible to the metropolitan bureau, but the members came from rural hideouts shortly before attacks and returned immediately afterward. This meant that the local cell network providing logistical support did not know who they were.[35] These attacks were distinct from Sendero's practices of cop killings and murders of local adversaries. Zone networks carried these out, using them to get arms and coerce recruits over an invisible line of no return. The first assassination attempt was the failed attack on the National Elections Board president in late April 1985. However, between October 1987 and April 1990, there was an eerie absence of major assassinations. This may have been due to Sendero's changing military priorities.[36]

In 1989, Sendero unveiled a new tactic in urban areas, the armed strike, which it had already used in the EMZs. It staged three armed strikes. The first was along the Central Highway. Citywide strikes occurred in July and on November 3, just before the municipal elections.[37] The media and analysts usually described Sendero's armed strikes as failures. Sendero, however, learns from its failures and identifies weaknesses in civilian society's defenses. One turned out to be the private bus-owners' federations, which control 90 percent of Lima's public transport. During the armed strike they were unwilling to risk their vehicles. Sendero also learned how to reduce Lima's food supply for brief periods.

Conclusion

A snapshot of the situation in mid-1990 shows that Sendero had secured its beachhead on the Central Highway and in Lima. Through infiltration, it paralyzed many of the grass-roots organizations along the Central Highway.

Its hyperactive curiosity and hunger for intelligence led its activists to penetrate a whole range of local groups (soup kitchens, school milk programs, evangelical groups, temporary emergency work programs, and political parties). It meant there were no free forums where the local community could debate resistance without being fingered by spies and sympathizers.

In shantytowns, Sendero unveiled a new, qualitatively superior stratagem, building on the experience over the previous six years in Huaycán and other shantytowns. It organized its own land seizure, with one hundred families paying ten dollars each for the right to participate. This pilot project resulted in two people killed. There were reports on the Central Highway that, with a waiting list of four hundred potential squatter families, Sendero was planning future larger seizures. Controlling a shantytown from its conception to its maturity gives Sendero influence in all aspects of daily life there. The early phases of a squatters' seizure take on paramilitary features to prevent police eviction or theft. This practice has obvious dividends for an organization that wants to train its members in military tactics and methods.

Due to the upheaval in the countryside brought on by political strife, drought, and economic collapse, migration allowed Sendero to gain a broader foothold in Lima. Displaced persons there totaled some 200,000 by 1990, according to human rights organizations. In Junín, Puno, and elsewhere in the hinterland, Sendero pushed strategies that set loose additional flows of forced migrants. The importance of kinship and place of origin in Sendero networks links up with Andean migrant practices. Sendero also recognizes that migration is one of the most grueling and "liberating" experiences of twentieth-century Peru.

On the labor front, Sendero had a spotty performance, losing its toehold in several unions that had served as its initial wedge (for instance, the Atlas Copco employees union). However, it was able to win the elections in Manufacturas Nylon and place cadres in the leadership of three other major unions. Polarized labor-management relations and the economic crisis provide Sendero with continuing opportunities in labor unions.

Across the range of its activities, Sendero shows some consistent patterns. It uses the local conflicts to push for polarization and armed violence. It harnesses processes of decline or anarchy, Peru's self-destructive tendencies, to the goals of its revolution. Prisons and courts, universities and secondary schools, striking trade unions and squatter settlements are foci of radicaliza-tion. By this approach, SL hopes to break down the organizations already in place and pick up those pieces that it may be able to turn to armed revolt. Frequently the government and its security forces do Sendero a service by increasing pressure on these same foci. This tactic also allows Sendero to concentrate its efforts on key leverage points within Peruvian society. Such a focusing of forces means that SL magnifies its presence and impact on grass-roots organizations well beyond its number of activists.

As an Ate Vitarte grass-roots leader says, Sendero takes for itself experien-ces of popular struggle. Peru's peasants, workers, and shantytown residents had worked for years to gain them. Sendero stripped them of their democratic and organizational underpinnings and turned them into weapons. It grabbed historic landmarks already in the popular domain, such as the Committee for Struggle and *El Diario*. It appropriated in some cases the long-standing practice of urban land invasions to turn them into "liberated territories." It radicalized strikes and protests where it could to turn out combatants for the revolution. It confiscated the survival mechanisms of extended migrant families and hometown circuits to turn them into extensions of clandestine cell networks.

This evaluation does not mean that Sendero has not suffered setbacks in Lima. The capture of Osmán Morote, widely believed to be SL's second-in-command, in May 1988 came from armed hubris — an underestimation of police intelligence capacity and a blatant disregard for security measures. The capture of an urban network in June 1990, implicating logistical and propagan-da apparati and safe houses, showed that counterinsurgency intelligence and surveillance work had improved during the second half of the 1980s. The Counterterrorism Agency (DIRCOTE) police intelligence unit had more resources in manpower, funding, and leadership.[38] Both cases highlighted Sendero's latent vulnerability in urban theaters of operation. However, the party assumed these costs as part of the "quota of blood" for forging a revolutionary fighting force. In addition, Sendero expected these losses and took precautionary measures against them.

As separate parts, Sendero's urban presence may seem insignificant. These parts, however, are integral to an overall strategy that augments its impact over time. With carefully laid plans, centralized command, organizational discipline, and meticulous care for detail, Guzmán's followers have strategic and tactical advantages over their political adversaries. While mainstream parties, trade union federations, and the government mustered forces to meet peak moments (the November 1989 March for Peace, for instance), they could not sustain a coherent policy over the medium term.

Throughout the period under review, Sendero found itself aided and abetted in Lima by a breakdown in the presence of the state, just as was occurring in the countryside. Not only could the state not expand its services and authority into areas of need, but it lost control over neighborhoods and services that it already had in place. Schoolteachers no longer had adequate monitoring, police no longer patrolled the streets, and corruption became the currency to make things work. Those political and social forces that wanted to work through the system found themselves frustrated. Sendero and others who worked outside the established order found a more open track.

Finally, a host of individuals and institutions, from the presidency down to organizations that claimed to back Lima's poor and marginalized, failed to grasp Sendero's changing scope and thrust in urban areas. Although evidence began to pile up after the 1986 prison mutiny and intensified in mid-1988, Peru's elites put little effective effort and resources into confronting this threat. It was as if the lessons of Ayacucho and the Andes had been in vain.

Notes

1. Guzmán interview, *El Diario*, July 24, 1988, p. 17.
2. This thesis is sustained by Raúl González in "El cambio de estratégia de Sendero y la captura de Morote," *Quehacer*, 53, July-August 1988, pp. 16-22; "Escalada Senderista: Fuerza o debilidad?" *Quehacer*, 61, October-November 1989, pp. 10-15; and "Sendero: Duro desgaste y crisis estratégica," *Quehacer*, 63, May-June, 1990, pp. 8-15.
3. A premise of this author's research has been to link concrete data from a specific geographic and social area to subversive practices and ideology. I followed events in Ate Vitarte from December 1987 to mid-1990, with additional research on preceding events. Aside from its strategic importance, the area had an invaluable resource: grass-roots leaders with historical perspective and a keen awareness of the Sendero

threat. This chapter would not have been possible without their insight. I retain the anonymity of my informants for their security.

4. Baltázar Caravedo, *Lima: Problema nacional* (Lima: Grupo de Estudios para el Desarrollo-GREDES, 1987), pp. 73, 77-78.

5. Marina Irigoyen, Teresa Chipoco, and Alberto Cheng, *Planificación con el pueblo: Una estratégia de gestión municipal, Ate Vitarte* (Lima: Convenio Centro IDEAS-Municipalidad Ate Vitarte, 1988), p. 22.

6. Caravedo, *Lima*, pp. 97-98.

7. Denis Sulmont, *El movimiento obrero peruano, 1890-1979: Reseña histórica* (Lima: Tarea, 1979), p. 157.

8. Caravedo, *Lima*, p. 41.

9. During this early stage, Lima terrorist activity was an efficient means to let Sendero's scattered followers know that the party had a national presence and was carrying out instructions.

10. Gustavo Gorriti, *Sendero: Historia de la guerra milenaria en el Perú*, vol. I (Lima: Apoyo, 1990), p. 112.

11. Gorriti, pp. 137-139. Also see Chapter 16, "La oferta de asilo a Guzmán," pp. 285-295, for a discussion of Presidente Gonzalo's health problems (psoriasis and other ailments), which meant that he had to spend long periods at sea level. Lima offers obvious advantages for hiding Peru's most wanted man.

12. Partido Communista del Perú (PCP), *Bases de Discusión* 5, p. 5. These documents were published en *El Diario*, January 3-8, 1988. The referencing refers to the order of the supplements and page.

13. Gorriti, *Sendero*, pp. 95-96.

14. See Partido Comunista del Peru, *Bases*, 3, for the party's separation of functions.

15. Jaime Urrutia, "La violencia en la región de Ayacucho," in *Los Niños de la Guerra* (Lima: Instituto de Estudios Regionales, "José María Arguedas," and Universidad Nacional de San Cristóbal de Huamanga, 1987), p. 16.

16. See Isabel Coral, "Ayacuchanos: Migrantes o refugiados de guerra?" *Los caminos de laberinto*, December 4, 1986, pp. 77-84, and "Refugiados ayacuchanos en Lima," in Urrutia's *Los niños de la guerra*; and Francisco Huamantinco Cisneros, *Los refugiados internos en el Perú: Un estudio de aproximación en dos asentamientos humanos de Lima* (Lima, 1990).

17. Jurgen Golte and Norma Adams, *Los caballos de troya de los invasores: Estratégias campesinas de la conquista de la Gran Lima* (Lima: Instituto de Estudios Peruanos, 1987), p. 72.

18. DESCO, *Violencia política en el Perú* (Lima: DESCO, 1989), p. 28.

19. See Gorriti, *Sendero*, pp. 253-283, for a detailed description of the Ayacucho prison break and a thorough analysis of "Desarrollemos la Guerra de Guerrillas," Sendero's first explanation of its insurrection. Guzmán imposed his decision on the party in March 1982 for an audacious surprise assault on the prison. Four years later, the prison mutiny in Lima was followed up by "Desarrollar la guerra popular sirviendo a la revolución mundial."

20. Irigoyen, Chipoco, and Cheng, *Planificación con el pueblo*, pp. 23-26.

21. Raúl González, "La cuarta plenaria del Comité Central del S.L." *Quehacer*, 44, December 1986-January 1987, pp. 49-53.
22. Partido Comunista del Perú, *Bases* 3, p. 5.
23. See Julio Calderón Cockburn and Luis Olivera Cárdenas, *Municipio y pobladores en la habitación urbana (Huaycán y Laderas del Chillán)* (Lima: DESCO, 1989).
24. César Rodríguez Rabanal, *Cicatrices de la probreza: Un estudio psicoanalítico* (Caracas: Editorial Nueva Sociedad, 1989).
25. José Enrique Larrea, *Poblaciones urbanas precarias: El derecho y el revés (El caso de Ancieta Alta)* (Lima: SEA, 1989). With the growth of grass-roots organizations in Peru over the past two decades, many of those who study and work with them have idealized the democratic features of the popular movement, especially since they have frequently focused on the most striking examples, such as Villa El Salvador.
26. Paradoxically, a constraint on Sendero's expansion along the Central Highway and elsewhere is the competition of MRTA. MRTA is the only other political force with the armed firepower to challenge Sendero.
27. Guzmán interview, *El Diario*, p. 36.
28. Ibid., p. 20.
29. See Jorge Parodi, "Los sindicatos en la democracia vacia," in Luis Pásara and Jorge Parodi, eds., *Democracia, sociedad y gobierno en el Perú* (Lima: Centro de Estudios de Democracia y Sociedad — CEDYS, 1988). Parodi's essay contains a fascinating appendix about the Cromotex plant seizure in which a police SWAT squad killed six workers. Néstor Serpa, a leader of the Cromotex union, first joined Sendero and later went over to MRTA.
30. See *Caretas*, May 2, 1988 and *Sí*, May 25, 1988.
31. Denis Sulmont, Javier Mujica, Vicente Otta, and Raúl Aramendy, *Violencia y movimiento sindical* (Lima: Red Peruana de Educación Popular y Sindicalismo, 1989), p. 34.
32. Hugo Salazar, "El teatro peruano de los 80," *Margines*, 5-6, December 1989, pp. 63-83.
33. The weekly magazine *Marka*, founded in 1975, was a symbol of the emergence of the socialist left as a national force. It became a daily in 1980 and was known as *El Diario de Marka*. However, the inconsistencies between professional journalism, readership, business management, and politicking were never resolved. The original shareholders and IU parties withdrew from the paper, leaving it to workers and political "adventurers."
34. Partido Comunista del Perú, *Bases* 4, p. 1.
35. *Peru Report*, June 1987.
36. Some analysts attributed this silence to a decline in the quality of Sendero's hit squads and manpower. However, after 1990 general elections, SL staged several elaborate assassinations that refuted this assumption. More likely, veteran cadres had been redeployed to the Central Sierra, the Upper Huallaga Valley, and elsewhere in the Andes to strengthen guerrilla columns.
37. *Perú 1989: En el espiral de la violencia* (Lima: Instituto de Defensa Legal), 1990, pp. 212-223.
38. For instance, DIRCOTE computerized its information in 1988. This measure and others improved the continuity of intelligence work since regular rotation of police personnel and expertise disrupted the accrual of intelligence.

8

SHINING PATH'S STALIN
AND TROTSKY[*]

Gustavo Gorriti

The cult of personality and purges of party leadership are common phenomena in the development of Communist orthodoxy, although they are certainly not the exclusive preserve of the left. Similar developments can be found in fascist movements as well as in many authoritarian governments and their corresponding parties.

Nevertheless, it is in Marxism-Leninism that the cult of personality has been carried to its most complete and most seductive levels. The cults of personality surrounding Stalin, Mao, Kim Il Sung, and Enver Hoxha during their lifetimes are specific manifestations of how orthodox Communism was defined for more than forty years (and still is in the case of North Korea).

---

[*]This chapter combines much of the article "The War of the Philosopher King," *The New Republic*, June 18, 1990, pp. 15-22, with permission of the author and the editors, with new material written for this volume. The new material covers the life and experience of Luis Kawata Makabe and the discussion of building and splitting the party. This material has been translated from Spanish by the editor and combined with *The New Republic* material to complete the chapter as it appears here.

This cult of personality in the orthodox Communist parties almost always developed after they took power, and was closely related to the struggles within the party leadership during the period when Communist Party authority was consolidating its control over the state. Throughout the revolutionary period of these Communist parties, especially those that had long and difficult guerrilla wars before taking power, the authority of the chief leader never spilled over into the excesses that often occurred afterward. Lenin in hiding, Mao in Yenan, and Tito during the partisan struggle were clearly the most respected first among equals of their organizations' leaderships. But outside of this modest distinction, revolutionary life retained a studied equality among the leaders. Once power had been won and consolidated, however, everything changed, and these competing leaders were among the first to suffer the consequences. Trotsky's relationship with Lenin, first, and with Stalin, later, is the clearest example on both counts.

Given this context, what is remarkable about the cult of personality within the Communist Party of Peru (Shining Path, Sendero, or SL) is that it has grown and developed during the party's clandestine, revolutionary period. What distinguishes Sendero from other Communist parties is that it had an autocrat at the helm from the very beginning of the armed struggle, while the goal of taking power was very distant in the minds of even the most optimistic activists. Leadership stability under one person made for a more efficient organization and a much more tightly controlled process of internal debate concerning differences in revolutionary doctrine and strategy, among other things. Sendero looked much more like a revolutionary party at a much earlier stage than other movements.

This chapter considers two of the Communist Party of Peru's key figures in the 1970s and 1980s, its Stalin and Trotsky, if you will, even though the comparison breaks down in some ways. Sendero's preeminent figure since the mid-1970s has been Abimael Guzmán Reynoso. The individual often identified with the Maoist leadership as second only to Guzmán in the early years in Ayacucho was Luis Kawata Makabe, who later fell from favor, like Trotsky, and was thoroughly humiliated rather than killed, unlike Trotsky. In these two personalities various insights concerning the dynamic and the development of Sendero can be derived.

Abimael Guzmán Reynoso

Abimael Guzmán's fervent disciples called him Dr. "Puka Inti," Quechua for Red Sun. Other followers of Guzmán, however, called him Shampoo, "because," as they said, "he brainwashes you." Even more than a decade since the once-obscure Puka Inti and his organization went to war, he is never depicted with a uniform or with a gun. In the few almost hagiographic propaganda posters Shining Path has produced, an idealized Guzmán leads endless columns of armed followers while clutching a book. He is much more than a warrior. As a 1982 Shining Path pamphlet on military matters puts it: "To wage war it is necessary to be a philosopher. Comrade Gonzalo's battle plans are political, not technical." ("Gonzalo" is the *nom de guerre* Guzmán assumed shortly after splitting from the main pro-Chinese Communist Party in 1970 to lead his own faction.)

Among Latin America's revolutionary movements, the Shining Path insurgency stands out. It is unrelated to other Latin rebellions, and it does not depend on any foreign country for support. Dispensing the same unconditional hostility to the Chinese, Soviet, Cuban, North Korean, and U.S. governments (to name just a few), Shining Path wages revolutionary war according to Maoist People's War doctrine, preserves its orthodox course through regular Cultural Revolution purging rituals, and maintains unity through a personality cult of gigantic proportions.

Before Shining Path went to war, Maoism in Latin America was usually associated with fringe student groups. No guerrilla organization had adopted People's War doctrine in an orthodox way. So when the Shining Path took up arms, the attempt seemed a doomed effort to graft the Chinese experience onto the entirely different Peruvian culture. To most people in Peru, including the large legal left, the movement seemed to be a crazy sect, hopelessly divorced from reality.

Yet the Shining Path insurgency has grown to proportions approached by no other rebellion since Peru became independent in the 1820s. The ragtag guerrillas of the early days, who had no military training and poor weaponry, have been replaced in several parts of the country by battle-hardened, company-size groups armed with machine guns and rifle-propelled grenades. This growth cannot be explained through the stereotype of Pol Pot — fanatics who are killing the very people they should be winning over. Although Sendero's murderous policies are all too real, there is clearly more than bloody fanaticism to them. The organization has a well-developed strategy, disciplined cadre, and, of course, Guzmán. It was evident from the beginning that Guzmán was the insurgency's key protagonist.

The metamorphosis from Abimael Guzmán to Presidente Gonzalo, the philosopher-emperor, was a long one, with tenacity playing a much larger role than intellectual brilliance. Born out of wedlock in December 1934 in Arequipa, Guzmán remained with his mother until his early teens. Then his father, a middle-class merchant, took him into his own family's custody in the city of Arequipa. He was sent to a Catholic high school, where he was known as an introverted student who excelled academically. Intellectual merit has always been respected in Arequipa, and this serious student was well liked.

After entering Arequipa's San Agustín University, Guzmán came under the influence of two older men who were decisively to affect his life. They were a philosophy professor, Miguel Angel Rodríguez Rivas, and the socialist-realist painter Carlos De la Riva. Rodríguez Rivas was a man of poor origins who had worked his way through high school and college. "He was very intelligent," recalls a former colleague, "but he was crazy...if his thinking suffered a deviation it could take him anywhere in the world, and he would follow it, thinking that he was dutifully following sacred Reason."

Rodríguez Rivas became a Kantian. He brought to his intellectual work an uncompromising intensity, rigorous methodology, an ascetic sense of discipline. He had a group of fiercely loyal disciples who were some of the best students, and his stern approach fired their enthusiasm and prodded them to work harder. But not everything was intellectual toil. As Professor Kant did with his disciples, Rodríguez Rivas got together with his own on Saturday nights for some hard-drinking, free-ranging philosophizing.

Abimael Guzmán became a junior member of the group. He was shy and retiring in his research, yet intellectually passionate. In an elitist group with a distinct sense of intellectual superiority over the rest of the academic community, Guzmán was seen as a gifted intellectual. He wrote some articles for the group's magazine, *Hombre y Mundo* (Man and World). The group, whose lofty goal was to forge through rigorous philosophical work the lever with which to change both man and world, soon became identified with the name of its magazine.

At about the same time Guzmán also came under the influence of Carlos De la Riva. De la Riva was an undiluted Stalinist, a Communist whose convictions were too fierce for the party to manage comfortably. As a painter of good technical skills and a fairly able writer as well, he could have succeeded in the conventional way in the meritocracy of Arequipa. He rejected it. He took social realism to heart, using his painting as a propaganda instrument and writing political pamphlets. De la Riva thought that if Communist parties were to achieve their goals, they must be unyielding, stoic, aggressive, yet smart; dialectic methodology ferociously carried out. To him, Stalin epitomized those qualities. And when the first signs of Khrushchev's de-Stalinization campaign began to shock Communist parties all over the world, he focused on the one country where the revolutionary fire still seemed to burn strongly: China. After a long trip to China, he wrote an enthusiastic book, *Where Dawn Is Born*. His thinking had a decisive effect on Guzmán. In late 1959 or early 1960, Guzmán became a member of the Peruvian Communist Party.

In January 1960 an earthquake caused great destruction in Arequipa. Rodríguez Rivas and the *Man and World* group decided it was time for Reason to come to the aid of Reality. Nobody knew the real extent of damage, so the group decided to do a census to apply relief efforts more effectively. It was a very thorough undertaking, which provided an accurate picture of both Arequipa's immediate needs and its poverty. For Guzmán, who participated in the project, this was a critical experience. Then Rodríguez Rivas made an ill-advised attempt to be elected faculty dean. He was soundly defeated. Bitterly disappointed, he quit his job and left Arequipa. The *Man and World* group disbanded.

Soon afterward, Guzmán graduated, with a thesis — dedicated to his mentor — on Kant's theory of space. What he retained from his relationship with Rodríguez Rivas was methodology, not substance: intensity in study and research, tenacious dedication to an objective, and asceticism. The substance came from De la Riva: orthodox communism, as developed and maintained in China. He would never swerve from that line.

In January 1962 Guzmán applied for a teaching appointment at the National University of San Cristóbal del Huamanga. Recruited by the new university president, Efraín Morote Best, he was named a few months later as a philosophy professor in the education program. Although the University of Huamanga was technically reopened in 1958 (it had been closed in 1886), it was in reality an entirely new and audacious education project for Peru. The idea was to use a modern, technically oriented university as an engine of progress in an abysmally poor and backward place. Its first president and guiding force, Fernando Romero Pintado, was a man of vision who believed that Ayacucho could become an education industry town that would prepare professionals appropriate for the region, mostly in areas such as farming, agro-industry, and mining. Both the university's research and the students would energize the region.

The university was fashioned on the American model of the time. Thanks to good fundraising, it could offer the best wages in Peru and attracted some of the country's top intellectuals. Several young U.S. and European professors also were hired. Political activity among the students, a decades-long tradition in Peru, was emphatically discouraged.

The university began to change Ayacucho for the better. At the same time, however, the very concept of change was called into question. The debate between reform and revolution that developed throughout Latin America in the 1960s was to take an extreme form at Huamanga. In 1961 the left, largely Communist-controlled groups began to increase their influence in the university. Romero unexpectedly lost reelection to the university presidency by a single vote, and Morote took over beginning with the 1962 academic year. A complex man of quick, acerbic wit, Morote had clear authoritarian tendencies. He would be torn between his desire to maintain the academic standards of the university and to help with the "politically progressive" measures of opening it up to masses of new students and allowing proselytizing work. Thanks to Guzmán, he never had much of a choice, and ultimately he would be overcome by events to a nightmarish extent.

When Guzmán arrived in Ayacucho, the local Communist Party organization was a sleepy group. Guzmán was put in charge of youth work and immediately set out to change things. Soon Communist students were conducting the kind of census in the Ayacucho barrios that he had helped organize in Arequipa. With accurate information about most neighborhoods, the young Communist activists were able to gain quicker and better results. Guzmán also tried to organize poor neighborhoods so that they would interact with the university, especially with student organizations.

His objective was clear: to use the university to recruit, educate, organize, and subsidize the growth of Communist cadres. Guzmán had the university create a teacher training school that was staffed mostly by Communist Party members or sympathizers. Those students who became early recruits proved an ideal way to forge a relationship with their towns and communities. Many would return home to lay the groundwork for revolutionary work. In the process he helped to destroy the academic excellence of the university. For him, it was a small price to pay.

In February 1964, after a discreet courtship, he married Augusta La Torre, the daughter of local Communist leader Carlos La Torre. Augusta was eighteen at the time, Guzmán twenty-nine. It would be a childless marriage (Guzmán had a daughter from a previous short-lived relationship), with Augusta remaining a devoted companion until her death, apparently in 1990.

The Sino-Soviet rift of December 1963 had a traumatic echo in Peru; at the beginning of 1964 the Peruvian Communist Party divided. The majority of the party's middle and high-level leadership went to the pro-Chinese camp. In Ayacucho, when old-time Ayacucho party leader Isaías Poma Rondinel proposed nominating Marx, Engels, and Lenin for the "symbolic presidium," Guzmán demanded the incorporation of Stalin as well. Khrushchev-era pro-Soviets just could not accept that. The final split occurred, with Guzmán emerging as leader of the Peking faction.

Guzmán had already achieved distinction in his dual role as university professor and the pro-Chinese faction's most important leader in Ayacucho. Still thin, with long hair, he had the appearance of an earnest young intellectual. He almost always wore a jacket without a tie and carried a book under his arm. His influence reached even Morote's household. Morote's older children Osmán and Katya became active followers of Guzmán. He was often surrounded by young students, most from very poor backgrounds, usually of Indian extraction, who eagerly made the jump from illiteracy to philosophy. He was opening up for them the secrets of the universe and their role in giving a sense to it, although some of his colleagues were skeptical.

In 1965 a Cuban-inspired guerrilla insurgency against the democratically elected government of President Fernando Belaúnde Terry (1963-1968) broke out in several places in Peru, including Ayacucho.[1] The pro-Chinese Communist group was pressed to make good on its revolutionary rhetoric and help the Castro-inspired group. That was not to be because the close ties between China and Cuba until 1963 had weakened considerably. As a result, the pro-Chinese groups were instructed not to cooperate with their pro-Cuban counterparts.

In Ayacucho Guzmán, who had begun to organize a military wing of the Communist Party, was hard put to maintain ranks with the party's youth; most wanted to join in the revolutionary enterprise, with its promise of immediate action rather than lengthy political work. At that juncture, Guzmán's arrest appeared imminent, and he was ordered by the party to go underground. He was sent to China, to cadre school. It was a decisive experience. The Cultural Revolution was just beginning and revolutionary zeal was burning again countrywide. He had the opportunity to see Mao while he was still alive, though from a distance. In cadre school he received thorough instruction in People's War doctrine. His predisposition to clandestine action was reinforced in a course on "open and underground work" given by a veteran of the struggle against the Kuomintang. He also remembered keenly his last class on explosives and demolition.[2]

When he returned to Peru, the pro-Chinese party's clandestine apparatus was in disarray. Several members had left to join the pro-Cuban insurgency, which had been crushed unmercifully by the Peruvian armed forces. He did not return permanently to Ayacucho until 1968, when another professor was sacked to make room for him. But by then he had the regional organization very much under control, as he was fighting both inside the party and against competing revolutionary groups, especially those with pro-Cuban tendencies.

The latter was a particularly tough fight. The Cuban revolutionary ideal still fired the imagination of young radicals throughout Latin America. The Cuban model was centered on the actions of small, highly mobile guerrilla groups that would erode the fighting capabilities of the armed forces and bring about the enthusiastic collaboration of the peasantry, which would then march from the Andes to the cities. The political direction of the insurgency had to rest on the guerrillas' military leadership. Cuba's blessing was a must.[3]

Nonsense, said Guzmán and the pro-Chinese cadre. He viewed the Cuban approach as a petit bourgeois militaristic deviation doomed to sure defeat, against which President Mao had written long ago when referring to the wandering guerrillas of Chinese history. In the People's War model, political work was central and military actions only a complement. Likewise the party had to control armed groups completely. The insurrection process itself was a gradual creation of ever-expanding base areas where the party acted as the new de facto government, strengthening itself while the government progressively weakened to the point of collapse.[4]

The discussions were bitter and vicious, but Guzmán prevailed. His prestige as someone equally well versed in the theory of dialectical materialism and the practice of party organizing had grown enormously. When lecturing, his delivery was now self-assured, emphatic. After his lectures, he would be followed by an enthusiastic cohort. He was Comrade Puka Inti.

The tremors of China's Cultural Revolution (1966-1976) reverberated in Peru, the country with the strongest pro-Chinese Communist groups in South America. However, they were badly split, and in 1967 a sizable group left the party and formed its own. Guzmán remained under party leader Saturnino Paredes, but most people thought it was only a matter of time before Guzmán's supremacy became clear.

In late 1968 Peru's armed forces, thinking the country was in a state of latent insurgency, overthrew President Belaúnde. Then, to everybody's surprise, they embarked on a left-wing reformist course, including nationalizations and a very bold agrarian reform. They opened up the jails, freed the few surviving former guerrillas, and made government bureaucrats out of them. Fidel Castro gave his wholehearted blessing. The pro-Soviet Communist Party applauded too, especially after the American military mission was expelled and huge quantities of Soviet weaponry were bought.

Guzmán and the pro-Chinese Communists sensed the reformist danger and opposed the military government tooth and nail. They condemned it as a fascist regime, and, though reserving their most bitter invective for those leftists who were cooperating with the government, tried to create bloody confrontations with it. They did not have to wait long.

In 1969 the military government tried to restrict free high school education to students with passing grades. Student protests in Ayacucho were quickly taken over by the pro-Chinese Communists, and then became violent. In June Guzmán was arrested and sent to Lima. The next day there were riots and hostage-taking in Huamanga and Huanta, followed by about a dozen deaths and then a general strike.[5] The military government backtracked and abrogated the education law. But Guzmán and others were accused of being saboteurs of the Agrarian Reform Law, and the pro-Soviet Communist newspaper accused them of being CIA agents. Guzmán was freed after one month but was put on trial. He would be detained again by the reformist military for short periods in 1979 and 1972.

Shortly thereafter, he broke with party leader Saturnino Paredes. After the usual barrage of mutual expulsions and Leninist invective ("Mr. Liquidationist," Guzmán called Paredes; "Mr. Opportunist," retorted Paredes), each set up his own shop, claiming to be the only Communist Party of Peru. Outsiders trying to differentiate one from the other used to identify them through their newspapers: *Red Flag* was Paredes; *Shining Path* was Guzmán.

Guzmán now had his own party, but the military regime was stealing the revolutionary organizations' thunder. It had captured the country's imagination and was carrying out the reforms they had demanded all along, including diplomatic relations with China, which began to grow less enthusiastic about the prospect of violent revolution in Peru. Shining Path continued its unconditional opposition to the military government, but for almost three years had to retreat. Guzmán used that time to reorganize the party from scratch. He contended that after the death of the party founder, José Carlos Mariátegui, in 1930, the party had deviated from its revolutionary course. It should go back to Mariátegui and rebuild the party. In doing so, it incorporated Mao's Cultural Revolution rituals with People's War doctrine. In order to justify armed insurgency, it defined Peru's society as semifeudal and semicolonial. Even other radical Marxist groups found that diagnosis ridiculous.

In the late 1960s and early 1970s, Shining Path virtually controlled the University of Huamanga. Guzmán used power in a cold, dispassionate way. For example, his former comrade Aracelio Castillo, who had remained with Paredes, was given a failing evaluation review at Guzmán's insistence. "You either use power or they will use it against you," Guzmán often said, and, "I don't have friends. I only have comrades." His lieutenants at the university did much of the proselytizing and carried out the often vicious attacks on Shining Path's opposition as it tried to form a coalition to unseat them. These subordinates were a talented group. There was Luis Kawata Makabe, a bright nisei whom everybody thought would be Guzmán's successor. There were also the children of Efraín Morote, no longer the university's president, and the Durands, and some of the Casanovas and the Cardenases. The party was their life, so they socialized and married among themselves. They were called "the Sacred Family," and the title was applied by extension to the rest of Shining Path's leadership. They were a disciplined group, but some were hard drinkers and others engaged in convoluted relationships, which eventually found expression in internal party politics.

Luis Kawata Makabe

If Guzmán is Shining Path's Stalin, then Kawata is its Trotsky. In the early years in Ayacucho before the break with Paredes and Red Flag in 1970, leadership of the Maoists was as often considered by outsiders to be in Luis Kawata Makabe's hands as in Guzmán's. Kawata, the son of Japanese immigrants, arrived in Ayacucho from the coastal city of Ica in 1960 with his brother Carlos, well before Guzmán himself, after the death of his father and his mother's second marriage. By 1961 he was already a teaching assistant in mathematics, and in 1962 he co-directed the preparatory program for prospective students at the university. By the time the Communist Party recruited him, Kawata was one who stood out among the lively, growing student population of Ayacucho.

Kawata was in every way the exact opposite of Guzmán; "Kabó," the nickname everyone called him by, was a laid-back nonconformist. In a student population that was mostly poor, Kawata was reasonably well off and quite generous with his friends. His nonconformist streak displayed a part of his character that could not be disciplined nor show reverence to those in authority. In the student culture of Ayacucho in the 1960s, political discussion was important, but so too was male companionship, alcohol, and complicated love affairs; Kawata excelled in all.[6]

Kawata is believed to have been recruited by Guzmán himself around 1965. At first Guzmán seems to have focused more on the promise than on the problems that a new recruit of Kawata's standing might entail. Nevertheless, before long Guzmán referred to Kawata as the prototype of "someone with great intelligence and able to give a great deal but who isn't sufficiently serious." Even so, during the first years after his recruitment, Kawata came to be considered Sendero's best orator and, for many, the only young leader with the capacity either to confront or to succeed Guzmán himself. This turned out to be an erroneous judgment; Kawata certainly had the necessary intelligence, but he lacked discipline. Nevertheless, during the years spent trying to gain control of the student movement in various Peruvian universities, especially Huamanga, Kawata was the most visible advocate of what was to become Shining Path.

The struggle among the various left groupings was complex, byzantine, and extraordinarily underhanded. It varied from verbal ambushes and insults over the proper interpretation of Marxist texts to late-night fistfights, aggressive handbills, and flyers bordering on the obscene. However, the principal weapon continued to be scholarly argumentation and persuasion. The object was to convince undecided students that Sendero's particular interpretation of Marxist thought was the only correct one and that all the rest were not only mistaken but condemnable, morally contaminated, and even traitorous!

Kawata excelled in this role. He had, as one of his contemporaries remembers, a standard pitch. It was a set lecture of about two hours in length that he developed during the period when one of his major tasks was to engage other left groups in debate and to give conferences in those universities where Sendero was attempting to expand its influence. The lecture was entitled "Matter and Movement." He drew a simple, complete, absolute system. He began with inorganic matter, the creation of the universe, and finished two hours later with today's society. He left students absolutely stunned.[7] Many converts would be able to tell you the exact moment during Kawata's presentation when their troubled intellectual meanderings were replaced by certainty and conviction. He almost always gave his speech dressed in black pants and shoes, his hair carefully combed. His voice and manner gave the listener the sense that he held something back, perhaps his gentle but stubborn iconoclasm.[8]

This trait had enabled him in earlier years to deal with any situation and get along with the ladies also, for he had a guitar and had learned to play it reasonably well in Ayacucho. Without any prompting he would start to strum. In later years and in more select circles, Kawata and Víctor Raúl Zorilla (also a Sendero leader, but not among the principal figures) livened up the parties. They became known as the "Red Angels," and they used to play and sing "He is coming, He is coming..." as they all awaited Guzmán's arrival. Sure enough, the doctor would eventually appear. After a while, when the party had become sufficiently lively, requests would multiply for a rendition of "Bésame mucho!" All eyes would focus on the Red Angels, who, smiling, would begin to sing this romantic ballad...in Quechua! It was always a musical triumph.

Guzmán and Kawata had very different views of the meaning of these festive gatherings. For Guzmán, the parties provided a release from the accumulated tensions of many days of intense and serious labor, a brief parenthesis of relaxation. They also provided a good way to get to know people as the effects of alcohol released them from their inhibitions. For the nonconformist Kawata, who combined both an artistic temperament and a tendency toward self-destruction, the parties were much more important.[9]

Even so, Kawata identified himself completely with the party and its doctrine; otherwise he could not have kept his party membership, much less a leadership position. Furthermore, he was for a long time one of the most effective representatives of the party within the university structure. Kawata was named in the early 1970s as professor of natural sciences for the students' all-important first year at the University of Huamanga. He soon became the focal point for Sendero opposition due to his open manipulation on behalf of the party and frequent neglect of his teaching responsibilities. "Rosa de Arancibía,"[10] who transferred from Huamanga in 1972 and had to retake some of her courses, including those taught by Kawata, remembers him saying that the only thing students had to know to pass the course were the Four Principles of Mao Zedong.

Victory and Defeat at the University

These were the years when Sendero controlled the student movement, the administrative structure, and the academic program of the university. Sendero exercised a totalitarian control that even then distinguished it from other Marxist groups and especially from the Maoists. This was manifested in a number of ways, but particularly with regard to gaining and retaining student recruits. Historically, university recruiters have been the life blood of the Marxist parties, but also the bane of their existence. Their youthful enthusiasm made them committed but ill-disciplined and fickle militants. Once they finished their studies, they usually abandoned their party commitment. This made it very hard for Marxist party leadership to incorporate students into their long-term planning.

Guzmán had his own approach for dealing with this problem. One aspect was to improve, strengthen, and discipline the institutional part of the partisan relationship. For example, membership in the Student Revolutionary Front (FER) was strengthened not only by party and Communist Youth control but also by participation in such "generated organisms" as the Youth Movement. A second aspect, perhaps more significant, was Guzmán's insistence that a substantial portion of the leadership also be engaged in teaching. He knew from his own experience how strong the ties between teachers and students could be. Thus he understood how great an impact the teachings of particularly admired professors could have on their disciples, especially those who could provide definitive answers to students' concerns. By ensuring that the teachers were at the same time the party leaders, Guzmán reinforced both activities. A third component involved Sendero with the daily routine of the students, especially their room and board, by gaining administrative control of those activities with the teacher-leaders or their followers. By ensuring that the daily activities of the university community revolved around the party, Shining Path could systematically harass opposition students and teachers.

Even outside the university community, especially in Ayacucho, there were regular activities with other mass organizations. The weekly *minkas* (an Indian tradition of cooperative work on specific projects) and a number of other events were coordinated with the nonuniversity groups that made up the "Popular Defense Front." They provided a form of cross-pollination that served, among other things, to strengthen and reaffirm commitment to Sendero. However, such activities also provoked a strong reaction by opposition elements well before the launching of the People's War in 1980. Not surprisingly, Kawata, as a prominent *apparatchik* and a vulnerable nonconformist, was a leading target of this opposition.

When the student coalition that opposed Sendero, the University Student Federation (FUE), began to gain strength beginning in 1972, one of the first Sendero victims of their reprisals was Kawata. He received a negative teaching evaluation and was removed from his position on the grounds that he had never completed his university degree. Shortly afterward, on July 17, 1973, a pitched battle broke out at the Student Residence between pro and anti-Sendero groups that lasted more than three hours. The FUE and its allies eventually triumphed, took over the Student Residence, and captured the Sendero activists. Kawata was their principal target, and in the heat of the moment, they might well have lynched him had they been able to find him. Since Guzmán did not happen to be in Ayacucho at that moment, Kawata became the symbol of the hatred directed at Sendero. They were not aware that for some time Kawata's position in the party had changed substantially.

The Fall of Kawata

The incident that precipitated Kawata's downfall seemed to have very little to do with his politics, and is one more example of how major historical events are often explained by a footnote. It occurred one afternoon when Abimael Guzmán, somewhat inebriated and accompanied by his equally drunk colleagues, Antonio Díaz Martínez and "Julio Arévalo Jiménez"[11] (who some years later would withdraw from Sendero), burst into Kawata's room after breaking the door down. In the room, they found a very worried Kawata with two women, one of whom, according to a number of interviews, was Guzmán's lover, even though both were married. There ensued a convoluted verbal altercation that culminated with Guzmán shouting Kawata out of the party. Although participants felt that everything would be straightened out once Guzmán calmed down and sobered up, he surprised everyone the next day by reaffirming Kawata's definitive expulsion. This marked the beginning of Kawata's personal Long March. Even though he continued to give lectures and to participate in gatherings connected to Sendero, his reduced status limited his impact.[12] Nevertheless, Kawata's continued presence fostered the impression among those not connected to Sendero, especially within the security forces, that he was a very important figure, perhaps even its true leader.[13]

The purging of Kawata left Guzmán's leadership virtually uncontested. Guzmán drove himself hard, and he began to suffer from two maladies that would plague him in coming years, psoriasis and erythremia. The latter would make it increasingly difficult for him to stay in Ayacucho or any other high-altitude place for extended periods. By hard work he gradually built and then reorganized his own highly disciplined political party, which survived both the reformist military government's high tide in the early 1970s and the growing strength of opposition forces in the university. But he did resign his professorship in 1976 and decided then to move many cadre to the countryside to expand political work in preparation for the armed insurgency fully four years before it began.

However, Mao's death and then Deng's coup in 1976 threw Sendero into confusion, since they had had a very close relationship with the Chinese for twelve years, sending cadre for training and receiving some financial assistance. It was hard for SL militants to realize that they were alone. For orthodox Communists, that was an unheard-of situation. For a time, they tried to keep bridges open with Mao's former ally, Albania's Enver Hoxha. But Hoxha's increasing attacks against Mao and his preference for Paredes' Red Flag made for a furious break. At this juncture, Guzmán and his party took an unexpected course: They came to see themselves as the center of world revolution. Maoist ideology had predicted the possibility of losing entire revolutionary countries to revisionist thermidorians. But by stressing the primacy of ideology, it showed that as long as an organized party maintained the correct line, Communism would recover and conquer in the end. Maoism had also tried to prevent capitalistic restoration with the Cultural Revolution, but in Guzmán's view it had failed because it did not go far enough. Since restoration had come through Communist leaders, it was clear to Guzmán that Stalin's and Mao's purges had not worked as expected. Therefore, cultural revolutions should be semipermanent affairs. Furthermore, since Communist parties had proven to be coup-prone, Guzmán believed the People's War's first stages should be as carefully planned as last. These adjustments to Maoism would be called the "Guiding Thought of Comrade Gonzalo."

In 1978-1979, while the military government was preparing to transfer power back to civilian rule and most Marxist groups were making the transition to elected legitimacy, the Shining Path alone prepared itself for war. The debate over whether to begin the armed struggle was not an easy one. Some veteran leaders confronted Guzmán and maintained that they were heading for collective suicide. But he humiliated and finally obliterated all opposition. A few were expelled in disgrace. The party followed Guzmán. His unexpected arrest in Lima in January 1979 proved to be only a minor irritant. Sendero hired a respected progressive lawyer and even managed to produce four generals (at least one was tricked) who supported his immediate release. As soon as he was free, he disappeared underground, where he has remained.

In March and April 1980, Shining Path had its last peacetime meetings. For those who faltered when considering the enormity of their task, Guzmán had a historical example. He read excerpts of Washington Irving's all-but-forgotten 1850 book, *The Life of Mahomet*, to show how several desert tribes when moved by an intense conviction could conquer a great part of the world in one generation. He was persuasive, and the war began a month later.

The insurgency grew steadily without any outside assistance. The quantity and quality of operations gradually increased and improved, from violent political demonstrations to military attacks. In a number of districts, especially rural ones, Shining Path eliminated the state's presence and became the de facto underground government. It was a strategy geared to gradually wrest control of territory and population from the Peruvian state.

With the start of the People's War, and in spite of all the security forces' misinformed assurances to the contrary, Kawata was once again out of Sendero. In part this was because he had been one opposing the launching of armed actions. Out of the party and living with his mother and his stepfather, Kawata turned himself in to the police in September 1980 after he had been linked in press accounts to Sendero attacks at that time. On that occasion, the police simply sent him back home. On February 17, 1981, however, the police arrested him as the alleged intellectual author of Shining Path activities. This time, shortly after his capture, newspaperman Patricio Ricketts went to interview him for *Caretas*. Although he did not succeed in getting the interview, he did get to see Kawata, and described him as follows:

> He was short and thin like a jockey, dressed in blue pants and a cream colored shirt with horizontal stripes. ..Kawata spoke with ease but carefully measured each word, looking from time to time at his fidgeting hands. He exercised an Eastern-like control over his emotions....Although he acknowledged his support for the thought of Mao Zedong and his long standing sympathy for Shining Path and his former relationship as a leader of FER-SL, he also asserted that he had nothing to do with the attacks and even opposed them.[14]

This may be how Kawata survived his opposition to Guzmán's strategy — by his silence both as to details of the organization and as to the specific nature of his differences. Unlike Trotsky, Kawata decided not to fight back. Like Trotsky, he was thoroughly humiliated and cut off from the party to which he had dedicated his life.

Kawata's most bitter experience occurred after he was sent to the prison island of El Frontón along with other Sendero suspects.[15] There, after two or three initial weeks of treating Kawata with considerable reserve, hostility toward him increased. Once the party's orders arrived, this hostility became a concerted campaign to break Kawata's will. Imprisoned party commissars approached Kawata from time to time in one or another of the prison's corners where he was trying to cope as quietly and discreetly as possible. Accompanied by their disciplined and obedient followers, they harangued him, shouted slogans, pointed at him, and called him "Traitorous Chinese Rat." They made life impossible for him in the Blue Block where the Sendero detainees were quartered and forced him to request a transfer to another section of the prison, El Chaparral, where collaborator and apolitical inmates were housed. A few of his old comrades and fellow dissidents defended Kawata; when the situation became impossible, they protected him and accompanied him to his new quarters. The attacks on these dissenters were not as severe; the most venomous and vitriolic were directed at Kawata.

The Sendero commissars were able to get into El Chaparral even though this section of the prison was supposedly off limits to them. They regularly made their rounds to virtually every corner of the island to make their party-line speeches. They would arrive, shout their slogans, and repeat the party phrases while shaking their fists until they became hoarse; all the while the other prisoners had to stand in silence, listen respectfully, and applaud at precisely the right moment. So the "Traitorous Chinese Rat" insults continued in El Chaparral as well. Kawata had no choice but to accept his fate in silence. Even in the midst of an embryonic revolution, Kawata became the Peruvian Deng Xiaoping.

Kawata's situation remained like this for some time. One afternoon in 1983, however, news arrived that Víctor Raúl Zorrilla, captured a few weeks before in Chimbote, was going to be brought to El Frontón the following day. The prisoners in the Blue Block immediately began feverish preparations to receive this loyal follower of Gonzalo. The news also raised Kawata's hopes, as he was to admit to some of his old friends years later at a nostalgic but painful gathering. He thought that he would be able to resolve his status at last with his former singing partner in the Red Angels and subordinate in the party. Obviously there was a problem, but these old friends could talk it out. He would be able to explain where he stood and would ask for an explanation for the expulsion from the party and for the humiliation imposed on him.

The next morning, the day Zorrilla was expected, the Sendero prisoners from the Blue Block gathered very early, all decked out with red flags. Kawata also went over accompanied by two or three of his closest companions, one of whom had also been a friend of Zorrilla. Although Kawata's presence provoked a number of hostile glances, no one taunted him, given the uncertainty now over his status.

When the launch was spotted on the morning horizon and when it landed, the red flags were unfurled and the staffs moved in unison, amid great applause and cheering. Zorrilla entered the yard of a Blue Block filled with the sound of Sendero anthems, marching cadres, and unfurled flags. When the Sendero formation fell into line to greet Zorrilla and shake his hand, Kawata decided to approach him. Upon coming up behind Zorrilla, Kawata touched him on the shoulder and called him by name.

Zorrilla turned around. He looked at Kawata totally stonefaced; there was no visible emotion. "How are you?" was all Zorrilla said, bare acknowledgment of some insignificant presence. Among the Sendero ranks a classic Marxist clapping began, slow and cadenced at first, gradually becoming a rapid staccato. Zorrilla turned around to join the clapping. Kawata had appealed his sentence and the appeal had been denied. He walked back to El Chaparral...alone.

Weeks later, Kawata was moved to the prison at Lurigancho. There he survived even worse abuses. At some point, however, with the help of family and friends, he gained his freedom. He returned to Ica, where he was able to support himself after a fashion as a teacher in a pre-university preparatory school, but aged rapidly. When he got together with his old Ayacucho friends in 1987, Zorrilla had already been dead for over a year, killed in the Lurigancho massacre of June 19, 1986. Kawata seemed to all those who saw him to be in a state of advanced deterioration. He had only a few of his teeth left and his skin was all dried out and stretched over his fragile face. His worn clothes also accurately displayed his misfortunes and current situation.

But Kawata refused offers of help to get out of the country. He told his friends that he had asked for an explanation for his expulsion from the party to which he had dedicated the best years of his life. "I don't understand what's going on," he said. "Let them explain things to me or let them kill me," he observed, and then added with a toothless smile, "Cheers!"[16]

Conclusion

Guzmán's status during these years had become even more exalted. He was called the "Fourth Sword" of world revolution. In the pledge that all new Shining Path members had to make, they promised Gonzalo, "Chief of the Communist Party of Peru and of World Revolution," to give their lives "for the triumph" of world revolution. At the same time, communities that resisted the Shining Path's rule were punished, sometimes with great ferocity.

Guzmán's primary strategic objective was to create an axis of Shining Path-controlled or influenced areas up and down the Andes Mountains from north to south. This was more or less achieved by late 1986. At the same time, Shining Path was active in Lima and in coastal areas. In 1987 it made a drive into the Upper Huallaga Valley, the world's most important coca-producing area, purporting to defend the *cocalero* peasants from the violence of narcotics traffickers as well as from police and U.S.-funded eradication workers. As the drug war intensified and American presence in the valley increased, Shining Path happily prepared to confront them, reasoning that if it can turn an insurgency into, in its words, "a war of national resistance," then "90 percent of the population would follow us."

Although it is doubtful that this scenario will materialize, the insurgency is likely to continue to grow, at least for a time. Its strength clearly is due as much to its own skills as to the weaknesses of the Peruvian state and the shortcomings of Peru's elites. After more than a decade of war, Shining Path has shown that it is possible to defy history's current. In Peru, at least, Communists are not yet a dying breed. As for Puka Inti, he will continue to produce many more deaths and destruction in the name of a better world. To his followers he is nothing less than the philosopher-emperor who will lead orthodox Marxist-Leninist-Maoists all over the world in a victorious reconquest of territory lost to the revisionists. He will most likely fall far short of that exalted objective.

But in the meantime, he is democracy's most formidable enemy in South America, and probably in the hemisphere.

As for Kawata, by early 1991 he was living in Germany, sharing lodgings and activities with other Sendero friends from the earliest days, friends who also had had problems with the party and had been pardoned, and were subsequently permitted to assist from abroad. Kawata, according to accounts of travelers who knew about him through common acquaintances, also was helping out. Unlike Trotsky, but like Deng Xiaoping, Kawata came back from his first purgatory at least partially forgiven. Unlike Deng, Kawata's patience did not serve him well.

He was one of a number of longstanding militants who were purged, expelled, and then permitted to return to help the party under severe restrictions, though his case is perhaps the most extreme. In practical terms, Sendero offered very little. But for those who had found a meaning to their lives in party activity and who had given the party what they considered their best years, there was nothing worse than ostracism and exile. For them, once they had completed their descent to purgatory, Guzmán let them come back. Once their resistance had been broken, Guzmán took advantage of what was left. As a close friend of Guzmán's once said, someone who had known him for many years and had been very close to him, "When he had an enemy, he was terrible. When he hated someone he didn't stop until that person was destroyed...taken apart, piece by piece. Then, at the last possible moment, he would pick him up and begin to put the pieces back together. This was the approach which produced his most blindly loyal followers."[17]

One might be able to contemplate the possibility that even in Guzman's most brutal purges to preserve the orthodoxy of the Communist Party of Peru and thus its dynamism, he has done Stalin or Mao one better. Instead of seeking out his Trotsky to kill him, Guzmán systematically broke his will to resist instead and then used what remained for whatever purpose suited him. As Guzmán's Trotsky, Kawata lives and serves, an example to all who might resist the discipline and the orthodoxy of the party that their only course is to march onward in lock step for the cause of Marx, Lenin, Mao, and Gonzalo.

Notes

1. On the 1965 guerrilla outbreak in Peru, see Richard Gott, *Rural Guerrillas in Latin America* (London: Penguin, 1973); Peru, *Las guerrillas en el Perú y su represión* (Lima: Ministerio de Guerra, 1966); Héctor Béjar, *Perú 1965: Apuntes sobre una experiencia guerrillera* (Havana: Casa de las Americas, 1969); General Armando Artola, *¡Subversión!* (Lima, 1976).

2. See author's "The War of the Philosopher King," *The New Republic*, June 18, 1990, p. 18 for additional details.

3. Gott, *Rural Guerrillas*; Regis Debray, *Revolution in the Revolution* (New York: Monthly Review Press, 1967).

4. Partido Comunista del Perú (SL), "Bases de discusión (linea militar)," *El Diario*, January 6, 1988.

5. On the 1969 riots, see Factor Ramos Solís and Jorge Loli Cabana, "Historia del movimiento popular en Huamanga," Universidad de San Cristóbal de Huamanga, Ayacucho, Senior thesis, 1979; Erik Cohen, "Power Structure and Urban Riots: A Case Study and a General Framework for Analysis," ms., Jerusalem, Hebrew University, Department of Sociology, unpublished paper, 1970; "Los sucesos de Huanta y Ayacucho," *Narración* (Lima), 1971.

6. Information about Kawata comes from a number of interviews with his contemporaries — classmates, some former fellow party members, and some political rivals — all friends. Most preferred not to be cited by name.

7. Interview with "José Alcázar" (a pseudonym), July 27, 1987.

8. Interviews with several of Kawata's former students and fellow professors.

9. Interviews, in August 1987, with the late Alicia Carrasco de Moya.

10. A pseudonym.

11. A pseudonym.

12. Various notations in the files of one or another of the government intelligence services deal with the presumed activities of Kawata in Lima, Ayacucho, and elsewhere (some of them surely apocryphal) on the following dates: April 19, 1976; June 12, 13, 14, and 28, 1976.

13. For example, in the Naval Intelligence Agency's Information Note 008-GNC-77, Kawata is described as the head of Sendero.

14. Patricio Ricketts, "Tiburón o loma?" *Caretas* (Lima), 638, March 2, 1981.

15. This discussion is taken from interviews with two of the participants in the August 1987 reunion with Kawata described below.

16. Interview with a participant in the gathering.

17. Interview in August 1987 with the late Alicia Carrasco de Moya.

9

THE ORGANIZATION OF SHINING PATH*

Gabriela Tarazona-Sevillano

Shining Path (SL or Sendero) stands out among guerrilla and terrorist groups worldwide for its strong and complex organization, with a substantial grassroots support structure. These defining characteristics have helped Sendero adapt to changing circumstances in Peru and maintain itself as a viable, expanding insurgency. The purpose of this chapter is to describe the major components of the organization and to analyze its strengths and weaknesses.

*The author served as a criminal affairs prosecutor in the Peruvian judicial system from 1984 to 1986. Much of the information for this chapter is based on notes taken on cases under investigation; interviews with officials whose identities are protected for reasons of confidentiality; and media accounts. Some portions of the chapter are derived from the author's *Sendero Luminoso and the Threat of Narcoterrorism*, Center for Strategic and International Studies (CSIS), Washington Papers 144 (New York: Praeger, 1990). With thanks to Ana María Bromley and Juan Malca Pérez of the Peruvian judiciary; Peter Duignan and William Ratliff at the Hoover Institution, Stanford University; and to John B. Reuter, Wes Hofferbert, and Lisa Jackson of Davidson College for their assistance.

National, Regional, and Local Levels

Shining Path is directed by the National Central Committee composed of Abimael Guzmán Reynoso and a few top lieutenants. Committee responsibilities include the setting of ideology, strategy, and policy for the entire organization. On an organizational flowchart, six regional committees are beneath the National Central Committee: Northern, Central, Southern, Primary, Eastern, and Metropolitan. Although each committee functions independently, all comply with national directives.

Each of these regional committees includes various departments and their subdivisions (provinces and districts). The only exception is the Metropolitan Committee, comprised solely of Lima and Callao. As Lima's present population now approaches seven million, the Metropolitan Committee is of special importance and does not extend to other departments. Regional committees handle the planning and evaluation of Sendero activities within their boundaries, from indoctrination to military operations. The regions themselves are further broken down into zones, sectors, and cells, each having its own military detachments.

Sendero leadership takes advantage of the ability of local people to best assess potential targets and the most effective times of attack in their respective areas. Hence the National Central Committee allows regional commanders a significant sphere of autonomy. This eliminates some of the cumbersome bureaucracy usually associated with layered organizations and enables the regional committees to react with greater speed and efficiency. Further, this process has led to military mobility and a high success rate for Sendero operations. By comparison, the Peruvian Army is slow to respond due to its top-heavy command structure. As a result, it has often experienced difficulty launching effective counteroffensive measures when presented with windows of opportunity.

Despite Sendero's considerable regional autonomy, it is able to act in national unison when situations so require, or when the national leadership deems it necessary. Coordinated attacks are planned several times a year, commemorating Guzmán's birthday (December 4), Independence Day (July 28), and Heroes' Day (June 19, honoring the 256 Sendero militants who died in the El Frontón and Lurigancho prison uprising in 1986). A combination of personal initiative and party unity forms one of Sendero's basic tenets; "In the party they teach us that we are not loose pearls," explained one captured militant, "but rather a pearl necklace."[1]

Intermediate Organizations

As of mid-1990, the police have determined that Sendero has developed entities for coordination and support between the National Central Committee and the regional subdivisions.[2] There are four new organs: the Department for Organizational Support, Group of Popular Support, Department of Finance, and Department of International Relations.

Among the duties of the Department for Organizational Support (DAO) are: (1) to transmit directives and reports from the Central Committee to the regional commanders; (2) to receive and send mail to and from regional commanders and militants; (3) to inform the Central Committee of requests, coordinating such requests with the other organs of coordination and support; (4) to reassign militants to new areas as deemed appropriate by the National Central Committee, and to give them specific duties; (5) to conduct studies on new developments in the social, political, and economic spheres using information received from the different regions; (6) to maintain the general archives of Shining Path, including the real identities of Sendero militants with their letters pledging themselves to the insurgency and to President Gonzalo, real documents of identification, and copies of the fake identities given to them.

The Group of Popular Support (GAP), an intermediate organ of Sendero, is divided into two branches: the *Intelligence Network* and *Popular Aid of Peru*. The *Intelligence Network* keeps the hierarchy updated with new developments in the pursuit of the popular war and counterinsurgency operations. This important subdivision channels reports to and from the regions, and is broken down into strategic intelligence and internal intelligence, of which the latter takes care of follow-up and support for released Sendero prisoners. Police sources believe that Delia Natividad Taquiri, known by her pseudonym of "Zulma," headed this department before her capture in June 1990.[3] *Popular Aid of Peru* is the most important support organization, and it will be discussed below.

The Department of Finance takes care of Sendero's finances, allocating funds as needed. It is still not known exactly what Sendero does with the large amounts of hard currency obtained through its activities in the coca and cocaine producing Upper Huallaga Valley (UHV).

The Department of International Relations reputedly takes care of Sendero's international activities, primarily to provide information and speakers for Sendero's sympathizers abroad. Sendero has support groups in France, Italy, and Sweden as well as a tiny support base in the United States located in the San Francisco area.[4]

Metropolitan Organization

As a result of the insurgency's emphasis since 1989 on urban strategy, the Metropolitan Region has become the focus of the movement's political and terrorist activities. Lima and Callao are distinguishable in name only, as the two cities are contiguous and comprise one large metropolitan area. For organizational purposes, Sendero has divided its metropolitan region into six zonal subregions. As of 1990, it appears that SL has extended its metropolitan region to include other provinces of the department of Lima located to the north, south, and east of the province of Lima itself (Huaral, Cañete, Huarochirí).

Sendero's Metropolitan Central Committee is composed of secretaries and a coordinator. These secretaries, all women from 1983 to 1985, also attend meetings of Shining Path's National Central Committee. Facilitating communication between the Metropolitan Central Committee and Lima's zone leaders is the coordinator. This position is of great importance; besides serving as an intermediary between the Metropolitan Central Committee and the zone leaders, the coordinator maintains lists of the true names of Sendero militants in Lima. Sendero members know each other only by their noms de guerre, which purports to protect their identities in case of capture. Although the coordinator's position was once located below the Metropolitan Central Committee on the organization's flowchart, it now appears that the coordinator may hold a seat on the committee itself.

Answering directly to the Metropolitan Central Committee secretaries are four "special squads." Each squad consists of three or four dedicated militants whose primary function is to carry out acts of sabotage or terrorism. Extensive study of numerous attacks and assassinations compiled by the government's Counterterrorism Office (DIRCOTE), the special police subdivision charged with the investigation of terrorist activities, has revealed that a common pattern characterizes most urban attacks. Each of the four special squads is utilized to perform a specific, predetermined role.

Attacks or assassinations are initiated by the "annihilation detachment" squad. Members of this detail typically pose as innocent-looking civilians — a couple, street vendors, students, and so on. They do not generally carry visible arms or explosives; these may be provided by "purveyors" at the moment of attack (the "purveyors" are separate entities who do not work within any particular squad). The second special squad, referred to as the "assault group," signals the commencement of action by creating a diversion in the immediate area of attack. This may entail throwing dynamite or homemade bombs, which creates confusion and provides the "annihilation detachment" with a moment of cover in which to carry out its mission. While the annihilation squad is in the midst of its attack, the third special squadron, the "containment detachment," steps in to neutralize any counterattack. Once the job is accomplished, the assault group escapes by melting into the crowd or climbing into getaway cars.[5] Then the fourth squad, called the "razing detachment," appears to complete the assignment by delivering a final shot to the head or chest — in the case of an assassination — and leaving a placard explaining the reason for the attack. Often, this fourth squad is composed of only one individual who, in many cases, is a woman.

The primary task of Sendero's Metropolitan Central Committee is to program Lima's six zonal committees and their four subsidiary divisions: zonal squads, sectors, subsectors, and cell militias. The responsibilities of each of these divisions are not as explicitly defined as those of the special squads; rather, they serve in a range of capacities. Police sources have determined that their work is directed in both political and military ways. Most serve primarily by disseminating Sendero material (for example, popular education) and by procuring whatever assistance they can for militants and other party members. The cell militia found in each metropolitan zone provide military support and backup to Sendero militants carrying out offensive maneuvers there.

Support Organizations

Sendero is assisted in Lima by a wide array of local support organizations. These groups are organized to recruit city residents from all walks of life. Once enlisted, new supporters are given a twofold mission: first, to participate in agitation and propaganda efforts; and second, to provide a wide range of support to the movement. Organizations that fall into this category include the following:

1. Laborers' and Workers' Class Movement (MOTC).
2. Laborers' and Workers' Class Struggle Committee of the Central Highway (CLOTCC). The Central Highway is Lima's major industrial area.
3. Class Struggle Committee of Argentina Avenue. Argentina Avenue is another of Lima's industrial sectors.
4. Popular Aid of Peru.
5. Students' Revolutionary Front (FER).
6. Neighborhood Class Movement (MCB).
7. Women's Popular Movement (MFP).
8. Youth Movement.
9. Popular Intellectual Movement.
10. Popular Peasant's Movement (MCP).
11. Shanty Town Movement (MPJ) or Shanty Town Revolutionary Movement (MRPJ).
12. Mariátegui Center for Intellectual Work (CTIM).
13. Popular Bases' Movement (MBP).
14. Agricultural Laborers' and Workers' Movement (MOTAG).

All these organizations are believed to be grouped under the general title of the People's Revolutionary Defense Movement (MRDP).[6] Beginning in early 1990, the MRDP was given a growing number of military assignments.

The most significant grass-roots support movement is Popular Aid of Peru, which first came to the attention of police in late 1987. Under this umbrella organization fall a number of smaller support groups that provide multiple types of assistance and service to the insurgency and those associated with it. Founded in 1982, the organization furnishes medical, legal, and other professional advice to the movement and assists with fundraising, transportation, food, and housing.

Authorities first learned of Popular Aid when a number of classified documents were captured from the apartment of a suspected Sendero commander, Roger Valle Travesano. The documents disclosed that Valle

Travesano, an attorney, was a member of the Association of Democratic Lawyers, an organization that provides free legal aid to those arrested for terrorist activities. The documents further revealed that Popular Aid had expanded from seventy-two members in 1982 to some six hundred members by 1986.

This popular assistance program coordinates its activities with those of the insurgency. According to Valle Travesano's documents, by August 1985 Popular Aid was to have reached the stage where it would take part in recruiting and organizing on a national level, in part by promoting demonstrations and other nonmilitary-type exercises. Its activities were to expand beyond Lima in 1986 to regions of the country that had experienced relatively little Sendero activity, such as Huaraz, Chimbote, and Ica. By mid-1990, Huaraz had become a significant area of Shining Path operations. This tactic of introducing the clandestine via the legitimate opened the way for Sendero indoctrination programs.

According to the Popular Aid organizational chart made up by DIRCOTE, the entire association is probably led by a six-member committee. Reporting directly to this committee is the Commission for Propaganda and Public Relations, a group working directly with intellectuals to develop mass propaganda for Sendero. In addition to this commission, Popular Aid has three other sections; the Department of Mobilization, the Department of Legal Defense, and the Department of Assistance.

Of these three sections, the Department of Mobilization is the largest. It has the tasks of mobilizing the masses in legal support of Sendero and of assisting prisoners and their families. It accomplishes the first by working closely with well established groups, such as MRDP, that are already integrated into the society. The second task, carried out by the Prisoners' Aid Committee, is to provide all necessary aid to captured members and their families and to the relatives of missing militants. It may also include legal pressure for prisoner visitation rights or for providing information on the whereabouts of missing Sendero militants or sympathizers. Another subcommittee tends to the needs of families of members killed in action, the "fallen heroes." Each of these groups is also charged with continuing education and indoctrination efforts.

The second branch of Popular Aid, the Department of Legal Defense, works as the primary source of assistance for captured Sendero members. The department is composed of three divisions: the Association of Democratic Lawyers, which provides free legal services to detained suspected terrorists; the Law Student Section, which provides free legal advice to Sendero members while working to cultivate interest in Sendero among fellow students; and the Organization of Lay Workers, probably made up of court-system personnel (clerks, messengers and secretaries). These serve by furnishing confidential information about prosecution plans in progress, by causing delays within prosecution proceedings, or by misplacing important files.

The final branch of Popular Aid is known simply as Assistance and is composed of Sendero sympathizers who prove more useful in their present occupations than they would as full-time militants. These individuals include electrical engineers who supply information about key sections of a region's electrical grid, security officials who allow militants admittance to sensitive areas, and other key personnel.

One particularly alarming case is that of Eva Gómez, a National Police Hospital psychologist. Gómez, a graduate of the Catholic University, worked in psychological evaluation of police officers who were to serve in emergency zones. In this post, she had access to extensive confidential records, including the backgrounds of police officers and their families, which she presumably passed on to key Sendero commanders. Gómez was arrested in late 1987 by DRICOTE.[7] Ironically, those who participate in Popular Aid activities do not necessarily face prosecution, as membership in a nonmilitary political organization is not interpreted as a criminal activity. In June 1987, a Lima judge ruled that prosecuting citizens for partaking in such activities would violate their constitutional rights.[8] As of early 1991, the state has chosen not to specifically penalize membership in such Sendero front organizations.

Indoctrination

Sendero's growth and expansion at the national level is due in part to its political work at the grass roots. Sendero's indoctrination is directed at the strata of society that traditionally have been excluded from Peru's economic mainstream, the rural and urban underclasses. The indoctrination is conducted in Popular Schools and provides Sendero a forum to increase class consciousness among the peasantry, working class, and students. This program — also called the political strategy of Sendero — began in Ayacucho in the late 1960s and grew into a national campaign during the 1980s. Sendero's ideology, tailored to its audiences, spreads by emphasizing the failures and inadequacies of the present state, the unjust and corrupt nature of the existing socioeconomic order, and José Carlos Mariátegui's Marxist interpretation of Peruvian reality.[9] The Popular Schools stress the need for the class struggle and outline Sendero's plans for the future New Democracy.

There are many historically unresolved grievances in Peru that the insurgency exploits to its advantage. In addition, the country's faltering economy lends itself particularly well to exploitation by Sendero. Inflation skyrocketed from 70 percent in 1982, to 1,722 percent in 1988, 2,775 percent in 1989, and 7,650 percent in 1990.[10] All Peruvians have been affected by a severe slump in buying power, with the lower and middle classes the hardest hit. The precipitous decline in real wages has led to widespread anxiety and an environment of general distrust that Sendero has manipulated to its advantage. Sendero propaganda speaks of the New Democracy in which all will have opportunity and a sense of identity and where ethnic and class separations will be erased.

Sendero's methods of indoctrination have developed along with the movement itself. It began in the early 1960s at the University of San Cristóbal de Huamanga in Ayacucho, where Abimael Guzmán went to teach philosophy and social science in the education program. Guzmán also conducted special study groups and seminars. Indoctrinated students returned to their native rural communities, often as teachers, and spread versions of Guzmán's theories among the peasants. This helped the movement to expand in the provinces of Cangallo, Víctor Fajardo, La Mar, and Huanta in Ayacucho, and in the province of Andahuaylas in Apurímac. Analysts concur that deterioration in socioeconomic conditions, isolation, indifference by the central government, and the weakness of mass organizations in most of these provinces gave Sendero a solid base there by the late 1970s.

In student circles, Shining Path took advantage of a preexisting national university student organization based in Lima, the Student Revolutionary Front (FER). Using the mechanisms of FER, well-trained Sendero cadres traveled about Peruvian campuses, encouraging the study of Mariátegui and exalting the theory of armed struggle. In the early 1970s, the impact of Guzmán's ideology upon the FER was apparent. By 1976, FER publications were virtually indistinguishable from those published by Guzmán and his group at the University of Huamanga.[11]

An important sector of the younger generation that is particularly susceptible to Sendero are the thousands of secondary-school students unable to enter the Peruvian university system. For example, of 217,679 students applying to public universities in 1987, 36,469 (16.7 percent) were accepted; of 95,131 students applying to private universities, 28,651 (30.2 percent) were accepted. This means that 247,670 applicants failed to enter the Peruvian university system in 1987 (close to 80 percent).[12] Many resent the lack of opportunity for advancement; finding employment in Peru's eroding economy is equally daunting. Shining Path offers an outlet for the resulting hostility these young men and women feel toward the system.

The urban underclass has become the focus of Sendero's efforts in recent years, resulting in the development of an array of support organizations grouped under the MRDP. These organizations have targeted specific sectors of the urban population and have often achieved success in areas where democratic organizations were weak. The MRDP organizations also serve to prepare their supporters for a "generalized insurrection," as disclosed by *El Diario* in January 1990.[13] The armed strikes that have occurred in Lima are fruits of these Sendero organizations' labors. By 1990, there was a SL campaign underway to form Popular Resistance Movements in the poverty-stricken settlements around the outskirts of Lima, with the goal of consolidating what Guzmán refers to as "iron belts" to squeeze the Peruvian capital.[14]

The Role of Women

Shining Path has unquestionably been strengthened by the recruitment of female members. Since the movement's start, women have played an important role, quite different from their historical role in Peru. Although many women do pursue higher education, society largely relegates them to more traditional secondary, passive roles. Most are restricted by keeping house, caring for men, and raising children. Even those who venture into the business world tend to hold secondary positions relative to their male counterparts. In many cases, especially in the lower classes, women are submitted to serious deprivation and regular abuse. For women, Sendero offers an escape, a promise to treat both its male and female members equally. Hence for the women fighting in Sendero's ranks, the struggle is imbued with higher stakes. They are fighting for more than just political and economic justice; they are fighting for equality.

Encouraging female participation in revolutionary struggles is not a new concept. Lenin spoke of the importance of women's participation in the Russian Revolution. Mao devoted lengthy paragraphs to the condition of women in China. Mariátegui wrote of the significance of women's roles in Peruvian society in the late 1920s. Guzmán has applied them all to the present Peruvian situation.

For example, female teachers in Sendero's popular schools emphasize that it is necessary for underclass women to be conscious of the double exploitation that they face — class and gender — and the importance of fighting for emancipation from both.[15] They teach that true female liberation will come only with the destruction of private property and the class antagonism it creates. Only then, they say, will the traditional home economic system that stupefies, oppresses, and removes women from the societal struggle be eliminated once and for all.[16]

In addition, Shining Path also emphasizes women's liberation within its own ranks.[17] In addition to holding such key positions as secretary of the Metropolitan Regional Committee, female militants are often assigned the most ruthless of all terrorist assignments. In examining major assassinations, police have found that it was a woman who, in most cases, delivered the final shot. Beyond ideology, Sendero's reason for assigning women to missions of this type lies deep within its organizational design. Assigning women difficult, dangerous, and mentally demanding missions allows them to prove themselves and enhances their self-confidence. Moreover, it serves to convince them and their colleagues of their capability of assuming leadership roles within the movement and within the future state. Women's participation in Sendero is designed to allow them to strike back violently against the system that restrained them for so long.

Hierarchy

Like any military organization, SL is structured hierarchically, its network operating on five basic levels. Most of the Sendero pyramid is made up of those at the bottom, the nationwide body of "sympathizers." Individuals in this category are generally those who have begun to develop an interest in the movement's ideology and to take part in demonstrations and/or to provide minor support in the form of money, medicine, clothes, food, arms, or explosives. While these sympathizers rarely participate in armed initiatives themselves, they may harbor arms or deliver messages for those who do.

"Activists" constitute the next tier of the organization. Members of this group are comprised primarily of students, workers, and members of the urban and rural underclasses. Though much more actively involved than sympathizers, most activists have not yet committed themselves irreversibly to the organization. Responsibilities of activists include setting up popular education programs, distributing leaflets and flyers, mobilizing the masses for demonstrations, and maintaining a spirit of civil unrest. While they themselves do not usually pursue violent actions, they are often accompanied by those who do.

The fully military component of the organization is found at the third layer on the structural pyramid, the "militant" level, and above. Sendero members must rise through the ranks, demonstrating their commitment to the insurgency, which often means participating in a terrorist act or some other violent, life-threatening activity. It is for this reason that Sendero has proven so difficult for the Peruvian police or armed forces to infiltrate. Militants are people who have pledged themselves to the insurgency, who believe that Sendero's ultimate success is of far greater importance than even their own lives. "The life of an individual is worth nothing," explains an imprisoned Sendero militant. "It is the masses that are important. When revolutionary blood is spilled, it is not in vain. That blood will fertilize new lives of combat for the revolution."[18] Militants comprise the Popular Guerrilla Army and are directly involved in all categories of violent actions.

The militants are directed by "commanders." These commanders, assigned by geographic zone and sector, are responsible for all military and political activities in their respective regions. Many commanders have both a political and a military chief working directly beneath them. The men and women classified as militants constitute the most ideologically committed individuals within the organization. It is their unusual degree of personal obligation — even fanaticism — that strengthens the insurrection. Unlike the soldiers who make up Peru's armed forces (a large percentage of whom are drafted),

Sendero's militants are fighting for ideological principles and the belief that Peru can have a more just future with Sendero at the helm. In short, they are fighting for themselves, their families, and their children. High-ranking commanders are also believed to have duties in the intermediate organs of Sendero discussed above.

Topping Sendero's pyramid of power are the National Central Committee members, known as the "cupola." This group consists of only a small number of the most elite members of the Shining Path organization. Most have participated in the movement since its emergence at the University of Huamanga. Operationally, the cupola directs all nationwide Sendero activities and advises regional commanders of policy changes and upcoming offensive operations. Central Committee members together form the intellectual workforce of the operation, making all the ideological and strategic policy decisions. Captured minutes from some of their meetings provide the only insights we have into the committee's operating procedures and membership. Most Sendero analysts believe that the cupola includes Abimael Guzmán, Julio César Mezzich, Osmán Morote (captured in June 1988), Maximiliano Durand (currently residing in France), Hildebrando Pérez, and Sybila Arredondo (captured, released for lack of evidence in 1989, and captured again in June 1990). The secretaries of the Metropolitan Central Committee are also thought to be members of the cupola, but their identities have not been disclosed.

Rising Through the Ranks

One of the organizational attributes that Sendero possesses is resiliency, being capable to date of generating and regenerating leadership. The insurgency continues to grow despite the Peruvian government's claims that it has captured or killed many top Sendero leaders. Shining Path's expansion suggests that the system is reinforced by a standing cadre of militants able to step into leadership positions as needed. The following example illustrates this point well. In 1986, a large number of known key leaders were being held in the Lurigancho and El Frontón prisons, and many speculated that the movement was being run from inside the prisons themselves. When 256 Senderistas were killed in major prison uprisings at these prisons in June 1986, it appeared that the organization might disintegrate, as many leaders were among the dead. Sendero may have been wounded by the sudden elimination of key members, but it did not fail. On the contrary, it quickly adjusted and soon went on the offensive again. After extensive study of the movement, police have concluded that Sendero's leadership is not limited to a few individuals, but extends through a well-trained hierarchical structure.

This ready supply of militants prepared to step into leadership positions demonstrates the power of Sendero's tiered membership. Before members assume leadership positions, they must prove their worth in the pyramid's lower rungs, beginning as sympathizers, activists, and militants. At each stage, individuals go through extensive indoctrination. This means that when individuals reach the upper levels of the organization, they already have both a profound understanding of the movement and valuable hands-on experience. An important goal is to increase individual self-esteem, a characteristic that is often lacking in members of the Peruvian underclasses. By assigning individuals to specific tasks, Sendero successfully reinforces self-worth, encourages a coordinated work ethic, and fosters a sense of "spiritual" attachment to the party among its members. Individuals in the group have a clear sense of purpose. Thus, by the time one climbs through the ranks, his or her emotional attachment to the movement has grown intense, bordering on fanaticism. Leaders who have risen from the masses also have a better understanding of the organization and its basic operating procedures. So it is the system itself that strengthens its membership and creates leaders thoroughly committed to the cause.

The 1990s

Strengths

Since initiating the "People's War" in 1980, Sendero has permeated the fabric of Peruvian society and has expanded to the national level. It has capitalized on continuing social and economic problems in Peru and has recruited actively among the youth and the marginalized, both urban and rural. Significantly, children are a major focus of the insurgency's indoctrination efforts, which gives Sendero an opportunity to prepare the next generation of cadres and illustrates the organization's long-term perspective.

Sendero's organizational structure has become more complex as the insurgency has grown, continuously adapting to meet changing needs. Since 1989, its "generated organizations" grouped under the MRDP have become active in armed actions as part of the movement's new urban emphasis. The diverse sectors of the population that these organizations try to relate to are of particular importance to Sendero for recruiting in urban areas.

In much of rural Peru, Sendero has advanced by stepping in to fill the power vacuum resulting from the reduction of central government presence and the withdrawal of traditional political parties from the most violent parts of the countryside. Shining Path finds itself virtually unchallenged in some rural areas. The alliance of convenience that Sendero has forged with drug interests in the coca-rich region of the Upper Huallaga Valley supplies the insurgency with tens of millions of dollars annually. This makes Sendero Luminoso financially self-sufficient and eliminates any need for foreign sponsors.[19]

Weaknesses

Shining Path has found the national labor unions hard to infiltrate. Two of Peru's most powerful and radical labor unions, the General Confederation of Workers of Peru (CGTP) and the Teachers Labor Union (SUTEP), have both resisted Sendero's pressure. On occasion, they have even expelled SL militants from their membership. These unions have traditionally been drawn to radicalism but not to terrorism. The resistance posed by Peruvian labor unions indicates that left organizations affiliated with corresponding parties participating in the democratic political process may well provide an effective deterrent to the advance of Sendero.

Peruvian analysts believe that Sendero may be behind in its calendar for taking power, and that this delay has created anxiety and fatigue among its rank and file.[20] While Shining Path doctrine calls for fifty to one hundred years of fighting, many of the insurgency's zealous followers might not have believed that the fighting would need to go on that long. The "People's War" was already been fought for more than ten years, and it has demanded a high degree of sacrifice from its militants. Sendero documents associated with the First National Congress of 1988 indicate that its leadership was pleased with the insurgency's development up to that point. They were also confident that the revolution would triumph by the early 1990s. Many believe that their more urban-oriented strategy was been staged to precipitate such an event.

In September 1988, the crumbling of the Peruvian economy and the loss of popular support for the García administration provided the insurgency with its best opportunity to date. The deterioration reached such a point that García's opponents demanded his resignation, and even a coup d'etat seemed possible. While the political forces of the nation worked to maintain the established democratic process, Sendero worked for the coup. Shining Path's position was that a successful coup would polarize Peruvian society, clearing the way for Sendero's march to victory with its revolution providing the only "just" alternative.

To destabilize the country politically, Sendero increased terrorism and sabotage aimed at the municipal electoral process of November 1989 and the presidential elections of April and June 1990. Militants proved how serious they were about stopping the elections by chopping off the voting fingers of some peasants in Huanta, Ayacucho. (Peruvians mark voting records using their ink-dabbed index fingers.[21] Assassinations of candidates for office, especially at the local level, sharply increased.

Despite Sendero's attempts, the coup did not occur. The population responded to the crisis by electing to the presidency a political newcomer with a new party representing the center. This was a double blow to Sendero: Turnout for the April 1990 elections was higher than the insurgency had expected, and the expected social polarization did not occur.

Immediately after these elections, Shining Path's internal squabblings manifested themselves. A dissident faction there decided to halt all military actions and publicly air their grievances at this time by distributing leaflets.[22] Some peasants even deserted Sendero. About one hundred in Huanta, Ayacucho, for example, asked to be reincorporated into their peasant communities in May 1990. They agreed to participate in government-sponsored peasant patrols in exchange for de facto amnesty from the political-military and judicial authorities.[23] The defectors offered their cooperation in apprehending their former fellow Sendero militants. This case suggests that Sendero may stand to lose its base of support in the Andean highlands. These peasants professed disenchantment with their continued suffering hunger and thirst and with always being on the run. They can no longer visualize the future for which the war is allegedly being fought.[24]

Is it likely that the Sendero threat will crumble? Not at all. As good Maoists believe, one line ought to prevail. It is likely that this will continue to be the military action line unless the Peruvian government capitalizes upon this problem and makes certain provisions for those who wish to defect. An example of Sendero's capacity to impose its single line occurred at Miguel Castro Prison in Lima in April 1990. Nine Sendero inmates who had earlier dared to critique the national command's orders to move forces from the provinces to Lima to increase armed actions engaged in self-criticism and pledged alliance to Guzmán, his ideology, and his strategy. However, two of the female militants were less flexible. Both Julia Liñan Toribio and María Huaman Cuajón refused to submit to the leadership, and stated that they felt these policies were clearly "vain sacrifices" of their fellow militants. As a result, SL prisoners expelled them from Sendero areas of the jail to join the ranks of common criminals. Upon seeing their predicament, six other Sendero militants then retracted their statements and were pardoned by Sendero leaders representing the dominant line. These leaders included Fiorella Montaño, Hilda Tulich, Renata Hear, Leonardo Gallegos, and Osmán Morote.[25]

Immediately following the appearance of the dissidents' leaflets in Ayacucho, Sendero staged a number of attacks to demonstrate that the insurgency's hard line was undeniably dominant. On the night of June 1, 1990, for example, fourteen synchronized Sendero attacks took place in the Peruvian capital. A car bomb exploded just 150 meters from the Palace of Government. Strategically placed bombs destroyed power lines, causing blackouts in several districts of Lima.[26] Many of the attacks were directed at political parties headquarters.[27]

Rural communities have also been targeted for Sendero's reprisals. In June 1990, Sendero targeted the small peasant community of Charchapata in Huanta, Ayacucho, because residents had formed a Civil Defense Committee.[28] Insurgents burned forty-five structures and brutally killed twenty people; among the dead were women and children. Similar incidents have occurred in rural villages such as Cuchullapcha and Pucará in Huanta, Ayacucho; Paracorral in Huancavelica; and Naymlap de Sonomoro in Satipo, Junín.[29] Such brutality has been common Sendero practice since 1983 when the Peruvian military took control of Ayacucho, Huancavelica, and Apurímac in an attempt to restore the state's authority. This practice of terrorism may ensnare Sendero as it alienates the insurgents from their rural base of support.

Conclusion

Sendero's vulnerability has been revealed by the resistance of labor unions, by rural disenchantment with the insurgency's violence, and by defection from within its own ranks. At the present time, among the government's most plausible policy options would be to facilitate, de jure, the desertion of Sendero members. Seizing this opportunity is crucial, as government forces could make good use of the knowledge defectors could provide. The Peruvian government, in designing its counterinsurgency strategy, should also address ways to alleviate Peru's profound socioeconomic problems. Otherwise, the Sendero challenge cannot be permanently squelched.

Notes

1. Laura Puertas, "Instruido para matar," *Caretas* (Lima), May 30, 1988, p. 28.
2. Information for this section was uncovered in a major police raid at one of Sendero's headquarters in Lima in June 1990. Scattered reports in the media have appeared in: "Año de purgas," *Caretas*, July 2, 1990, pp. 38-40; "Cris: El enlace," *Caretas*, July 9, 1990, pp. 34-37.
3. See "Cris: El enlace," p. 37.
4. In France, Sendero is known to have held conferences, meetings, and fundraising activities at the University of Paris. In Italy, Sendero's propaganda focuses on the youth, such as in secondary schools. See *Caretas*, June 15, 1990, p. 6. Sweden has granted political asylum to many Sendero sympathizers, where it is believed they have formed a cell. In the United States, leaflets have appeared in the San Francisco area requesting contributions that were distributed by the Support Committee for the Revolution in Peru. Responses were directed to a post office box in Berkeley. See *Caretas*, July 31, 1989, p. 1.
5. Author's notes; also see "Sendero urbano," *Caretas*, March 23, 1987, p. 12.
6. Information pertaining to the variety of support organizations forming the MRDP resulted from documents seized as a result of the capture of Osmán Morote in June 1988. The existence of individual support groups has been known by DIRCOTE since 1987, but their common bond with the MRDP was not clear until then. See "Organos de fachada," *Caretas*, March 23, 1987, p. 16. The author updated this list with an interview at the National Attorney's Office of Peru in 1990. For another media report, see "El bunker de Abimael," *Oiga* (Lima), June 11, 1990, p. 74.
7. "El socorro de Sendero," *Caretas*, January 11, 1988, p. 14. Also see "Sicóloga de Hospital Policial es senderista," *Expreso* (Lima), December 30, 1987, p. 18.

8. The issue of aiding the insurgency by nonmilitary means has been the subject of much controversy in Peruvian legal circles.
9. José Carios Mariátegui (1895-1930) was Peru's first Marxist analyst. His writings, in particular *Siete ensayos de interpretación de la realidad peruana* (Lima, 1926), strongly influenced Shining Path's characterization of Peru.
10. Statistics for 1982 from David Scott Palmer, "Peru," in *Yearbook of International Communist Affairs 1983*, ed. Robert Wesson (Stanford: Hoover Institution Press, 1983), p. 123. Inflation figure for 1988 from DESCO, *Resumen Semanal* (Lima), 501, December 23, 1988-January 5, 1989, p. 1. Inflation figure for 1989 from *El Comercio* (Lima), January 5, 1990, p. A2; and for 1990, from *Resumen Semanal*, 601, December 21, 1990-January 3, 1991, p. 1.
11. Piedad Pareja Pflucker has documented the relationship of the FER with Guzmán's ideology. See *Terrorismo y sindicalismo en Ayacucho, 1980* (Lima: Empresa Editora Ital Perú S.A., 1981), pp. 79-81.
12. Data from Instituto Nacional de Estadística (INE), *Perú: Compendio estadístico 1987* (Lima: INE, May 1988), p. 80.
13. Cited in "El bunker de Abimael," p. 74.
14. Ibid.
15. José Gonzales, "Sendero de mujeres," *Sí* (Lima), April 6, 1987, p. 83.
16. Ibid.
17. The Peruvian Constitution of 1979, Article 2, asserts the equality of gender under the law, but tradition persists in certain sectors of the populace.
18. José María Salcedo, "Con Sendero en Lurigancho," *Quehacer*, 39, February-March 1982, p. 64.
19. While fund-raising activities are carried out abroad, these are really only symbolic and reflect Sendero's ideological commitment to international solidarity.
20. See "Sendero y los volantes," *Caretas*, May 21, 1990.
21. "Sendero y Fujimori," *Caretas*, April 16, 1990, p. 54.
22. See "En Ayacucho: Sendero anuncia retiro temporal de lucha armada," *Expreso*, May 18, 1990, p. 3. "Sendero Luminoso habría acordado suspender las acciones armadas," *El Comercio*, May 18, 1990, p. A6. "Sendero y los volantes," *Caretas*, May 21, 1990, pp. 30-32, 83.
23. As of early 1991, Peruvian law does not provide any mechanism to accommodate deserters. Terrorist offenders (such as these who were previously enlisted in the ranks of Sendero) are considered criminals under the law and receive no special treatment. However, in the absence of such legal mechanisms, the defectors are added to the ranks of the peasant patrols to assist counterinsurgency efforts rather than being handed over to political-military and judicial authorities.
24. Aida Meza, "Centenares de senderistas se entregan en Ayacucho," *Expreso*, May 24, 1990, pp. 22-23.
25. See "Sendero Luminoso y elecciones: La pelea," *Caretas*, April 10, 1990.
26. "Estalló coche-bomba a espaldas de catedral" and "Terroristas incursionan en la capital: atentados contra torres causaron apagón en Lima," *Expreso*, June 6, 1990, pp. 1, 8.
27. "Subversivos quisieron crear caos con 14 antentados dinamiteros. Participaron unos cincuenta terroristas sincronizadamente," *El Comercio*, June 3, 1990, p. A12.

28. The Civil Defense Committee is a government-sponsored counterinsurgency program in the highlands of Peru; Indian communities are grouped in one territory to defend themselves with peasant patrols from Sendero's attacks.

29. For information on these massacres, see "Brutal arremetida de Sendero: Asesinaron a veinte comuneros en Huanta," *Expreso*, June 4, 1990, p. 13; Vicente de Szyszlo, "Muertos sin rostro: Hombres, mujeres y niños fueron mutilados," *Caretas*, May 7, 1990, p. 45.

10

MAKING REVOLUTION
WITH SHINING PATH[*]

Tom Marks

Many gaps remain in our understanding of insurgency.[1] Perhaps the most vexing is that we continue to comprehend only imperfectly the manner in which would-be revolutionaries are able to garner support. This is particularly true of movements such as Shining Path (SL or Sendero) that engage in practices which would seemingly alienate potential followers. It remains virtually an article of faith that to achieve success, an insurgent movement must win the "hearts and minds" of the people. The clandestine mechanisms of rebellion, continues the argument, are so dependent on popular assistance that they cannot possibly survive in an environment where the populace is controlled through repression.

Yet there lies the problem. Sendero obviously engages in widespread use of terror and views it as a key tactic of people's war. How can such a movement

*Material for this chapter was collected during field work in Peru in August 1989 and has been supplemented and updated by correspondence with sources. Peruvian realities necessitate that no person quoted be identified by name. I have earlier drawn upon this research for the publications under my name in the bibliography.

grow, we must ask, if brutality is its main tool? Or is our befuddlement simply a product of our lack of data? The answer, I believe, lies in the relationship among the mechanisms of terror, recruitment, and infrastructure, and the manner in which these change over time in relation to the maintenance of the insurgent movement.

Analytical Perspectives

Insurgency as a phenomenon has been academically peripheral in recent years. Instead, scholarship concerning revolutions and would-be revolutions has emphasized the importance of structural factors over deliberate (purposive) action.[2] "Revolutions are not made; they come," writes Theda Skocpol.[3] Groups, in other words, do not *make* revolution; rather, they contend within a context of economic, social, and political breakdown. Such emphasis leads researchers to focus on the "deeper" causes of revolution rather than on the ideological designs of those who would be king. Although the structural perspective may be the dominant paradigm of the movement,[4] there is considerable dissatisfaction with the downplaying of deliberate action.[5] The Viet Minh's success against the French, for example, can be understood only by examining various strategic and tactical features. This will reveal that the mechanics of organization were a key factor, as was the use of terror.[6] Similarly, in the Chinese Revolution, structure did set the parameters for action, but both of the main contenders for power, the Kuomintang and the Chinese Communist Party, were able to maneuver tactically in response to distinctive local situations in myriad strategic variations.[7]

To venture into the specifics of these would be to explore insurgency. For our purposes here, let me use the following definition: Insurgency is guerrilla warfare in support, strategically, of a political goal, operationally, of a political infrastructure, and tactically, of local political domination. Such a definition recognizes both the political nature of the insurgent campaign and its symbiotic relationship with force. An insurgency, then, is a political campaign backed by threatened or actual violence. It is the conscious effort to supplant one political structure with another. Taken to its logical end, insurgency becomes that which Sendero claims to be waging, revolutionary war, the conscious effort to make a revolution by seizing state power using politico-military means.

Thus it is that the raison d'etre of insurgent military power, in whatever form, is the projection and protection of its political infrastructure. How exactly to achieve this has been related by various revolutionaries. Mao Zedong, for instance, whose doctrines Sendero professes to follow, set forth a three-step process (strategic defensive, stalemate, and offensive) and found it necessary, in the end, to transform his guerrilla armies into massive conventional forces to remove the last vestiges of Kuomintang power. Fidel Castro, in contrast, found a Cuba so decayed that minimal guerrilla action was all that was needed to bring the edifice crashing down. Regardless of the force level required to achieve the political aim in these cases, it was dictated by the need to protect the alternate political system being constructed and not by military concerns per se.

Basis for Insurgency

In the case of Sendero, its inspiration is Maoist. Precise articulation varies in particulars from the Chinese model but faithfully reproduces its essence: People's war is to be used to gain control of the countryside for the purpose of encircling the cities. Hazleton and Woy-Hazleton have described this strategy as follows:

> Sendero has made very few public statements about its agenda and strategy, but [SL leader} Guzmán's plans for a protracted armed struggle have Sendero's activities evolving through several stages. The first stage was one of "agitation and propaganda," in which Guzmán and his followers recruited, trained, and organized cadres in the isolated Andean highlands. In 1980, when democracy was being restored in Peru, Sendero initiated its second stage of creating the social and material bases of a people's army. It also made its presence known through attacks on public buildings and other symbols of authority. Liberated zones were created in which Sendero imposed its antitechnological, subsistence peasant model by brutal methods, destroying farm equipment and crops, closing regional markets, and killing informers and reluctant supporters. In 1982, Sendero launched its so-called third stage, which was to initiate an armed struggle in the rural areas and gradually move into urban areas to create the conditions for the fourth stage — a people's war.[8]

Though the Hazletons have more recently judged that Sendero has altered this strategy in favor of "a quicker, urban-based revolution,"[9] this is doubtful.

It may well be the case that SL has chosen to emphasize both urban and rural components of people's war. To claim that the original strategic blueprint has been abandoned is, I would argue, a misinterpretation of the evidence.

Regardless, when analyzing the manner in which Sendero has implemented its strategy, analysts tend to emphasize its unique trajectory.[10] This is surprising, since, allowing for differences in particulars, there is little in Sendero's growth or approach that would set it apart from other Maoist movements. While Sendero may depart quite radically from the *foco*-type insurrections frequently attempted by Latin American rebels, including Peruvians, its tactical, operational, and strategic aspects are not unique when viewed in international perspective (and particularly when compared to Maoist-inspired movements in Asia).

Further, in analyzing the movement, it seems clear that the composition of Sendero membership is also similar to that of revolutionary movements elsewhere. As James Scott has perceptively noted, all insurgent movements necessarily contain two elements: leadership ranks comprised of members drawn from society's elite and followers taken from the masses.[11] The same "causes" motivate them but in very different ways. The leadership normally perceives injustice and attempts to deal with it in ideological terms. The followers, in contrast, who historically have been drawn overwhelmingly from the peasantry,[12] attempt to deal with injustice directly by correcting those immediate wrongs they identify. If the ideological approach of the leadership is able to hold sway, insurgency will result. The movement will go on to pursue political goals. If, however, the resolution of immediate grievances dominates, as normally desired by the rank and file, rebellion will result.[13]

In the case of Shining Path, it is the ideologically motivated leadership that has prevailed. It is quite clear that Sendero is not a peasant rebellion that has been "captured." A radical core at the University of Huamanga in Ayacucho, led by education program professor Abimael Guzmán Reynoso, gained control of the university in the 1960s and broke away from the national Maoist movement at about the same time. From this university base, Sendero carried out for more than a decade patient organizational work in the countryside with the peasantry. Only in 1980 did it move from organizing to violence. The principal target was Ayacucho's infrastructure, from power lines and clinics to community leaders and teachers, the glue that held society together.

"Sendero has an ideology," observes an analyst, "to destroy society in order to build a new society. They don't want to modify. It's easier to build anew than to change what exists."[14]

However, the armed columns that sought to implement this vision were not comprised of the peasantry they claimed to represent. Notes an official of an embassy in Lima:

> Sendero has sympathizers in most areas, as well as armed individuals in towns. But the heart and soul of the movement remains youth from the disenfranchised, landless, former middle class. Frequently, the youth who join Sendero will have university training and be twenty to twenty-five years old; their parents will often have held land. All the modalities are present in Peru for a popular uprising, but one has not happened. This [Sendero] is not a *campesino* movement. True, it can recruit from disenfranchised peasants, but at least fifty percent of Shining Path columns come from the middle class whose parents were small landowners. Almost all are Spanish speakers. It is not a European movement, however; neither is it pure Indian. It is mestizo. It's not certain there ever was a real link between Sendero and the illiterate, landless peasants of the sierra. The cadre were drawn from the universities. In fact, politico-social leaders *seem to have been* the movement. Most areas where Sendero has been most successful have had no government presence at all. Isolation, therefore, had a great deal to do with [SL's] success. Our sources tell us that most *campesinos* look at Sendero with the same suspicion with which they view the government: "they are foreigners telling us what to do." Some of their own young are drawn to the movement but not the population in general.[15]

Adds a Peruvian analyst:

> The full time Sendero elite is very small and has a college education. But the typical militant is an eighteen-year-old Indian with only a grade school education, if that. He will have an agricultural background. Yet Sendero is not an Indian movement. How can Sendero be an Indian uprising? Its main targets have been Indians, more than the white population. If it was an Indian uprising, it would strike against the white minority. Its support group is among the Indians. But the basic question is what the hell are they after? A lot support Sendero because they are young kids who have been indoctrinated; Sendero takes them and puts the fear of God into them.[16]

The conclusion of these two analyses is consistent with that seen in other insurgent movements: leadership from society's elite and followers from the masses. However, Sendero's armed columns also field a large proportion from the elite, which implies a movement that is more "activists taking advantage of social causes" than "societal causes producing activists." In short, the wrong folks are doing the rebelling. It is not the poor and the dispossessed who are fighting for a better life — it is their social betters fighting, they claim, on their behalf.

Insurgent Infrastructure

It is not difficult, therefore, to see the role terror must play in the movement. The lower classes everywhere are notoriously suspicious of elite causes. Some catalyst must push them into membership. In Peru, terror has served that purpose; but it is not aimless killing.

Cautions the embassy official:

> Sendero is brutal but not indiscriminate. It is not committing genocide. We are not witnessing pent-up rage exploding. Rather, we are seeing carefully designed and calculated terror. They target individuals in advance, then execute them in ways which have symbolic meaning. Sendero's most recent tactic is the "armed strike." Cadres pass out leaflets that in seventy-two hours there will be a strike. Subsequently, Sendero will kill several who violate the strike, bomb several businesses, and burn some transport. Horrible methods of execution will be used, ways which are symbolic in a mythological sense. For example, one of the most common is to slice the throat of the victim, because then the soul cannot escape from the mouth.[17]

What makes such terror so effective is the absence of anywhere to turn for help. "There has traditionally been no government presence in many areas," says the editor of a leading Peruvian news magazine. "Hence, as one source puts it, there are no liberated areas, only abandoned areas."[18]

In such a vacuum it takes only a few armed individuals to establish Sendero's writ. Contacts are made with a community through acquaintances or relatives. This gives Sendero sufficient local presence to make a number of converts, who then form the nucleus of a Popular Committee. The committee's leadership normally consists of five individuals, with a political commissar at the head. This leader is assisted by individuals charged with: (1) security (organizes mechanisms of control and defense; all movement, in particular, is controlled); (2) production (determines matters of provision and logistics, especially which crops will be grown); (3) communal matters (administers normal societal functions such as justice, marriage, and burials); and (4) organization (classifies the population by sectoral group: children, juveniles, women, peasants, or intellectuals; these divisions are then used for study sessions and other activities).[19]

This political organization exists in the open and maintains influence in part through its ability to call upon a Sendero armed column for support. This is the force that normally carries out acts of terror. Such actions are particularly intimidating, because the local Communist Party organization of Sendero remains underground in clandestine three-person cells (each has a secretary, subsecretary, and an information specialist). The result is that no one knows for sure who is informing on them. This paralyzes attempts to fight back. Given the virtual absence or intermittent nature of the government's presence, there simply is no one to whom villagers have recourse.

Shining Path's approach illustrates the importance of scale and the changing relationship among the elements of terror, recruitment, and infrastructure. Peru is sufficiently large and diverse that there are innumerable marginal areas in which subversive political activity can operate with minimal fear of government intervention. Ayacucho was just such an area during Sendero's years of preparation before the outbreak of armed action. During this period Sendero expanded its political sway largely through persuasion. In the process it benefited from the political space provided by the military government's (1968-1980) efforts to mobilize the peasantry behind its reform measures without the capacity to implement them effectively in a region Lima did not consider important.[20] Sendero garnered considerable sympathy and support among the population of Ayacucho during this interlude by addressing grievances initially raised by the military itself.

Nevertheless, the moment came when Sendero's leadership felt that it must resort to force to consolidate the gains made and to expand further. The infrastructure already in place was the vehicle for expansion. Terror and guerrilla action served to protect it and to give it power. At this point the mechanisms of organization — of infrastructure — became paramount. An alternative political body had come into existence. Those who joined no longer did so purely in response to grievances but instead for a more complex mixture of motives, ranging from desire for advancement to fear. "Human factors considerations," in other words, became salient.[21] At one extreme, potential recruits saw the movement as a viable alternative for social participation; at the other, they simply recognized that this organization had for all intents and purposes become the state and thus had to be obeyed. It socialized and controlled.

When a region targeted by Sendero is deemed to have a sufficient number of Popular Committees, a Support Base can be declared. In mid-1989 there were eighty Popular Committees and twenty Support Bases operating in the departments (states) of Ayacucho and Huancavelica. One function of the Support Bases is to control and divide farm production, with half going to the people and half to Sendero for stockpiling and use during operations.[22]

Hence there exists an extensive dual web enmeshing the people: the overt system of sectoral organizations, coordinated by the Revolutionary Front for the Defense of the Village (FRDP), and the covert system of the party, with its cells. These party cells, in turn, are coordinated by Local Committees (CL), which themselves fall under Sub-Zones (SZ) belonging to Zone Committees (CZ), and finally to Regional Committees. Each Regional Committee is headed by a secretary and subsecretary, working with five other staff members responsible for military operations, logistics, security, agitation and propaganda, and administrative organization. Peru's size makes these Regional Commands quite independent. Ayacucho is one of six regions nationwide and includes neighboring departments of Huancavelica and Apurímac. Ayacucho has its own Regional Command and is called "the Principal Area," because Sendero began there.

Not at all clear are the lines of command between the political infrastructure and Sendero's military component. In a normal Communist guerrilla movement, the primacy of politics dictates a chain of command that is quite standard — all military formations are controlled by party organizations. A district guerrilla unit, to illustrate, would report to and take orders from the district party apparatus. In Sendero, however, where Guerrilla Zones (ZG) are defined by operational necessity, they may straddle any number of SZ. Within each ZG is found the classic guerrilla tripartition, which Sendero labels the principal force, the local force, and the base force. Together, these comprise the Popular

Guerrilla Army (EGP). Local forces gain manpower from the most promising base force personnel, and the principal force draws from the best of the local force. Senior authority is supposed to lie with the political commissar of the ZG, but there have been increasing reports of military commanders taking charge. Like the tension between the leadership and the followers, Sendero also must grapple with the issue of who wields the power: those who "talk" or those who "fight"? Invariably, military ascendance results in a bloodier conflict, because decisions begin to be driven by consideration of force.

As for those who do the actual fighting, as many as half of any Sendero military unit are women. This high percentage of female combatants has prompted a number of explanations. Some note that women join as a route to freedom from the horrible conditions of marriage most must endure in the highlands.[23] An alternative possibility was offered by a longtime aid worker in the sierra: "Women are not mistreated per se there. There is a great deal of beating both ways. In truth, it is women who control the purse strings. They function as equals, so it's perfectly logical that they should simply join Sendero like anyone else, not because they're particularly downtrodden."[24]

Conduct of Operations

Men or women, the numbers involved are not very large. Peruvian intelligence estimates that in Ayacucho in mid-1989 the principal and local forces fielded about 250 personnel each, the base force, 750.[25] Only the principal force appears to have high-powered firearms, normally AK-47s, as well as RPG-7s captured from the police. The essential formation is the column, which operates with no fixed table of organization and equipment. Groups of ten to fifteen are the norm, with larger units formed by consolidation. All of these combatants must be party members.

Constantly moving, the columns travel nomadically from village to village. That such small numbers are able to have the impact they do amid a population in Ayacucho of over half a million stems from their training, their arms, and their sense of mission. With combat power serving as a shield, the Sendero political organization has the capacity to organize the communities that the government often lacks.

Relates an experienced journalist: "There is at least one instance where two thousand villagers were brought together by three columns of forty armed men, then given various courses of instruction. It's unclear as to what precisely the course content was, but plays and so forth were held. Several Sendero cadre reportedly got drunk and were strongly disciplined."[26]

If they were only "strongly disciplined," they were lucky. Sendero's puritanical regulations are more often enforced with savage discipline. This same mode of behavior that has ultimately proved the movement's undoing in many areas of Ayacucho. In at least several recorded instances, whole villages have risen up and, using homemade weapons, often no more than sharpened stakes, wiped out or chased away the Sendero cadre. They have then appealed to the government security forces for assistance in meeting Sendero's inevitable attempt to exact retribution. Such help has often been slow in coming, but coordination and use of militias is improving.

Faced with this new situation, Sendero has had to push its expansion efforts into areas other than the Ayacucho heartland. "The Upper Huallaga is the key area right now," states one of Peru's top military leaders, "although Ayacucho is the heart and soul of the movement. The Upper Huallaga is being used as Sendero's training camp and source of major financing. They are putting together their armed forces there. Providing security for the drug lords is good training."[27] Capitalizing on ill-will aroused by government coca eradication efforts, Sendero has been able to establish a mass base. Unlike the 10- to 15-person columns of Ayacucho, actual companies (60 to 120 individuals) have been formed in the Upper Huallaga. Deals with druglords have provided M-60 machine guns, 81 mm mortars, and grenade launchers. In the Upper Huallaga, Sendero has turned to a more military-oriented approach. Observes one interviewee, "There are strong indications that...the military component of Sendero has been overshadowing the political, and that the columns themselves are not very well coordinated."[28]

Here and in some other parts of the country, Shining Path has been able to establish a certain base of support. However, it is not substantial nationwide, and it does not appear to be growing rapidly. "There is no groundswell of support [for Sendero]," a Peruvian analyst states flatly.

> The Inca's "Last Rebellion" explanation is bullshit. Many people attempt to vote with their feet, to flee areas under Sendero control. But SL does have a sizable level of support, though all of this base is not necessarily active. If you put them as a political party, they would be, for sure, a minority party, a tiny party even, but in some areas of

the country they might be as much as 20 to 30 percent of the people there. These, to be sure, are not the most populated areas (e.g., Ayacucho, the Upper Huallaga Valley). In other words, Shining Path is an armed party. They are not a tiny band of conspirators. They do have a social base.[29]

This social base allows Sendero to survive. As it presses to incorporate others into its mass base, violence assumes greater proportions. Continues the analyst:

> Sendero is very consistent in its approach to popular war, though it may be noted it is using much more the Viet Cong methods than the methods of early Mao. Terror and coercion are for it very important ways to gain support, going hand in hand with propaganda and agitprop. Persuasion versus terror is an incorrect dichotomy in analyzing their methods. *Indoctrination* holds the key. The "propaganda of the deed" is very important. The perception of strength goes a long way to being a magnet. True, there are cases of sheer coercion. Yet, generally, there is a good balance between indoctrination and coercion.[30]

That, in the final analysis, is the key. As long as Sendero can continue to use violence as a tool, as opposed to an end unto itself, to facilitate the functioning and expansion of the infrastructure, the movement will remain viable. We might do well to compare the Peruvian case with that of Vietnam to get a sense of how Sendero's approach might be able to succeed under certain circumstances.

When the United States committed combat units to South Vietnam in 1965, the country was on the verge of collapse. In this process, the North Vietnamese Army (NVA) itself was not yet an important element, though aid coming down the Ho Chi Minh Trail was. Regardless, neither of these factors was key. What had happened during the decade after the departure of the last French troop transport from the South in 1955? Why was Diem's regime already in complete collapse before U.S. forces arrived? And before the NVA arrived in strength, for that matter? The answer was that the Viet Cong had already put the South on the ropes. While North Vietnam provided leadership, technical personnel, and some heavy weapons, the strength of the Communist movement in the South prior to 1965 came from revolt against Saigon. What were some of the reasons that led a sizable portion of the South Vietnamese population to support the Communists irrespective of their ideology and notwithstanding their widespread use of terror? A major factor was that Viet Cong terror was highly selective and therefore effective. The Vietnamese Communists keep their "blood debts" at a relatively modest level, and they tied assassinations and bomb blasts to causes that people could back. By doing so, they maintained popular support.

Conclusion

We can learn from the example of Vietnam when analyzing Sendero. In interpreting violence that accompanies an insurgency, the English language limits us. The word "support" implies freely given, as in "By winning the hearts and minds we can gain the *support* of the people." While correct semantically, this construction has led to an operational fallacy. There are those, ideologues for instance, who give their support because they are committed to ideals. Most people, however, sit on the sidelines until compelled to do otherwise. They give their support when it becomes in their *interest* to do so.

Terror is but one tool for creating such an interest. It may show what happens to traitors; it may remove threats quietly from the area of operations. Simply because it is used does not mean the populace is terrorized by the perpetrators. Quite the contrary can also be true. Terror can send a message that is accepted by the inhabitants as painful but necessary. The argument for necessity is provided by propaganda. Further, in its most powerful form, terror can serve as the instrument of vengeance for pent-up popular frustrations, as it appears to have done in revolutionary China. "Collaborators, traitors, exploiters, and criminals" can be dispatched with the approval of the masses.

Providing it is not abused, then, terror, while it may alienate some, also fortifies others. At the margins, it can push an undecided group into support it would otherwise not give. Once involved in the actual mechanisms of such support, the role terror originally played in the process is forgotten.

On the other side of the coin, the use of terror by the security forces has generally been ineffective or has had disastrous consequences for them, because they claim to represent a higher standard of conduct and morality. Democracy, in particular, draws its strength from its ability to deliver justice to a society of voluntary participants. Thus, actions that put the lie to that principle may actually serve to undermine the legitimacy of democratic government.

The insurgents, committed to total war and the need to eliminate certain elements of the foe, are subject to a different set of rules. They, too, must act in the interests of the people, but in the interests of the "revolutionary people." The nonrevolutionary remainder becomes as much the foe as the security forces and may be dealt with accordingly.

These realities of terror must be understood if Shining Path is to be dealt with, because in Peru terror dominates every discussion of the movement. The dominant explanation given for the growth of the guerrillas is their brutality. Yet this explanation is inaccurate insofar as it treats the role of terror in isolation. The total insurgent movement, particularly its use of political means to achieve political ends, is the most significant aspect of the war now being waged by Sendero — with force available when needed to make a point.

Notes

1. A particularly useful definition of the term is offered by Raj Desai and Harry Eckstein, "Insurgency: The Transformation of Peasant Rebellion," *World Politics*, 42:4, July 1990, pp. 441-465: "insurgency is a syncretic phenomenon — one that joins diverse elements in an explosive mix. It combines three elements: first, the 'spirit' of traditional peasant 'rebellion'; second, the ideology and organization of modern 'revolution'; and third, the operational doctrines of guerrilla warfare" (p. 442). The authors elsewhere observe that insurgency is "the mix of millenarian zeal, revolutionary ideology and organization, and guerrilla warfare" (p. 463).
2. For a summary review, see Jack A. Goldstone, "Theories of Revolutions: The Third Generation," *World Politics*, 32:3, April 1980, pp. 425-453. A benchmark work is Theda Skocpol, *States and Social Revolutions* (New York: Cambridge University Press, 1979). Also useful is Walter L. Goldfrank, "Theories of Revolution and Revolution Without Theory: The Case of Mexico," *Theory and Society*, 7, 1979, pp. 135-165.
3. Skocpol, *States*, p. 17.
4. Goldstone, "Theories of Revolution."
5. One early work in reaction to Skocpol's structural perspective is representative: see Bruce Cumings, "Interest and Ideology in the Study of Agrarian Politics," *Politics and Society*, 10:4, 1981, pp. 467-495.

6. This issue is discussed explicitly in Truong Buu Lam, *Resistance, Rebellion, Revolution: Popular Movements in Vietnamese History* (Singapore: Institute of Southeast Asian Studies, 1984), esp. pp. 37-48.

7. An illustrative work is Kathleen Hartford and Steven M. Goldstein, eds., *Single Sparks: China's Rural Revolutions* (Armonk, NY: M.E. Sharpe, 1989).

8. William A. Hazleton and Sandra Woy-Hazleton, "Terrorism and the Marxist Left: Peru's Struggle Against Sendero Luminoso," *Terrorism*, 2:6, 1988, p. 481.

9. William A. Hazleton and Sandra Woy-Hazleton, "The Influence of Sendero Luminoso After One Decade of Insurgency," Paper presented to the International Studies Association, London, April 1, 1989.

10. See, for example, James Anderson, *Sendero Luminoso: A New Revolutionary Model?* (London: Institute for the Study of Terrorism, 1987).

11. James C. Scott, "Revolution in the Revolution: Peasants and Commissars," *Theory and Society*, 7:1 and 2, January-March 1979, pp. 97-134.

12. Virtually our entire body of literature derives its data and premises from instances of *peasant* rebellion. Discussion in the literature centers on two principal questions: (a) Why do peasants actually become involved in rebellion/revolutionary action? and (b) Which particular peasant strata are most prone to participate in such activities? Good overviews are contained in Cumings, "Interest and Ideology"; J. Craig Jenkins, "Why do Peasants Rebel? Structural and Historical Theories of Modern Peasant Rebellions," *American Journal of Sociology*, 88:3, November 1982, pp. 487-514; and Theda Skocpol, "Review Article: What Makes Peasants Revolutionary?" *Comparative Politics*, 14:3, April 1982, pp. 351-375.

13. Though rarely dealt with explicitly, a significant issue in the literature is the precise relationship between peasant rebellion and insurgency. While Scott, in "Revolution in the Revolution," has dealt with the subject theoretically, his insights have not yet inspired a body of empirical work. But the point is crucial. If an insurgency is viewed as essentially a coalition of various local rebellions, analysis will focus on the sources of peasant unrest. If, however, leadership tightly controls and regulates the insurgency, recruiting from different social strata, then analysis shifts to the mechanisms of organization. These two perspectives are not value-neutral. In the first case, rebellion comes from "within"; in the second, it comes from "without." The first suggests a certain inherent legitimacy in the uprising; the second, a manipulation by outsiders. Predictably, a fusion of the two approaches, with special attention paid to the evolution of organization over time, yields the most satisfactory results. This, fortunately, is the methodology adopted by major works on Sendero.

14. Interview by the author in Lima, August 15, 1989.

15. Ibid.

16. Ibid.

17. Ibid.

18. Interview by the author in Lima, August 17, 1989.

19. For a comparable analysis of Sendero infrastructure, see Anderson, *Sendero Luminoso*.

20. See Cynthia McClintock, "Peru's Sendero Luminoso Rebellion: Origins and Trajectory," in Susan Eckstein, ed., *Power and Popular Protest: Latin American Social Movements* (Berkeley: University of California Press, 1989), pp. 61-101.

21. See Andrew R. Molnar et al., *Human Factors Considerations of Undergrounds in Insurgencies* (Washington: The American University, 1965).
22. Interviews by the author in Ayacucho, August 23-25, 1989.
23. Interview by the author in Lima, August 17, 1989.
24. Interview by the author in Lima, August 20, 1989.
25. Interview by the author in Ayacucho, August 23-25, 1989.
26. Interview by the author in Lima, August 20, 1989.
27. Interview by the author in Lima, August 26, 1989.
28. Interview by the author in Lima, August 18, 1989.
29. Ibid.
30. Ibid.

11

SHINING PATH AND THE MARXIST LEFT[*]

Sandra Woy-Hazleton and William A. Hazleton

For the political left in Peru, the 1980s was a decade of unprecedented expansion in strength and influence, tempered, however, by the tension of ideological definition and the reality of armed conflict. The two main claimants to revolutionary leadership — Shining Path (SL or Sendero) and the United Left (IU) — had a similar intellectual heritage and sought support from the same sectors of society. Their goals and means were diametrically opposed, however. The major difference was that IU opted to participate in the political system and SL wanted to destroy it. The IU's electoral strategy succeeded to the point of giving the Marxist coalition a real chance to win the 1990 presidential elections.[1] Shining Path's guerrilla war had expanded concomitantly, claiming over 20,000 lives through 1990 and putting a majority of Peru's population of 22 million under government-imposed states of emer-

---

[*]This chapter is based in part on earlier work of the authors: "Sendero Luminoso and the Future of Peruvian Democracy," *Third World Quarterly*, 12:2, April 1990, pp. 21-35; and "Terrorism and the Marxist Left: Peru's Struggle Against Sendero Luminoso," *Terrorism*, 11:6, 1988, pp. 471-490.

gency. Sendero's effort to disrupt the 1990 presidential elections nationwide failed. However, IU's collapse as an electoral vehicle for the left in those elections revealed weaknesses that were to prove debilitating for the future of Peruvian democracy.

The left's participation in electoral politics has been important to Peru for several reasons. First, the IU coalition provided significant representation for large sectors of the population, with its local and regional strength reflected in leadership of key popular organizations and a large number of elected officials. Second, the left parties have been outspoken defenders of civil and political liberties and of human rights. Furthermore, the legal left was a significant barrier to Sendero's success; where left organizations were strong, Sendero made few inroads. For these reasons, SL has made the legal left a key target in its guerrilla war. This chapter explores Sendero's decade of struggle against the United Left and its effect on Peru's political system.

Origins of the Contemporary Political Left

Virtually all left political groups in Peru can trace their intellectual origins to the two leading figures of twentieth-century Peruvian politics: José Carlos Mariátegui and Víctor Raúl Haya de la Torre. However, with the exception of the original Peruvian Communist Party (PCP) and the American Popular Revolutionary Alliance (APRA), most of Peru's left parties are of recent origin. They began with the guerrilla insurgency of 1965 or with the opening to the left by the reformist military government (1968-1980).[2] As the country returned to civilian rule between 1978 and 1980, the political left was seriously divided. Perhaps the major cleavage in the transitional period was whether or not the leftist factions would participate in the system. After lengthy internal debate, all but one opted for electoral politics. The exception was Shining Path.

The Electoral Path

The rest of the left did not believe that conditions were ripe for revolution. They thought the moment was propitious to continue to organize the popular sectors, with a high probability of electoral success. The left provided six of the thirteen groups entering candidates in the June 1978 Constituent Assembly elections; they won 30 percent of the vote and twenty-eight of one hundred seats. Buoyed by this success, they tried but ultimately failed to form a united coalition for the 1980 general elections.[3]

Campaigning independently, five leftist parties together garnered only 14 percent of the presidential vote and 19 percent of the senate vote, even though illiterates voted for the first time (increasing the electorate by 17 percent).[4] The clear lesson was that disunity cost representation. So the leftists joined forces (as the United Left) in the November 1980 municipal elections, capturing 24 percent of the total vote. This made IU the second largest political force in Peru, a position it maintained through the 1980s.

Forces of Unity and System Support

The United Left stayed together for ten years for several reasons: (1) the loose structure allowed cooperation as an opposition bloc, but imposed little authority on component units; (2) electoral success at the local and regional levels provided the impetus for continuity and coordination; and (3) divisive questions were avoided. The organization was run by a weak National Directive Committee (CDN) comprised of prominent politicians, each of whom headed his own political group. Until 1987 unity was personified by Dr. Alfonso Barrantes Lingán, IU mayor of Lima (1983-1986) and president of the CDN. Then, the position was weakened by rotating leaders. The CDN was a coordinating body, not a policymaking group. IU's structure allowed members to preserve their identity at the expense of centralized leadership. This gave the coalition flexibility and contributed to greater success in municipal elections than in national elections.

As might be expected, IU did much better in opposition to the government in power in Lima than as a contender for that power. IU's main concern had been government respect for civil and political freedoms guaranteed in the 1979 constitution. IU had been especially sensitive to the application of antiterrorism laws that restricted legitimate activities of a political opposition and to electoral mechanisms that curtailed representative government. Hundreds of IU members were detained without trial after being picked up in massive sweeps for terrorists. Because most of those picked up were longtime political organizers, IU charged that the administration was deliberately seeking to undermine their mobilization efforts. IU strongholds in Lima's lower-class neighborhoods were subject to particularly brutal raids by police seeking subversive cells. Such insensitive mass roundups made it difficult for the legal left to challenge Sendero's characterization of the regime as repressive.[5]

IU's championing of human rights concerns in parliament and through public demonstrations was viewed by government parties (Popular Action — AP, 1980-1985, and APRA, 1985-1990 and Cambio-90, 1990-) as expressions of pro-Sendero sentiment. However, IU had viewed itself as a competitor with Sendero for the support of the poor and for the mantle of revolutionary vanguard. It favored human rights causes on their own merits and to protect itself.

Under the APRA's Alan García Pérez, IU's position became more complicated. First, electoral success increased pressure for greater party unity. However, attempts to define IU's program more concretely placed the coalition more and more in the role of "loyal" opposition.[6] IU head Barrantes advocated a pragmatic relationship toward APRA, supporting those initiatives that served IU's overall goals in order to increase its chances for victory in 1990.

However, the strong leadership required for victory in 1990 was not forthcoming. Barrantes was the early choice to head the coalition. Opposition grew as he showed little concern for critical organizational details and compromised too much, leading to his resignation in May 1987. Efforts to make IU a more representative party organization between 1987 and 1989 were quite successful. Party representation within IU was preserved even as the power of the grass-roots organizations was increased. Of the 3,153 delegates attending the first National Congress in January 1989, 75 percent were elected from local committees and 25 percent were selected from the component parties, the culmination of 400 district congresses and 60 provincial events.[7] Democracy and diversity triumphed over unity and strength.

Forces of Disunity and Violence

Ideological cleavages also contributed to the left's failure to take advantage of the opportunity provided by the 1990 national elections. From the beginning the coalition was divided into moderate and radical factions on the basis of three ideological issues: (1) conditions for revolution in Peru, (2) the role of violence to achieve political objectives, and (3) the relative efficacy of legal participation or guerrilla warfare.

The moderates held that a transition from popular democracy to socialism was possible through nonviolent means because a government controlled by elected left representatives could bring about that transformation. They refused to reconcile IU with violence by arguing that the coalition's primary concern should be to stop Sendero, which would in turn bring an end to militarism and repression in Peru.[8] Thus the moderates denounced terrorism and guerrilla warfare as antipopular, and they condemned the goals and methods of Shining Path. They did not, however, deny the necessity of violence under certain circumstances — such as protecting popular gains against encroachments by either the government or Sendero. This position led to a strategy of including all who wanted to participate. It also meant a willingness to observe the rules of democratic politics.

For members of the radical faction, electoral politics are secondary to the task of radicalizing the population. They view the moderates' commitment to democracy as undermining IU's ideological underpinnings. They believe doctrinal purity is more important than electoral success, so they have been willing to exclude groups from participation. They also deny the possibility of building socialism from within the existing system and specifically reject cooperation with the government.[9] In July 1988, a radical faction of the United Mariateguist Party (PUM) adopted the position that "revolution is imminent and the party must develop an armed branch for self-defense and eventual insurrection."[10] Making confrontation an immediate priority was a direct challenge to the IU moderates.

Such differences drove a wedge between participants at IU's January 1989 party congress. Although the plenary adopted a moderate program, the moderate faction was convinced that the new IU leadership was more radical and would not carry it out. Therefore, the moderates formed the Socialist Accord (AS) in February 1989 to restructure the IU from within by holding new internal elections.[11] With two sets of candidates a formal split was only a question of time. This occurred in October 1989 when Barrantes announced his presidential candidacy in a new political party — Socialist Left (IS).[12] By creating a separate organization to run for president, Barrantes tried to eliminate the far left in the belief that the majority of IU supporters would rally to his position. But the split in the party removed any chance that the left would claim electoral victory in 1990.

The Revolutionary Path to Power

When Shining Path appeared in 1970, it was judged to be a deviant strain so far from the mainstream left that it would quickly expire. SL's ability to withstand military repression, expand operations, and challenge the legal left forced a reassessment. In part, this was due to the failure of two successive elected governments to implement viable socioeconomic reforms and an effective counterinsurgency strategy. But SL also persisted because it was able to: (1) modify its agenda and structure and absorb new followers, (2) target expansion in areas where competition is weakest, and (3) escalate the use of political violence in Peru.[13]

Modification of Means, Not Goals

Sendero is a product of isolation. Beginning in the 1960s, Dr. Abimael Guzmán Reynoso nurtured his philosophy and trained his followers within the confines of a remote provincial university.[14] Convinced of Sendero's unique mission, Guzmán eschewed both Soviet and post-Mao communism, denounced Peru's Marxist left as "parliamentary cretins," and dismissed the Revolutionary Movement of Tupac Amaru (MRTA) as "objective allies of reaction."[15] SL therefore has remained isolated from other revolutionary movements and possible sources of external support.

SL's goal, discussed in a few political tracts by Guzmán, was to mount a general uprising in the Andean highlands that would in turn bring about the collapse of urban society and destroy the regime in Lima. Toward this end, Sendero systematically intimidated and eliminated representatives of authority around its rural base. This included elected officials, nationally funded teachers and medical workers, and even church leaders. The resulting power vacuum allowed the group to carve out liberated zones in which it attempted to redistribute wealth, impose "people's justice," and block all but subsistence economic activity.

Sendero's sense of political mission and all-encompassing doctrine was attractive to some highland peasants who had long been neglected by the urban, coastal elite. Sendero's harsh discipline was considered better than no attention, and, as the armed struggle accelerated, victims of military repression swelled the ranks of SL.

The government of Belaúnde Terry created an emergency zone, eventually including thirteen provinces, under the direct control of the military. The armed forces were unable to eliminate Sendero, but the challenge to the guerrillas' Andean base forced SL to revise its strategy. At their first plenary session in September 1987, SL's leaders endorsed a strategic shift, which they had begun earlier, from protracted rural warfare to an accelerated, urban-based revolution.[16]

Many doubted that the close-knit, clandestine organization could make this transition from Ayacucho, but Sendero decentralized and expanded its membership. The result was more dispersed incidents of political violence, giving the impression of strength and bringing greater attention to the group.[17] Urban activity was different; SL could no longer expect to win by default after intimidating a few officials but had to compete with other political groups. This necessitated a transition from a clandestine, cadre organization to one that was more visible and broader based.

Forces of Change: Competition and Expansion

The composition of SL began to change after the 1986 prison riots in which at least 256 inmates, many committed Sendero leaders, were massacred. A backlash of sympathy was generated for the party on the left. These new elements were accustomed to political organizing, and they chose to champion SL's cause in familiar ways. Thereafter, Sendero became more visible and competed directly with mass organizations controlled by IU and with MRTA.

Sendero held meetings on university campuses, members distributed pamphlets and sent revolutionary messages to the media, and activists marched through Lima. A pro-Sendero demonstration on Labor Day in May 1988 was claimed to be "the march without fear," marking a new stage in the popular struggle.[18] That July the elusive Dr. Guzmán gave his famous interview to *El Diario*. At this time, Guzmán ruled out any cooperation with the politicians and targeted existing popular organizations as "obstacles to the revolution."[19]

Sendero's campaign against the popular organizations was two-pronged, to disrupt their activities and to create alternative political mechanisms. Party members sought to gain control of neighborhood, professional, and union organizations by shouting down speakers at meetings and demanding support for the armed struggle.[20] They also incited repressive violence during otherwise peaceful demonstrations and protests.[21] Sendero created a network of popular organizations. The People's Revolutionary Defense Movement (MRDP) was composed of at least eight organizations to mobilize sympathizers, including the Movement of Class Conscious Workers and Laborers (MOTC) and the Neighborhood Movement (Movimiento Barrial).[22] MOTC's goal was to replace "revisionist" demonstrations for salary and benefits with "combative" strikes that emphasize the class struggle.[23]

Sendero's move to the city weakened the movement's internal security. The first real intelligence break for the government came with the capture of Sendero's second-in-command, Osmán Morote Barrionuevo, in June 1988. The Morote case was only a qualified success, however, in that an inept court system cleared some of the charges against him, triggering violent right-wing reaction with the formation of the "Comando Rodrigo Franco" death squad.[24] In June 1990 and March 1991, police broke Sendero's urban communication network and, in what appeared to be a heavy blow to the organization, found safe houses with extensive archives, plans, schedules, videotapes, and records.[25]

Sendero's success in competing for political support was mixed. In areas with strong popular organizations, such as Puno, Cuzco, the sierra mining areas, and industrial Lima and Callao, Sendero has made few lasting inroads. In areas with less extensive organizational experience, such as the central and southern Andean ranges and the Upper Huallaga Valley (UHV), the guerrillas met with less opposition and attained some measure of influence.

Sendero's move into the UHV not only expanded its range but also brought new influences upon the guerrillas. In the highlands, Sendero could isolate peasants by severing ties with research institutes or development projects, and create autarchic communities. But coca presented a completely different reality. The coca fields are intricately tied to the Colombian drug cartel and international distribution networks.[26] In addition, the United States launched a "war on drugs" that defined the guerrillas as part of the problem.

Sendero portrayed its mission in the region as protecting indigenous culture and livelihood from the crop substitution and eradication programs of Peruvian police and U.S. Drug Enforcement Agency (DEA) officials. Nevertheless, SL had to use terror to control the population, and its relations with the drug dealers were complex. The drug traffickers, being pragmatic and brutal, paid "taxes" to Sendero for protection as long as the guerrillas were in control, but they paid the military as well. Estimates were that SL received 10 percent of the price of every kilo of coca paste, which greatly enhanced the organization's resource base.[27] An alliance with the drug traffickers may have been difficult for Sendero to control, however, because of the potential for corruption and the absence of shared ideological goals.

On the other hand, intervention by the United States enhanced Sendero's position. The $3 million U.S.-built base at Santa Lucía was to be a "model" in the war on drugs. But the Huey helicopters and U.S. agents in fatigues have led both American and Peruvian reporters to note its eerie Vietnam look; SL encouraged that comparison. On the first foray from the base, nineteen coca laboratories and twelve airfields were destroyed.[28] Sendero predicted that there would be a war between the Peruvian people and "the U.S. interventionist forces." While Luis Arce Borja's estimate of "at least 100,000 victims in the next two years"[29] was a gross exaggeration, the numbers of confrontations did increase dramatically.

Forces of Violence

To achieve its overall goal of popular revolution, SL set in motion a spiral of violence that accelerated during the García administration. From 1985 to 1986, terrorist attacks more than doubled nationwide, from 695 to 1,327. After three years of undiminished activity, the number of attacks rose sharply, to 2,113 in 1989 and to 2,154 in 1990. The increase in political deaths each year since 1987 gave another dimension to the generalization of violence in Peru. How much could be directly attributed to Shining Path was hard to determine. All attacks not claimed by another group were counted by the government as the work of SL, which no doubt inflated the totals. For example, the national coordinator for human rights estimated that, of the 782 deaths they attributed to political violence between January and March 1990, Shining Path was responsible for half, while other guerrilla groups accounted for less than 10 percent. Government forces and *rondas campesinas* were responsible for 37 percent. Regardless of the perpetrator, the majority of the victims of this deadly crossfire were Andean *campesinos* and civilians, whose death rate was 75 percent higher in 1989 than in 1988.

Some civilian deaths were due to increased military action, but the civilian fatality rate was primarily an indicator of Sendero activity. Analysts, with peasant corroboration, argue that SL's use of terror was not indiscriminate but part of its revolutionary strategy of control. Heavy retribution was visited upon those who were seen as obstacles or who refused to conform to the ascetic life style. In fact, between January and December 1989, 76 percent of Sendero's victims (995) were *campesinos* or poor urban dwellers.[30] Another target was government officials. Some 166 public officials were assassinated between January and December 1989, while only 261 had been killed in the previous eight years.[31] At least eighty districts and four provinces had no municipal authorities, and political parties found it difficult to recruit candidates for office in many areas.[32] In addition, SL killed two congressional deputies in 1989 and in 1990 two former cabinet officials, one deputy, and forty-two other high-ranking government authorities were murdered.[33]

Finally, Sendero attacked domestic and foreign research and development programs. By mid-1989 more than 70 percent of the public works projects in the Central Sierra had been abandoned because ninety-five government engineers had been killed.[34] The number of foreigners killed pales in comparison to indigenous victims, but foreign governments and businesses withdrew all nonessential personnel from Peru, undermining confidence in the regime as well as hindering assistance.

Beginning in 1989 there were more direct confrontations between the armed forces and the guerrillas involving a larger number of combatants on both sides. The result was a marked rise in the number of deaths both for the security forces and for the guerrillas, as well as a rise in reported human rights violations. From 1988 to 1989 deaths of government forces rose from 266 to 339, and in 1990, 298 military and police officials were killed.

Some sources argue that the number of guerrilla deaths was exaggerated by the military merely to demonstrate its effectiveness. A more disturbing interpretation of the fatality count was that it included many innocent civilians. In August 1989 Amnesty International (AI) issued its second report critical of Peru's human rights violations, claiming that the security forces were responsible for the disappearance, torture, and death of many civilians. For three years in a row, Peru had the highest number of forced disappearances of any nation in the world. In 1987 there were 78; in 1988 that number rose to 170; and in

1989 there were more than 300 cases reported.[35] AI also condemned Shining Path for its campaign of assassination, sabotage, and armed attacks, charging the group had "spread a veil of terror on the country."[36]

The government's inability to mount an effective counterinsurgency strategy spawned paramilitary groups wishing to take matters into their own hands. Of the four or five groups claiming to combat left-wing terrorism, the Comando Rodrigo Franco was the most prominent, initiating thirty-five attacks in 1988-1989 and murdering nine persons it claimed were SL militants or sympathizers.[37] The most significant rival to Sendero, however, was the Tupac Amaru Revolutionary Movement (MRTA) on the left. At Sendero's national congress in February 1988, MRTA was described as "the principal enemy of the revolution...that must be confronted because there cannot be the triumph of two revolutions."[38]

Concrete ties between the radical parties of IU and MRTA were denied, but there was certainly some support and relations strengthened as the overall national situation deteriorated.[39] MRTA was the product of radical splits from mainstream left political parties.[40] Although it used violence, MRTA frequently reevaluated its position and held out the possibility of peaceful, conciliatory activity. Like IU, MRTA criticized Sendero's campaign of political assassination because it gives legitimacy to the government's military counteroffensive.[41]

In contrast to Sendero, MRTA was a middle-class, urban-based group. Although MRTA operated in the countryside and mounted armed attacks against both the military and Sendero in the UHV, much of its activity was in urban areas, especially Lima. MRTA usually staged actions with an explicit message of attracting support and obtaining funds rather than instilling fear in the population.[42] It sought publicity for its actions and has forged external as well as internal ties with other groups. The number of deaths and destructive incidents attributed to the group grew under García despite early offers of a truce.[43] In 1990 the group assassinated the ex-minister of defense, Enrique López Albújar, for his role in the killing of MRTA members in April 1989, and Judge César Ruiz Trigoso, whom they claimed supported antilabor policies.[44]

Impact on 1989 and 1990 Elections

Shining Path's goal for 1989 and 1990 was to undermine the democratic system by sabotaging the November municipal and April general elections. Although they failed to halt the process, the guerrillas affected the conduct of the campaigns and the outcome in specific areas. Sendero launched an especially intense campaign in the five weeks before the municipal elections. In what became known as "Red October," more than 360 persons were killed, including 28 government officials, 11 mayors and vice-mayors, 2 district lieutenant governors, and 1 governor. Less deadly perhaps, but no less intimidating, were the car bombs, fires, and violent attacks on political party offices and meeting halls as well as candidates' homes and workplaces. At least 260 of the candidates seeking office withdrew before the election.[45]

In March the second highest monthly total of terrorist incidents (309) was recorded. These attacks had a chilling effect on campaigning, which perhaps hurt IU more than other parties. Candidates took stringent security measures by limiting their public appearances and often not publicizing them in advance. This forced greater emphasis on television advertising; the conservative Democratic Front (FREDEMO) spent thirty times more than IU.[46]

To stifle participation, Sendero called for an election boycott backed by armed strikes. Poll workers were frightened into refusing to cooperate, electoral cards were stolen, transportation was stopped, and electricity was cut off on election day. In response to these provocations, the government increased protection for voting tables, provided transportation, and extended polling hours. García also eliminated the use of indelible ink to signify who had voted because SL was known to cut off marked fingers.

The municipal results indicated widespread frustration with traditional parties. Novelist Mario Vargas Llosa and his new right-wing coalition, FREDEMO, captured thirty of forty-one districts in Lima and led the nation with 37 percent.[47] Independents attracted almost 30 percent of the vote: Television personality Ricardo Belmont was elected mayor of Lima with 45 percent. The big losers were APRA, which received 21.5 percent, and the left, with IU and IS together polling only 20.3 percent. Even so, IU still emerged as the second most important party, winning a plurality in thirty-eight of the provinces compared to APRA's nineteen.

In January 1990 virtually all political analysts predicted a Vargas Llosa presidency. At that time the only question was whether he would win outright or be forced into a runoff with one of the major contenders — Alfonso Barrantes, Henry Pease, or Luis Alva Castro. In late February the media first noticed a candidate who had been consigned to the "others" category — Alberto Fujimori, an obscure nisei agronomist, who registered a 3 percent preference as leader of a grass-roots party called CAMBIO 90 (or Change in 1990). By mid-March, with a 9.5 percent preference, he moved ahead of Henry Pease. Political pundits felt Fujimori had "little chance of catching the contenders, but could take sufficient votes to force a second round."[48]

The results of the April 8, 1990, election astounded pollsters; Vargas Llosa received only 27.61 percent of the vote and Fujimori was second with 24.62 percent. The left was thoroughly defeated with Pease mustering only 6.69 percent, but still outdistancing Barrantes's 4.07 percent. Newspapers called it a "political tidal wave," the "greatest upset in Peruvian electoral history."[49] Fujimori's surprise showing was seen as a signal that the people were tired of the old, worn-out politicians and their parties. CAMBIO 90 was a loose coalition of people who wanted new approaches to seemingly intractable problems. Fujimori offered an alternative for those worried about FREDEMO's austerity program but who were disillusioned by APRA failure and corruption and the left's political in-fighting. In fact, the vote for the left was so low in areas of traditional strength (Cuzco, Puno, Pasco, Tacna), it was clear that CAMBIO 90 had received an influx of previously IU votes.[50]

Mario Vargas Llosa's failure to avoid a run-off cost him the presidency in June as the center and left coalesced against FREDEMO and gave Fujimori 57 percent of the vote to Vargas Llosa's 34 percent. IU and IS actively campaigned to defeat the "shock policies" of FREDEMO even though they worried about CAMBIO 90's lack of a specific government plan. The moderates rejected a spoiled vote option called for by radical parties, feeling it played into SL's call for a boycott.

Sendero's greatest impact was in Ayacucho and in the Mantaro and Upper Huallaga valleys. This impact could be measured in terms of absenteeism and blank and null votes. Absenteeism was highest in the emergency zones, with Huánuco 50.1 percent, Junín 49.5 percent, and Ayacucho 47.5 percent in the first round. The percentages were high not only because of threats, but also because of forced migration from the area and failure to register.[51] Null and blank votes are important indicators of antisystem pressure on the democratic process because the constitution says that an election in a district is void if one-third of the ballots are blank or spoiled. In the first round there were some very high percentages of invalid votes, but this diminished in the runoff. Nationwide, the invalid votes in the first round were 15.35 percent compared with 9.55 percent in the runoff.[52] The temptation to see this as a victory over Sendero was played up heavily in the media. Certainly, democracy was reinforced with the successful conduct of the election, but predictions of the guerrilla movement's decline may be premature.[53]

Conclusion

Trends identified in the 1990 elections included popular frustration with the traditional parties, a desire for "independent" leaders, and weak support for democracy. With each new political, social, and economic era, the left confronts defining questions. The answers that provided a measure of cohesiveness and direction in the 1980s were no longer appropriate, so the revolutionary left began the 1990s in disarray. The electoral left had been unable to translate its presumed leadership of the popular sectors in power. At the same time, SL's armed campaign stalled. It had already expanded into those areas easiest to control and now faced stiffer popular resistance and internal challenges, wrought by growth, in a new generation of militants. In 1992, both the electoral and armed branches of the left suffered critical blows to their organizations and leadership. In April the Fujimori *autogolpe* undermined the representative democratic institutions in place since 1980, and in September, SL founder Abimael Guzmán was captured.

The questions for the left continued to be: (1) whether or not to participate in elections, (2) how far to pursue peaceful cooperation in government participation and/or opposition alliances, and (3) whether or not to support violence in efforts to overthrow the system or in efforts to defend past gains. IU split into "a thousand pieces" in responding to these questions. The more radical components refused to participate in Fujimori's constituent congress elections in November 1992 and called on their followers to cast blank or spoiled votes. The moderate groups formed an electoral coalition, Movement of the Democratic Left (MDI), which ran a dismal campaign and won only 4 percent of the vote.[54] Individuals from IU had some success regionally in the January 1993 municipal elections, but the bloc structure of the 1980s must be reevaluated in light of the reconstituted government, challenges to progressive elements of the 1979 Constitution, and in response to a population that Julio Cotler described as "disoriented, depoliticized, with disbelief in institutions."[55]

The traditional parties were shaken by popular support for Fujimori's concentration of power. His successes in economic stabilization and guerrilla pacification gave him leeway to turn his anti-democratic dissolution of Congress into a new political system that featured a strong executive, allowed reelection for the president, weakened congressional representation, restricted labor rights, and opened the economy.[56]

Sendero's strength in the 1980s had been relative to the government's weakness. However, Guzmán's capture and humiliation, the roundup of many inner-circle leaders, and the decline of urban incidents bolstered Fujimori's control and support. The movement's strength was also undermined by internal divisions over urban/rural strategies and leadership.[57] Nevertheless, the viability of democracy in Peru remains tenuous and support for the governing administration is perhaps more fragile than electoral outcomes indicate.[58] In fact, Gonzalo "Thought" still lives and the conditions that bred it continue unabated.

Notes

1. In late 1988 popular polls were projecting that IU might become the first Marxist coalition elected to power since Allende in Chile. *Resumen Semanal*, December 16-22, 1988, p. 5.

2. Among the books that treat the origins of the current Peruvian left in some detail are Ricardo Letts, *La izquierda peruana* (Lima: Mosca Azul, 1981); Jorge Nieto, *Izquierda y democracia en el Perú 1975-1980* (Lima: DESCO, 1980); Enrique Bernales, *El Parlamento por dentro* (Lima: DESCO, 1984); and Eugenio Chang-Rodríguez, *Opciones políticas peruanas 1985* (Lima: Centro de Documentación Andina, 1985).

3. For more information on the coalition formation, see Sandra Woy-Hazleton and Stephen M. Gorman, "The Peruvian Left Since 1977: Ideology, Programs, and Be-

havior," Paper presented at the annual meeting of the American Political Science Association, September 2-5, 1982, pp. 29-37.

4. Ibid., p. 42.

5. *Andean Focus*, August 3, 1989, pp. 7-8.

6. IU's plan of 1985 included the following points: (1) debt moratorium of five years and the formation of a debtor's club, (2) reduction of profit remissions abroad and recuperation of national property, (3) fulfillment of promises to the Unitary National Agrarian Council (CUNA), (4) labor amnesty and labor stability, (5) respect for autonomous organizations, (6) civilian supremacy over the military, (7) political amnesty, and (8) decentralization. *Resumen Semanal*, November 22-28, 1985, p. 3.

7. *Resumen Semanal*, January 13-19, 1989, p. 2.

8. *Resumen Semanal*, May 29-June 4, 1987, p. 1.

9. *Resumen Semanal*, August 19-25, 1988, p. 4.

10. This was at the PUM's Second National Congress, July 25, 1988; translated in *U.S. Joint Publication Research Service* (*JPRS*), September 22, 1988.

11. *Resumen Semanal*, March 3-9, p. 4; March 10-16, p. 3.

12. For more detail on this controversy, see Sandra Woy-Hazelton, "Peru," in *Yearbook on International Communist Affairs 1990* (Stanford, CA: Hoover Institution Press, 1990), pp. 131-132.

13. Henri Favre, "Perou: Sentier Lumineux et Horizons Obscurs," *Problèmes d'Amérique Latine*, 72, 2e trimestre, 1984, pp. 3-27; Cynthia McClintock, "Sendero Luminoso: Peru's Maoist Guerrillas," *Problems of Communism*, 32, September-October 1983, pp. 19-34; and "Why Peasants Rebel: The Case of Sendero Luminoso," *World Politics*, 37, October 1984, pp. 48-84.

14. For insight into this period of Sendero development, see David Scott Palmer's works, particularly "Rebellion in Rural Peru: The Origins and Evolution of Sendero Luminoso," *Comparative Politics*, 18, January 1986, pp. 137-146, and "Terrorism as a Revolutionary Strategy: Peru's Sendero Luminoso," in Barry Rubin, ed., *The Politics of Terrorism: Terror as a State and Revolutionary Strategy* (Washington: Foreign Policy Institute, Johns Hopkins School of Advanced International Studies, 1989), pp. 129-153.

15. Gordon H. McCormick, *The Shining Path and Peruvian Terrorism* (Santa Monica, CA: Rand Corporation, 1987), pp. 17-18.

16. See Raúl González's discussion in *Quehacer*, 50, January-February 1988, pp. 47-59.

17. See Palmer, "Terrorism as a Revolutionary Strategy," p. 139; and Gabriela Tarazona-Sevillano, *Sendero Luminoso and the Threat of Narcoterrorism*, Center for Strategic and International Studies (CSIS), The Washington Papers 144, (New York: Praeger, 1990), pp. 55-77.

18. *Resumen Semanal*, April 22-May 5, 1988, p. 3.

19. *Andean Focus*, August 3, 1988, p. 3.

20. The most overt attempt was made within the Unitary Peruvian Teachers Union (SUTEP), which has 200,000 members nationwide. Teachers located in remote areas are often the only representatives of authority, so they are under great pressure to cooperate with Sendero. When they went on strike with other government employees for cost-of-living increases in June 1988, Sendero urged them not to settle at all. *Latin America Weekly Review* (London) (*LAWR*), June 23, 1988, p. 8.

21. At one IU rally in Lima, Sendero militants exploded dynamite, wounding four workers, and directly assaulted several others, including pro-Moscow Peruvian Communist Party (PCP) leader Jorge del Prado. *Resumen Semanal*, January 22-28, 1988, p. 2.
22. See Tarazona-Sevillano, *Sendero Luminoso*, pp. 62-67.
23. *Resumen Semanal*, January 22-28, 1988, p. 2; *Quehacer*, 53, July-August 1988, p. 17.
24. Manuel Febres Flores, Osmán Morote's lawyer, was assassinated in July by the group named for an Aprista official killed in Ñaña in 1987. Group members announced they would kill a terrorist for every Aprista murdered. *Resumen Semanal*, August 5-11, 1988, p. 3; December 2-15, 1988, p. 2.
25. *Resumen Semanal*, June 1-7, 1990, pp. 1-2.
26. Roger Cohen, "Cocaine Rebellion," *Wall Street Journal*, January 17, 1989, p. A1.
27. Ibid.
28. The Peruvian government desires foreign military assistance for counterinsurgency operations, but the United States, in supplying it, is concerned mainly with stopping the flow of coca. See Waltrud Queiser Morales, "The War on Drugs: A New U.S. National Security Doctrine?" *Third World Quarterly*, 11:3, July 1989, pp. 147-169; Cynthia McClintock, "The War on Drugs: The Peruvian Case," *Journal of Interamerican Studies and World Affairs*, 33:2-3, Summer/Fall 1988, pp. 127-142.
29. Interview with Luis Arce Borja, "There is no other way," by Anita Fokkema, in "Fatal Attraction: Peru's Shining Path," *NACLA Report on the Americas*, December/January 1990-1991, p. 25.
30. *Boletín Informativo*, November 1989-January 1990, p. 1.
31. Ibid.
32. For example, of the six district mayors of the province of Leoncio Prado in Huánuco, three were murdered and three resigned after receiving death threats. *Resumen Semanal*, June 30-July 6, 1989, p. 4; June 9-15, 1989, p. 2; *Andean Newsletter*, 31, June 12, 1989, pp. 5-6.
33. *Resumen Semanal*, April 21-27, 1989, p. 1; May 5-11, 1989, p. 1.
34. *LAWR*, June 22, 1989, p. 8.
35. *Andean Newsletter*, 37, December 4, 1989, p. 6; *Boletín Informativo*, 5, November 1989-January 1990, p. 1.
36. *Resumen Semanal*, August 18-24, 1989, p. 2.
37. *Andean Newsletter*, 35-36, November 9, 1989, p. 8.
38. *Quehacer*, 53, July-August 1988, pp. 18-19.
39. MRTA's "Robin Hood" tactics — stealing trucks of food to distribute to the poor communities — appeals to the disaffected youth of the urban middle class. In fact, the youth representatives to the PCP's Ninth Congress were alleged to be MRTA members. *La República*, Lima, March 13, 1988, translated in Foreign Broadcast Information Service (FBIS), *Latin American Report*, March 22, 1988, p. 27.
40. MRTA was created in late 1983 when a faction of the PSR split to form the PSR-Marxist-Leninist. Then four splinters of the Leftist Revolutionary Movement (MIT) joined the PSR-Marxist-Leninist to create an armed alternative to Shining Path.
41. *Resumen Semanal*, January 30-February 19, 1987, p. 2.
42. See James Anderson, *Sendero Luminoso: A New Revolutionary Model?* (London: Institute for the Study of Terrorism, 1987), p. 1.
43. *Cambio*, September 5, 1987; *Resumen Semanal*, September 25-October 10, 1987, p. 6.

44. *LAWR*, January 25, 1990, p. 9, and *Andean Newsletter*, December 10, 1990, p. 5.

45. *LAWR*, November 16, 1989, p. 3.

46. Estimates were that FREDEMO spent thirty times what IU did, twice APRA, and six times IS on television advertising. *Caretas*, June 29, 1990, pp. 11-14; *FBIS*, February 27, 1990.

47. *Resumen Semanal*, November 25-December 1, 1989, pp. 1-3.

48. Alberto Fujimori is the son of Japanese immigrants who went to Peru in 1934. He studied agronomy at La Molina, the National Agrarian University in Lima; at the University of Wisconsin; and at Strasbourg, France. He was rector of La Molina from 1984 to 1989, when he quit to run for president. For polling information see *Latin American Regional Report, The Andean Countries*, March 9, 1990, p. 6.

49. *Resumen Semanal*, April 6-11, 1990, p. 1.

50. *Resumen Semanal*, May 18-24, 1990, p. 5.

51. Ibid., p. 6.

52. *Resumen Semanal*, May 11-17, 1990, p. 2.

53. Carlos Iván Degregori has written of the "fourth stage" of internal problems. He felt the passing of the tenth anniversary with no major celebrations indicated the organization's decline. Certainly there have been a growing number of captures, deaths, and desertions. Indications are that there is a struggle between the "red" and "black" factions over the efficacy of continued terrorism. The younger, more radical members favor more military operations, while the older, "black" factions favor political and social activities. *Sí*, May 21-28, 1990, pp. 16, 83; Madrid EFE, May 14, 1990, translated in *FBIS*, May 16, 1990, p. 43.

54. *Resumen Semanal,* November 18-24, 1992, p. 2.

55. Inter Press Service, February 15, 1, *Lexis/Nexis*.

56. *Washington Post,* November 2, 1993, *Lexis/Nexis.*

57. See *Quehacer* 79, September-October 1992, "Sendero: El Principio del Fin?," pp. 30-53 and *Quehacer* 81, January-February 1993, "La Caida de Abimael Guzmán y El Destino de Sendero Luminoso," pp. 80-89.

58. While Fujimori's supporters won 38 percent of the votes and thus occupied 44 of the 80 congress seats, a total of 51 percent of the population voted blank, for opposition parties, spoiled their ballot, or abstained. (*Resumen Semanal,* December 1992, p. 1). Similarly, the approval of the new constitution by referendum on October 31, 1993 was, according to preliminary results, by a margin of 55-45 percent. However, support was regionally skewed with Lima's 61 percent approval balanced by losses in 12 of the 24 departments and defeats in those areas most affected by poverty and terrorism (EFE Madrid, October 31, 1993, *Lexis/Nexis*).

12

THEORIES OF REVOLUTION AND THE CASE OF PERU*

Cynthia McClintock

In 1991 and especially in 1992 prior to the September capture of Abimael Guzmán, some analysts of the Shining Path (SL or Sendero) were forecasting a victory for the guerrilla movement within five years or less. Most believed that a revolutionary victory was possible. Said Peruvian analyst Enrique Obando: "The state is on the verge of defeat. The armed forces could tumble down at any moment."[1] Warned Gustavo Gorriti: "If they [the Shining Path] continue this way, they will be able to beat the Peruvian state."[2] Concluded a U.S.-based analyst: "The Shining Path has become a direct threat to the government of Peru."[3] In 1989, SL inflicted more deaths, controlled a greater percentage of national territory, and was approved in opinion polls by a larger percentage of citizens than the guerrilla movement in El Salvador.[4]

*I would like to thank the U.S. Institute of Peace for a Jennings Randolph Peace Fellowship during 1990-1991, which facilitated research and writing for this article. Jocelyn Nieva, research assistant at the Institute, greatly helped in the preparation of the manuscript.

Was a Shining Path victory possible in Peru? What are the necessary factors for a revolutionary triumph in Latin America in the late twentieth century? This chapter presents two perspectives that, not surprisingly, offer very different answers to these questions: the perspective of mainstream scholarly theory, primarily by North American analysts, and that of Shining Path itself. Necessarily brief, this chapter can only highlight the most important points of both. Moreover, issues not fully addressed by either perspective may have been critical both to Sendero's expansion and to its weakening after its leader's capture.

Mainstream Theories of Revolution

Relative to many topics in the comparative politics field, scholarly consensus about the reasons for revolutionary triumph is strong. While emphases vary, there is no factor that one set of analysts believes facilitates revolution while a second group thinks impedes revolution. There are no sharp disagreements among analysts about the definition of revolution, either. Perhaps the most cited is Samuel Huntington's: "the broad, rapid, and violent expansion of political participation outside the existing structure of political institutions."[5]

From the work of scholars of revolution, can we infer an answer to the question of Shining Path's taking power in Peru? For most, the answer would be a clear and emphatic "No," primarily because the character of Peru's state does not fit the type described in the academic literature as vulnerable to revolution. Yet some scholars, especially those who are as interested in the emergence of revolutionary movements as in actual revolutionary takeover, would qualify their "No."

Especially during the 1980s, scholarly analysis has highlighted the personalistic dictatorial regime type as essential to multiclass protest and revolutionary victory.[6] "The ballot box...has proven to be the coffin of revolutionary movements...Avowedly socialist revolutions — which according to classical Marxism were supposed to follow after and build upon the achievements of bourgeois-democratic revolutions — have occurred only in countries that never established liberal-democratic systems in the first place."[7]

These scholarly conclusions are empirical in character, based on historical evidence. In Latin America, among the four twentieth-century cases of revolution — Mexico (1910-1917), Bolivia (1952), Cuba (1959), and Nicaragua

(1979) — three were governed by longstanding personalistic dictators who had repressed electoral processes: Porfirio Diaz in Mexico, Fulgencio Batista in Cuba, and Anastasio Somoza in Nicaragua. Bolivia was ruled by a military junta. Writes Cole Blasier: "In each case, a dictatorial figure or group openly and cynically denied the electorate the opportunity to select its own leadership....Capitalizing on what became ultimately moral issues, the revolutionary leaders succeeded because they were able to mobilize, or neutralize, the great mass of the population in a struggle against despotic regimes."[8]

Reviewing the Cuban and Nicaraguan experiences, Robert Dix is even more emphatic.[9] Whereas Blasier believes that societal problems and widespread perceptions of foreign domination by the United States were important preconditions for the Latin American revolutions, Dix argues that the socioeconomic characteristics of the countries where revolutions succeeded were no different from those in the countries where they failed. Dix contends that the necessary and sufficient catalyst for Latin American revolution is "a personalistic dictator — isolative, repressive, antinational, and corrupt — who over time turns a whole nation against him and his...associates."[10]

There are, however, some limitations to the empirical, historical approach to revolution. First, analysts are working with a very small number of cases of revolution.[11] Theda Skocpol's work is built around three cases: France, Russia, and China. In two of these countries revolutions occurred prior to World War II, when arguably revolutionary conditions were different.[12] Other studies are about revolutionary movements against colonial regimes or monarchies, of which there are few today.

In addition, some analysts (including especially Marxist scholars) have excluded Mexico and Bolivia from the cases of Latin American revolution on the grounds that the extent of social change was insufficient.[13] With these exclusions only two cases, Cuba and Nicaragua, remain.

Therefore, some scholars ask whether or not the history of revolutionary experiences can be a precise and complete guide to the future of revolutions.[14] They point out that governmental authorities as well as revolutionary leaders study past revolutions in order to glean lessons for the present. In particular, scholars analyzing the world's most recent cases of revolution, Nicaragua and Iran, as well as such ongoing revolutionary movements in El Salvador and the

Philippines, tend to highlight the importance of several new variables.[15] One of these is the significance of the international context not only in terms of interstate military pressures or international captialist penetration, as was most common in the previous literature, but also from the standpoint of superpower politics. For example, comparing the revolutionary success in Iran and Nicaragua, Farideh Farhi emphasizes the importance of "permissive world context" — in these cases, the relative tolerance of revolution by the United States under President Jimmy Carter.[16]

The inability of the revolutionary movement in El Salvador to take power during the 1980s also suggested to various scholars the importance of superpower policy — in this case, the intolerance of revolution by the United States and a "non-permissive" world context.[17] Furthermore, although the Salvadoran revolutionary movement did not triumph, it almost did — and its regime was not the personalistic dictatorship specified as necessary for revolution by theorists. To date, scholarship on El Salvador has failed to develop a consensus as to why a revolutionary movement became strong there.[18]

With ongoing peasant-based revolutionary movements in several countries, including Peru, various scholars encourage greater attention to analysis of the origins of these rebellions.[19] The rationale is that the event of peasant rebellion is itself significant and that a greater emphasis on societal rather than state (for example, dictatorships) factors may be necessary.

Several theories of peasant rebellion are now classics. James Scott focuses on peasant rebellions in Southeast Asia and argues that, as population grew, as capitalism expanded, and as the state imposed new fiscal claims on the peasantry, peasants became more susceptible to subsistence crises. Especially in cohesive villages with strong communal traditions, peasants threatened by a subsistence crisis believe that their fundamental social right of survival has been rejected by elites and, morally enraged, they revolt.[20] Scott perceives small holders as the most rebellion-prone peasant group. However, Jeffrey Paige contends that the peasant classes most disposed to insurrection are hired laborers or sharecroppers who have nothing to lose.[21] Samuel Popkin suggests another variation: that the key to rebellion is the capacity of the revolutionary organizations to provide attractive benefits to peasants, who are essentially rational utility-maximizers.[22]

Popkin's emphasis on revolutionary organization and ideology and their importance in the Iranian and Nicaraguan revolutions has led several scholars to raise a third research concern: the importance of revolutionary ideology. Traditionally, mainstream scholarship has downplayed the role of ideology; in various key works revolutionary ideology is not even discussed.[23] However, analyzing the significance of Islamic ideas in Iran and liberation theology in Nicaragua, Farhi contends that worldwide concepts are important.[24] Raj Desai and Harry Eckstein criticize the "secondary status" accorded to "professional revolutionaries and their strategies" and argue that, when twentieth-century revolutions have triumphed, insurgents were "stirred" and "mobilized" by "innovative" and "visionary" ideas that replaced the "regressive, passive, millenarian" orientations of earlier revolutionary moments.[25] Following this approach, we turn next to the ideology of Shining Path, before evaluating the validity of both mainstream scholarly theory and Sendero ideology for Peru.

Shining Path's Theory of Revolution

Needless to say, Sendero's interpretation of the revolutionary process is different from that of mainstream scholarship.[26] Shining Path's thinking follows Mao's during the period of the Cultural Revolution — what is often called "Gang-of-Four Maoism." In the 1988 interview of Shining Path leader Abimael Guzmán Reynoso in *El Diario*, Guzmán acknowledges that "the principal contribution [of Sendero] is to establish Maoism as the third and superior stage of Marxism" and "to apply in the most faithful way possible the universal truths of Marxism-Leninism-Maoism to our concrete reality."[27] Although the name Shining Path is taken from a statement by Peru's first prominent Marxist, José Carlos Mariátegui, Guzmán had almost nothing to say about Mariátegui in the interview except that "if he were alive today, he would be a Maoist."[28] Shining Path's Maoism took on its distinctiveness in part from extended stays in China during the Cultural Revolution (1966-1976) by Guzmán and several of his key lieutenants.[29] Three key elements include: (1) characterization of society as "semifeudal," implying that the peasantry will be the primary social base of the revolution and that democracy is impossible; (2) the fundamental role of political violence in the revolutionary process; and (3) Gang-of-Four Maoism as an invariable truth.[30]

For Mao, China had changed from a feudal to a "semi-colonial" and "semi-feudal" society by the 1930s and 1940s. "In their aggression against China the imperialist powers...hastened the disintegration of feudal society and the growth of elements of capitalism."[31] However, given the "collusion of imperialism with the Chinese feudal forces," the development of Chinese capitalism was "arrested" and "uneven." It was essentially "bureaucratic capitalism introduced by a weak national bourgeoisie, who serve as the intermediaries of imperialism and whose activities are of a comprador and usurious character, rather than productive."[32] In this context, the Chinese people, particularly the peasants, become more and more impoverished, and the peasants become the key social base for revolution.[33]

Shining Path's analysis of Peruvian society is identical:

> Contemporary Peru is a semifeudal and semicolonial society in which bureaucratic capitalism is unfolding; a delayed capitalism subjected completely to imperialism, in our case Yankee imperialism, and accordingly does not develop the great productive forces of our country, but rather damages it....[Bureaucratic capitalism] is totally opposed to our national interests, to the most essential and most urgent needs of the masses of our people.[34]

Just as in Maoism, the semifeudal character of Peruvian society implies for Shining Path that the peasantry, especially the poorest peasantry, must be the principal revolutionary force.[35] Whereas other Peruvian marxists perceive considerable variation amony recent Peruvian governments and often praise the military regime's 1969-1975 agrarian reform in some way, for Guzmán they have all been "facist, corporatist and reactionary."[36] In Peru's semifeudal context, Guzmán and key Sendero intellectual Antonio Díaz Martínez view agrarian reform and development projects as benefiting the professionals employed in these programs but not the peasants.[37]

A second important similarity between Maoist and Shining Path ideology is the emphasis upon violence both as revolutionary strategy and as socialization: "From the barrel of a gun grows political power."[38] Philip Mauceri notes the significance of violence for Mao: "violence takes on an almost mystical quality, not only destroying the old but creating the new. For Mao, revolutionary violence is an immense force which can transform many things, or open the way for their transformation."[39] Similarly, for Sendero, "popular war is the principal form of struggle,"[40] just as "the war itself forges the militant."[41] Adulation of bravery in revolutionary war is prominent throughout Shining Path tracts. Several publications begin with the citation, apparently from Mao, that "He who is not afraid of being cut into a thousand pieces is bold enough to bring down the Emperor."[42] A poem commemorating Shining Path militants who died in a massacre in Lima's prisons in June 1986 reads: "Glory to the fallen heroes, long live the revolution! Blood does not drown the revolution, but irrigates it!"[43]

Given such adulation of violence, it is not surprising that Shining Path dismisses nonviolent electoral and legislative activities as "rotten":

> What do elections imply? Is it in the people's interest to vote? Looking at Peru's experience, what revolutionary transformation has the people achieved through voting or in parliamentary activity? Every triumph has originated in the acts of popular struggle, and it is on the bases of its results that laws have been promulgated that recognize the masses.[44]

Shining Path's criticism of parties of the United Left (IU) is often virulent:

> [There is] the opportunist group run by the calloused revisionist Jorge del Prado [leader of the pro-Moscow Communist Party] and his clique, servile followers of the imperial cudgel of Brezhnev, the boss of Russian revisionism and grand puppet-master of revisionism at the world level...these are enemies of the revolution...Yesterday's "enemies" of Deng Xiaoping who now adore him can do no other than attack us for fighting the Yankee imperialist partner of their new boss.[45]

As Guzmán's invective indicates, Sendero is certain that it is the sole repository of Marxist truth. For the rest of Peru's Marxist left, the dogmatic sectarianism of Shining Path is an especially serious error.[46] The left believes that Shining Path's dogmatism transforms it into a type of fundamentalist religious sect, where absolute truth is opposed by absolute falsehood. This sectarianism is so extreme that other Marxists are frequent targets of Shining Path.

How Do These Theories Apply to Peru?

Key questions raised by both scholarly theory and Shining Path ideology relate to the potential for revolution in Peru. The most salient disagreement between the two schools is the nature of the Peruvian state. A second core issue is the potential appeal of an ideology that is as based on violence and as sectarian as Sendero's. A final question, the world attitude toward revolution in Peru in the 1990s, is a crucial concern in the most current scholarship and is also becoming more important in Shining Path documents.

Peru's Regime Type, 1980-April 1992

For mainstream scholars, Peru's state was democratic, not the dictatorial type that was vulnerable to revolution. Yet for Shining Path it was fascist and reactionary. Which characterization most closely approximated reality?

In scholarly practice, regular elections are the necessary and almost sufficient condition for the democratic standard.[47] Since 1980 three free and fair presidential elections had been held in Peru, as specified in the 1979 Constitution. Political competition had been broad, with greater participation by Marxist parties than in any other Latin American country. Human rights violations by the Peruvian military occurred primarily in remote highlands villages against peasants; no leftist leader had been killed by the military during an electoral campaign.[48] Political debate in the media was vigorous; even a pro Shining Path newspaper circulated relatively freely in the 1980s. Some decentralization had been achieved, municipal officers were elected, and in 1990 "regions" were established and elections held for representative assemblies in each.

The electoral process had engaged the citizenry. Indeed, rates of electoral participation in Peru were among the highest in Latin America.[49] By 1985 more than 80 percent of Peru's eligible population was registered to vote, and turnout was over 90 percent; in 1990, in a context of widespread pressures by the Shining Path against voting, about 80 percent voted in each of the two rounds of the election.[50] Since the early 1980s in Lima, when citizens have been asked their preferred political regime, between 70 to 80 percent opt for a democratic system, while only between 5 to 20 choose a socialist revolution and a mere 2 to 10 a military regime.[51] In addition, majorities generally assessed the incumbent government as at least somewhat democratic.[52]

However, Sendero considers the electoral process meaningless because the semifeudal and semicolonial class structure predetermine Peru's governments as repressive and exploitative. To what degree is SL's characterization of

Peru's class structure as semifeudal and semicolonial accurate? By virtually every indicator, Peru does not resemble prerevolutionary China. Peru's population in the 1980s was about two-thirds urban and three-quarters literate, with only about one-third of the labor force in agriculture; by contrast China was just 10 percent urban and 10 percent literate in about 1950, with more than two-thirds of its labor force in agriculture.[53]

Post-1968 Peru cannot be described as "feudal." The 1968 land reform swept large landlords from the countryside, and sharecropping or rental arrangements also disappeared. In contrast, prior to the Chinese revolution, about 30 percent of the land was owned by a gentry that did not work or live in peasant villages, but rather rented its land in exchange for half the crop.[54] Nor is Peru colonial. Spanish rule ended in Peru about 170 years ago, and Peru has never been invaded by the United States or a European power; in recent years, Peru has strictly regulated foreign investment and trade.[55] In contrast, during the nineteenth century China suffered repeated foreign invasions. Concessions were forced upon it by Great Britain, and "spheres of influence" were carved up by European powers and Japan. Japan defeated China in an 1895-1896 war and invaded the country during World War II.

Given the stark differences between Peruvian and Chinese society during the relevant periods, what caveats about the inapplicability of Shining Path ideology to Peru should be noted? Most important, despite the contrasts between Peru and China at the national level, Peru is a geographically diverse country marked by extremely sharp and overlapping regional, ethnic, and class cleavages. Although the home region of Sendero, Ayacucho, does not continue to suffer from feudalism or colonialism, the area is extremely poor and has become poorer in recent years; not only does the Lima-centered government fail to provide resources to remote highlands areas such as Ayacucho, but this government is widely perceived to be exploiting these areas through its pricing and credit policies.[56] In such areas of Peru, citizens are much more likely than in Lima to define democracy as equality and popular participation (rather than freedom and elections), and they are also much more likely than in Lima to reject the democratic label for Peru's post-1980 governments.[57]

Also, even among Peruvians who have upheld liberal-democratic ideas and who have accepted the electoral process as the key basis for political legitimacy, doubts about these beliefs have increased as Peru's recent popularly elected administrations have performed so poorly. The approval ratings of President Belaúnde (1980-1985) and of President García (1985-1990) were barely above the 20 percent mark in the latter parts of their terms, and the rating of President Alberto Fujimori (1990-1995) was below that of his two predecessors at the same point in their administrations. The legitimacy of Fujimori was weakened in particular by his breaking of his key electoral promise (that he would not impose an economic "shock" program) almost immediately after his inauguration.

Shining Path's Appeal

Assuming with the most recent scholarly theorists as well as Shining Path that ideology is relevant, how attractive can SL's extremely sectarian, pro-violence doctrine be? On the one hand, it is clear that, for the vast majority of Peruvians, Sendero beliefs and tactics are anathema. For example, reflecting upon his experiences with SL, a one-time member of the organization writes how "It always frightened and saddened people when there was Sendero killing."[58]

On the other hand, for certain individuals the fundamentalism and the violence of Shining Path are apparently satisfying. Stereotypical Shining Path militants are the sons or daughters of highland-born peasants, one of the first members of their family to finish secondary school and perhaps even attend a university; subsequently, their aspirations are blocked and they feel frustrated by the inequities in Peruvian society and uncomfortable both in their parents' traditional Andean world and in the urban Western world.[59] For these disoriented individuals, Shining Path offers a simple, coherent vision of the world; believing that SL is the caretaker of absolute truth, they can be certain that their lives will not be lived in vain.[60] For some, Shining Path's violence affords a satisfying revenge. Explains one analyst: "Sendero is a compensation for impotence."[61] Comments another: "For the first time in their lives, they [SL] can command respect. They are the ones who instill fear."[62]

The World Context

Analysts of revolution, especially those comparing and contrasting revolutionary outcomes in Iran, Nicaragua, and El Salvador, have emphasized the importance of a "permissive world context" to revolutionary triumph. Shining Path has not discussed the world context in any detail, but recently it has denounced as interventionist the U.S. anti-drug program and the proposed U.S. military aid to Peru.[63]

Overall, the world context with regard to Shining Path was permissive. In contrast to U.S. policy toward El Salvador, for example, neither the Reagan nor the Bush administration indicated significant concern about Shining Path prior to 1992. U.S. economic aid to Peru was only about $75 million annually during the 1980s, increasing to about $100 million in 1991, at most 6 percent of total U.S. aid to the region.[64] (By contrast, El Salvador received about $300 to $400 million annually, for a population roughly one-quarter that of Peru's.[65]) U.S. military aid to Peru was extremely low, averaging under $1 million annually.[66] While the United States proposed a $34.9 million military aid package to Peru in 1990 and 1991, the primary stated objective of the aid was to help the Peruvian government in the war against drugs, not the war against Shining Path.[67]

Why did the United States not seek to bolster the Peruvian government against the country's revolutionary movement? First, the geopolitics of Shining Path in Peru are very different from the geopolitics of revolutionary movements in Central America. Peru's location is relatively far away from the United States. Second, United States-Peru relations have tended to be tense since the late 1960s. Under General Juan Velasco Alvarado (1968-1975), the Peruvian government not only expropriated most of the country's large haciendas as well as several major U.S. companies, but also began to purchase significant quantities of arms from the Soviet Union.[68] Moreover, as Shining Path expanded in the latter years of the García administration, García maintained his anti-free-market economic policy as well as his nationalistic position on Peru's debt service, policies that disgruntled both the Reagan and Bush administrations. Third, the primary U.S. concern in Peru was the "war against drugs." As the producer of more than half the coca that is eventually transported to the United States as cocaine, Peru became a priority theater. In the view of some analysts, the antidrug effort was at odds with effective counterinsurgency in the coca-growing region.[69]

Conclusion and Postscript

After the capture of Guzmán in September 1992, Sendero was greatly weakened. In the view of virtually all analysts, Sendero no longer presents a direct threat to the Peruvian state.

Accordingly, should it be concluded that mainstream theorists of revolution were correct? Not necessarily. The factors highlighted by these theorists as important to the thwarting of revolutionary movements were not more evident in Peru in 1992 than previously. Indeed, after the April 1992 *autogolpe,* Peru was less rather than more democratic by the conventional scholarly criteria. And although international concern about Shining Path was rising in 1992, the U.S. government was reducing rather than increasing official support for Peru in the aftermath of the *autogolpe.* Rather than validate the mainstream theories of revolution, the importance of Guzmán's capture to the undermining of Sendero highlights the significance to the revolutionary outcome of the organizational capabilities of both the state and the guerrilla movement. In the case of Sendero, the organization's centralization, which had appeared as an advantage, facilitating discipline and cohesion, became a serious flaw in the wake of the leader's capture.

However, although the threat from Sendero is probably ended, another revolutionary movement may emerge in Peru five or ten years hence if the socioeconomic problems that originally ignited the revolutionary flames are not ameliorated. The Peruvian experience suggests that, in contrast to conventional wisdom, a constitutionally democratic regime type is not by itself a barrier to revolution. At some future date, amid a context roughly similar to Peru's during the 1980s, a regime that political analysts had labeled democratic may fall to a Sendero-like movement.

Notes

1. *Newsweek,* August 19, 1991, p. 29.
2. *The New York Times,* November 11, 1991, p. A1.
3. Gordon H. McCormick, *The Shining Path and the Future of Peru* (Santa Monica: Rand, 1990), p. 5.
4. Cynthia McClintock, *Politics, Economics, and Revolution: Explaining Guerrilla Movements in Peru and El Salvador, 1980-1991* (Washington, D.C.: U.S. Institute of Peace, forthcoming), table 1.1.
5. Samuel P. Huntington, *Political Order in Changing Societies* (New Haven: Yale University Press, 1968), p. 274. Comparable definitions are provided by Cole Blasier, "Social Revolution: Origins in Mexico, Bolivia, and Cuba," in Rolando E. Bonachea and Nelson P. Valdes,

eds., *Cuba in Revolution* (New York: Doubleday, 1972), p. 19; and Robert H. Dix, "Why Revolutions Succeed and Fail," *Polity*, 16:3, Spring 1984, p. 423.

6. See Jeff Goodwin and Theda Skocpol, "Explaining Revolutions in the Contemporary Third World," *Politics and Society*, 17:4, December 1989, pp. 489-509; Huntington, *Political Order*; Jack A. Goldstone, "Theories of Revolution: The Third Generation," *World Politics*, 32:3, April 1980, pp. 425-453. Manus I. Midlarsky and Kenneth Roberts, "Class, State, and Revolution in Central America," *Journal of Conflict Resolution*, 29:2, June 1985, pp. 185-187.

7. Goodwin and Skocpol, "Explaining Revolutions," p. 495; Huntington made the same point in *Political Order*, p. 275.

8. Blasier, "Social Revolution." p. 32, and pp. 48-49.

9. Dix, "Why Revolutions Succeed and Fail."

10. Ibid., p. 433.

11. Goldstone, "Theories of Revolution," pp. 450-451.

12. Theda Skocpol, *States and Social Revolutions* (New York: Cambridge University Press, 1979).

13. Barry Schutz and Robert O. Slater, *Revolution and Political Change in the Third World* (Boulder, CO: Lynne Rienner, 1990). Also James M. Malloy, *Bolivia: The Uncompleted Revolution* (Pittsburgh: University of Pittsburgh Press, 1970); and Mark Wasserman, "The Mexican Revolution: Region and Theory, Signifying Nothing?" *Latin American Research Review*, 25:1, 1990, pp. 231-242.

14. Walter L. Goldfrank, "Theories of Revolution and Revolution Without Theory: The Case of Mexico," *Theory and Society*, 7, 1979, p. 161.

15. Farideh Farhi, "State Disintegration and Urban-Based Revolutionary Crisis: A Comparative Analysis of Iran and Nicaragua," *Comparative Political Studies*, 21:2, July, pp. 231-256; Gary Hawes, "Theories of Peasant Revolution: A Critique and Contribution from the Philippines," *World Politics*, 42:2, January 1990, pp. 261-298; Timothy P. Wickham-Crowley, "Understanding Failed Revolution in El Salvador: A Comparative Analysis of Regime Types and Social Structures," *Politics and Society*, 17:4, December 1989, pp. 511-537; Midlarsky and Roberts, "Class, State, and Revolution," pp. 163-193; Dix, "Why Revolutions Succeed and Fail," pp. 438-442; Matthew Soberg Shugart, "Patterns of Revolution," *Theory and Society*, 18, 1989, pp. 249-271.

16. Farhi, "State Disintegration," pp. 241-245. The term "permissive world context" was first coined by Goldfrank, "Theories of Revolution," pp. 148-149.

17. Dix, "Why Revolutions Succeed and Fail," p. 441; Midlarsky and Roberts, "Class, State, and Revolution," p. 192; Shugart, "Patterns of Revolution," p. 261; Wickham-Crowley, "Understanding Failed Revolution," p. 528.

18. See articles cited in note 13.

19. See Hawes, "Theories of Peasant Revolution," and Cynthia McClintock, "Why Peasants Rebel: The Case of Peru's Sendero Luminoso," *World Politics*, 37, October 1984, pp. 48-84.

20. James C. Scott, *The Moral Economy of the Peasant: Rebellion and Subsistence in Southeast Asia* (New Haven, CT: Yale University Press, 1976).

21. Jeffrey M. Paige, *Agrarian Revolution: Social Movements and Export Agriculture in the Underdeveloped World* (New York: Free Press, 1975).

22. Samuel L. Popkin, *The Rational Peasant: The Political Economy of Rural Society in Vietnam* (Berkeley: University of California Press, 1979).

23. Theda Skocpol in particular discards a role for ideology. See Theda Skocpol, *States and Social Revolutions: A Comparative Analysis of France, Russia, and China* (New York: Cambridge University Press, 1979), pp. 168-171. Reviews of the literature on revolution include Goldstone, "Theories of Revolution," and T. David Mason, "Dynamics of Revolutionary Change: Indigenous Factors," in Schutz and Slater, *Revolution and Political Change*, pp. 30-53.

24. Farhi, "State Disintegration and Urban-Based Revolutionary Crisis," pp. 248-252.

25. Raj Desai and Harry Eckstein, "Insurgency: The Transformation of Peasant Rebellion," *World Politics*, 42:4, July 1990, pp. 441-466.

26. Discussions of Shining Path ideology include David Scott Palmer, "The Revolutionary Terrorism of Peru's Shining Path," paper prepared for the Ford Foundation-sponsored project "Terrorism in Context," Martha Crenshaw, director, January 1990; Vera Gianotten, Tom de Wit, and Hans de Wit, "The Impact of Sendero Luminoso on Regional and National Politics in Peru," in David Slater, ed., *New Social Movements and the State in Latin America* (Amsterdam: CEDLA, 1985), pp. 171-202; Gustavo Gorriti, "The War of the Philosopher-King," *The New Republic*, June 18, 1990, pp. 15-22; Raúl González, "Gonzalo's Thought, Belaúnde's Answer," *NACLA Report on the Americas*, 20:3, June 1986, pp. 34-36; Raúl González, "Ayacucho: Por los caminos de Sendero," *Quehacer*, 19, October 1982, pp. 36-79; Santiago Pedraglio, *Armas para la paz* (Lima: Instituto de Defensa Legal, 1990), and Colin Harding, "Antonio Díaz Martínez and the Ideology of Sendero Luminoso," *Bulletin of Latin American Research*, 7:1, 1988, p. 65.

27. Luis Arce Borja and Janet Talavera Sánchez, "La Entrevista del siglo: El Presidente Gonzalo rompe el silencio," *El Diario*, July 24, 1988, p. 45, 5.

28. Ibid., p. 4.

29. See Arce Borja and Talavera Sánchez, "La Entrevista del siglo," p. 46; Gorriti, "War of the Philosopher-King," p. 18, and Harding, "Antonio Díaz Martínez," esp. p. 70.

30. Philip Mauceri, in a draft chapter on the ideology of the Shining Path, also discusses at length the link between Maoism and Shining Path ideology. He highlights the questions of semifeudalism and the role of violence, but emphasizes the issue of the cultural gap between city and countryside rather than sectarianism as a third key ideological component.

31. Mao Zedong, "The Chinese Revolution and the Chinese Communist Party," in Bruce Mazlish, Arthur D. Kaledin, and David B. Ralston, eds., *Revolution: A Reader* (New York: Macmillan, 1971), p. 282.

32. Ibid., p. 283. See also Harding, "Antonio Díaz Martínez" p. 71.

33. Harding, "Antonio Díaz Martínez," p. 71; and Ross Terrill, *Mao: A Biography* (New York: Harper Colophon Books, 1980), p. 81. See also Mao Zedong, "Report on an Investigation of the Peasant Movement in Hunan," in Mazlish, Kaledin, and Ralston, eds., *Revolution: A Reader*, pp. 264-281.

34. Comité Central, Partido Comunista del Peru, "No votar! Sino generalizar la Guerra de Guerrillas para conquistar el poder para el pueblo!" (Lima(?): Ediciones Bandera Roja, February 1985), p. 2.

35. Comité Central, Partido Comunista del Peru, "Desarrollemos la Guerra del Guerrillas!" (Lima(?): Ediciones Bandera Roja, February 1982), p. 27; and Arce Borja and Talavera Sánchez, "La Entrevista del siglo," p. 9.

36. Comité Central, "Desarrollemos la Guerra de Guerrillas!" pp. 2-4; Arce Borja and Talavera Sánchez, "La Entrevista del siglo," pp. 29-32.
37. Harding, "Antonion Díaz Martínez," and Colin Harding, "The Rise of Sendero Luminoso," in Rory Miller, ed., *Region and Class in Modern Peru* (Liverpool, England: University of Liverpool, 1986), pp. 179-207.
38. Terrill, *Mao: A Biography*, p. 151.
39. Mauceri, draft paper, pp. 220-221.
40. Arce Borja and Talavera Sánchez, "La Entrevista del siglo," p. 10. See also virtually any other Shining Path publication. Perhaps the most emphatic statement is in Comité Central, "Desarrollemos la Guerra de Guerrillas!" pp. 22-23.
41. Arce Borja and Talavera Sánchez, "La Entrevista del siglo," p. 13. Guzmán's statement here about the socialization role of violence is more detailed than other publications.
42. For example, Comité Central, "Desarrollemos la Guerra de Guerrillas!" p. 2.
43. Comité Central Partido Comunista del Peru, *Glória al Día de la Heroicidad!* (Lima: Ediciones Bandera Roja, 1987), p. 33.
44. Comité Central, "No votar!" pp. 7-8.
45. Comité Central, "Desarrollemos la Guerra de Guerrillas!" p. 10.
46. Raúl A. Wiener F., ed., *Guerra e ideología: Debate entre el PUM y Sendero* (Lima: Ediciones Amauta, 1990), is especially revealing on this point.
47. Scholars often define democracy in loftier terms, but ten apply the label to countries despite high levels of human rights violations and other limitations. See, for example, Larry Diamond, Juan J. Linz, and Seymour Martin Lipset, eds., *Democracy in Developing Countries: Latin America* (Boulder, CO: Lynne Rienner, 1989); and Terry Lynn Karl, "Dilemmas of Democratization in Latin America," *Comparative Politics*, 23:1, October 19920, pp. 1-22.
48. The Coordinadora Nacional de Derechos Humanos publishes regular reports of human rights violations by victim and perpetrator. See its *Boletín Informativo*, 5, November 1989-January 1990, for data for the year 1989.
49. Cynthia McClintock, "The Prospects for Democratic Consolidation in a 'Least Likely' Case: Peru," *Comparative Politics*, 22:2, January 1989, pp. 127-148.
50. The figure that is hard to calculate is the total eligible population, for various reasons. Figures are from Fernando Tuesta Soldevilla, "Cartilla de Información Electoral," mimeo, Lima, May 1990, and Cynthia McClintock, "Peru: Precarious Regimes, Authoritarian and Democratic," in Diamond, Linz and Lipset, eds., *Democracy in Developing Countries*, p. 346.
51. See McClintock, "Prospects for Democratic Consolidation," p. 140, for details about this survey item and application. The survey research firm, Datum, has provided me with results for the item through March 1990.
52. Contrast Datum survey, November 1987, for Lima and my own surveys in Huancayo and Virú, primarily among peasants.
53. For China, Matthew Soberg Shugart, "Patterns of Revolution," *Theory and Society*, 18, 1989, p. 254. For Peru, Inter-American Devlopment Bank, *Economic and Social Progress in Latin America, 1989* (Washington, DC: IADB, 1990), p. 412.
54. Skocpol, *States and Social Revolutions*, p. 148.

55. Abraham F. Lowenthal, ed., *The Peruvian Experiment* (Princeton, NJ: Princeton University Press, 1975), esp. pp. 302-349; and Cynthia McClintock and Abraham F. Lowenthal, eds., *The Peruvian Experiment Reconsidered* (Princeton, NJ: Princeton University Press, 1983).

56. McClintock, "Why Peasants Rebel," esp. pp. 58-72.

57. These results appear in my nonrandom surveys in various poor agricultural settings of Peru, Huancayo, and Trujillo. They are reported in McClintock, "Why Peasants Rebel," p. 62, and McClintock, "Prospects for Democratic Consolidation," p. 137.

58. Carlos Iván Degregori and José López Ricci, "Los hijos de la guerra: Jóvenes andinos y criollos frente a la violencia política," in DESCO, ed., *Tiempos de ira y amor* (Lima: DESCO, 1990), p. 201.

59. For commentary by scholars who knew Shining Path militants during the 1970s or early 1980s, see Gianotten, de Wit, and de Wit, "Impact of Sendero Luminoso," esp. pp. 189-192; Degregori and López Ricci, "Los hijos de la guerra," and Degregori's commentary to a journalist in Kathryn Leger, "Peru's Leftist Rebels Gain Ground," *Christian Science Monitor*, May 2, 1989, p. 3; and Henri Favre, "Violencia y descomposición social," *Debate*, 11:57, September/October 1989, pp. 31-33. For data on socioeconomic characteristics of Shining Path militants, see Dennis Chávez de Paz, *Juventud y terrorismo: Características sociales de los condenados por terrorismo y otros delitos* (Lima: Instituto de Estudios Peruanos, 1989).

60. A report on the attitudes and behavior of Shining Path militants in a Lima jail suggests the degree of psychological satisfaction that Shining Path ideology and discipline has given members. See Scott Malcomson, "On the Shining Path," *The Village Voice*, May 5, 1987, pp. 24-31.

61. Psychoanalyst César Rodríguez Rabanal, cited in Leger, "Peru's Leftist Rebels Gain Ground," p. 3.

62. Carlos Iván Degregori, cited in Leger, "Peru's Leftist Rebels Gain Ground," p. 3.

63. See recent Shining Path publications, including English publications such as Committee to Support the Revolution in Peru, "Stop U.S. Intervention in Peru!" Berkeley, CA, n.d.

64. Agency for International Development (AID), *U.S. Overseas Loans and Grants and Assistance from International Organizations: Obligations and Loan Authorizations, July 1, 1945-September 30, 1988* (Washington: Agency for International Development, 1989), esp. pp. 35 and 60. See also subsequent editions of this annual report by AID.

65. Ibid., p. 49.

66. Ibid., p. 60.

67. See the discussions of the aid package in Eugene Robinson, "U.S. Drug Effort Runs Into Latin Resistance," *Washington Post*, September 14, 1990, p. A22; Eugene Robinson, "U.S. Efforts Against Coca Run Into New Peruvian Drug Policy," *Washington Post*, November 4, 1990, p. A29.

68. U.S. Arms Control and Disarmament Agency, *World Military Expenditures and Arms Transfers 1989* (Washington: USGPO, 1990), p. 117, for 1984-1988 data. See other editions for other years.

69. Cynthia McClintock, "The War on Drugs: The Peruvian Case," *Journal of Interamerican Studies and World Affairs*, 30: 2 and 3, Summer/Fall 1988, pp. 127-142.

Conclusion: The View from the Windows

David Scott Palmer

As we try to understand the Shining Path (Sendero or SL) insurgency both in the Peruvian context and as an example of revolutionary movements in different parts of the world at different historical moments, the array of considerations that must be taken into account is daunting indeed. Each of the chapters in this book contributes to our understanding. Different authors with different backgrounds and experiences look at different parts of Sendero in different parts of the country and consider different facets of its internal and external relationships. It is not surprising that some of their conclusions differ also. Like the fable of the blind people touching various parts of an elephant and then describing what they felt, our individual analyses illuminate distinctive features of the SL phenomenon. Each conclusion, however valid for the particular component under study, may be in tension with or even seem to contradict another.

The following questions illustrate these tensions or contradictions.

On the one hand, did continuing high national turnout for elections imply that Sendero was not making headway in its quest for power through violent revolution? On the other hand, did high abstention rates and high levels of spoiled or blank ballots first in scores, then in hundreds of districts, indicate just the opposite?

Did Chuschi's decision to cast its lot with the government and request (and receive) a police post show that Shining Path leaders and cadres really did not understand how peasant communities work and what was required to get and to keep their support? Or was Pacucha's experience of keeping its options open because of Sendero's continuing ability to move about rural Andahuaylas and to be responsive to at least some of the communities' needs more representative? Or perhaps rural reality in terms of SL was best expressed by the willingness of thousands of small farmers in the Upper Huallaga valley (UHV) to support the organization as long as it could protect their livelihood and to go with the government when it could not?

Did Sendero work the interstices of Peruvian society to its advantage, or did it fail to distinguish between the different constellations of societal complexities to its disadvantage?

Was Sendero's selective terror the key mechanism that broke down resistance and generated support, or was it the factor that alienated the affected family or neighborhood or community and drove it into the arms of the government at the first opportunity?

Has Sendero's ideology represented a slowly and painstakingly derived formulation for Peru of the universal Marxist theory of history, or has it been a secular religion that attracted and held those disillusioned with society's alternatives? Or has Sendero ideology simply been a mask for a few to gain control over the many?

Has the large and diverse electoral left represented a bulwark against Shining Path or stepping-stones to it?

Did Sendero's cult of personality and pursuit of the one correct line (that is, Guzmán's) demonstrate its hydrocephalism and its vulnerability? Or did it facilitate the building and the maintenance of a strong organization likely to survive its founder?

Did the restoration and maintenance of procedural democracy until 1992 inhibit Sendero's advance or facilitate it?

Has SL's obsession with careful preparation at the periphery and with a long-term strategy for taking power given it greater capacity to succeed or has it made the organization increasingly irrelevant to the center?

Have government successes against the insurgents reflected institutional capacity or the ability of a few individuals? What about insurgent successes against the government?

Depending on where one is looking, and when, and at what level, and with what particular disciplinary or political lens, the answer to many of these questions, specifically addressed in one or more of the preceding chapters is...yes. This is why the concern for Peru's complexity is so important and why the Sendero phenomenon must be viewed from several windows. From the array of information and insights derived from this approach, often in tension and conflicting, sometimes reinforcing, what general conclusions can be drawn?

The observations to follow sort out these tensions in a summary, encapsulated form. They also take into account the significant developments of 1992-1994, which have enabled us to deepen our understanding of Sendero and its prospects.

1. Shining Path is fundamentally the creation of one person, Professor Abimael Guzmán Reynoso. Therefore, the movement was from the beginning indelibly stamped with his personality — dogmatic, uncompromising, totally committed, diligent, compulsive, dominating. At the same time this made the movement vulnerable should he be removed. Since Guzmán's unexpected capture in September 1992 Shining Path has simply not been the same. Incidents and levels of political violence have declined sharply — to about 50 percent of 1992 levels in 1993 and to about 25 percent in the first quarter of 1994 compared with the same period in 1993. National and regional organizations have lost focus and direction; many are scrambling just to survive. More recent Sendero operations frequently have appeared to lack the careful planning, precise implementation, and strategic genius that often characterized them before.

The initiative has shifted so dramatically to the government that Guzmán has been reduced, from prison, to desperate measures to try to regain contact with his compatriots. These included recognizing the authority of the Peruvian head of state and a call for peace negotiations. President Fujimori used Guzmán's gambit for his own purposes. One of these aims was to gain more popular support in order to secure a favorable vote for the new constitution in an October 1993 referendum. This was successful, though by a much closer margin than expected. Another goal was to drive a wedge between Sendero factions to further weaken the organization's capacity for action. The danger, given Guzmán's importance to the movement, was that it restored lines of communication that might permit SL's key ideologue and strategist to restore direction and purpose to the organization and revitalize its capacity for violence.

2. Sendero is derived from the university, not from the peasantry. This means that its perspective on the armed struggle is fundamentally intellectual and ideological rather than practical and developmental. Ideology has been Shining Path's greatest strength — the glue that binds its militants and justifies its violence — but also its greatest weakness — blinding SL leaders to the complexities of Peruvian society and the vast differences across its base. Clearly one ideological size does not fit all.

This became apparent with the large-scale defections of peasants and the poor as soon as Sendero's vulnerabilities became evident and as the central government began to reassert its control. Given a choice, most of SL's would-be beneficiaries have returned to the government's fold, however uncertain. The government sponsored *rondas campesinas* (self-defense forces) often proved to match more closely peasants' perceptions of their immediate needs than anything Sendero was prepared to offer. The *rondas'* success indicated the preference of the rural dweller to side with authority rather than rebel when given the opportunity. With the reduction of rural violence in 1993, tens of thousands of Peru's internal refugees — estimated to number from 200,000 to 600,000 — began to return to their villages and communities. The peasants' first goals were peace and security, and most believed that Shining Path's prescriptions would bring the opposite.

3. SL's provincial, that is, Ayacucho, origins gave the organization and its members a distinctive perspective on Peruvian reality that influenced both their interpretations of society and their approach toward trying to resolve its problems. That is to say, they tend to see Peruvian reality from a rural, provincial perspective; subordinate, marginalized, poor, with low state priority and response to their needs. Such an institutionalized and historically based lack of focus on Peru's periphery and its needs keeps central authority vulnerable in Peru.

The Fujimori government reversed several decentralization initiatives begun by his immediate predecessors. While the 1993 Constitution significantly reduced central government's involvement in the Peruvian economy, it also reconcentrated political authority in Lima. Municipalities soon had access to fewer resources and less control over those remaining. Social welfare projects, designed to offset some of the cumulative negative effects of years of economic erosion and reduction of government capacity, had ambitious goals and an expanding budget but were administered by a small staff, through FONCODES, run directly out of the Office of the President itself. Such an approach virtually guaranteed the continuation of a central authority, or top down, perspective on Peru's problems rather than a provincial, or bottom up one. The resulting lack of responsiveness to local needs gave Sendero continuing opportunities to work the periphery to its long-term benefit.

4. Shining Path's strategy and tactics are more important than the factual basis for the party's official interpretation of Peruvian reality. Therefore, ridiculing SL because it misunderstands Peruvian social and economic history misses the point. The destruction of Peru's status quo and how best to go about it is what Sendero is really about. Given the reverses experienced by Shining Path between late 1992 and early 1994, it is easy to lose sight of the leadership's obsession with strategy and tactics. Though forced into a defensive mode by government intelligence and military successes, Sendero leaders appear to have reformulated their strategy to make the most of their substantially reduced options. The government, by giving imprisoned leaders some room to maneuver for its own purposes, runs the risk of letting SL back into the political violence game.

5. For SL the struggle for power is fundamentally political, not military. Thus actions are usually taken more for their political impact (that is, how they affect the state or people's perceptions of it) rather than for their military effect. This is a main reason why the government's successes, particularly the capture of key leaders and cadre, witness protection, and a limited amnesty program, rather than annihilation via military operations, has been such a devastating blow for Shining Path. The guerrillas have lost the political and psychological advantage they enjoyed for so many years and which they worked diligently to build up even before launching their people's war in 1980. In this context the *rondas campesinas* fulfill a political as well as a defensive military

objective by helping local communities to organize themselves. Strengthening municipal governments would accomplish the same political purposes. However, the central government has moved in the opposite direction, probably because most local authorities elected in the most recent January 1993 local vote were not supporters of President Fujimori. Such a recentralization strategy could well be counterproductive and play directly into Shining Path's hands.

6. Sendero's ideology served first (before the late 1970s) to distinguish and legitimize the party within the Marxist intellectual tradition of the university and then (beginning in the late 1970s and early 1980s) as a credo — a secular religion — to attract and to give certainty and meaning to the lives of people at society's interstices who became its militants. The displaced seem to be SL's métier — Sendero gives them an identity. However, the guerrilla organization is much less sensitive to community needs and to the differences between neighboring villages. Shining Path's vision of the New Democracy is based on giving the displaced a "home," not on improving the status of those wanting to return to community and tradition.

This "dispossessed" segment of the Peruvian population has grown enormously in recent years, and will remain subject to extremist appeals as long as government authorities cannot respond to its needs. Some refer to this population as "Peru's time bomb." As of 1994, at least, neither the country's recently restored economic growth nor its social welfare program had begun to have any discernible impact on this significant group.

7. The larger political context — whether military or civilian, left or right — was that of the center and not of the periphery and was, therefore, largely irrelevant to SL's development. Sendero is a movement from the geographical, social, economic, and political periphery that took advantage of the relatively open natures of both the military regime and the return to procedural democracy, but did not develop either because of or in spite of them. From the beginning Sendero has set its own agenda, has operated on its own timetable, and has chosen its own targets. Shining Path's independence of action was quite dramatically affected by Peruvian government successes against the organization and its leadership in 1982 and 1983. These successes forced Sendero back to a defensive posture and to its original long-term strategy for gaining power. Indications of reduced capacity at the periphery included much

lower levels of local election disruption in January 1993 (about 20 local officials killed and 100 districts disrupted) than in November 1989 (over 120 local officials killed and 400 districts disrupted).

8. Shining Path uses terror to further its revolutionary ends but it is not a terrorist movement. The insurgency has rarely engaged in indiscriminate violence and should not be compared with Pol Pot and the Khmer Rouge in this regard. Nevertheless, Sendero's selective terror and intimidation has turned off large segments of potentially sympathetic populations. Some went along when the guerrillas had the capacity to enforce their threats. With an ascendant government between late 1992 and early 1994, however, such tactics worked against Shining Path's ultimate objectives. Part of SL's internal debate raging in 1994 concerned how to deal with the issue of selective terror.

9. Sendero's capacity and ability vary widely from command to command and from local area to local area, so its degree of success varies also. It makes many mistakes and has paid for them dearly, as in the loss or capture of key personnel or the loss of support of peasants or workers. The capture of SL leaders, cadre, and documents was a devastating blow that affected the organization's operations and capacity in most parts of the country. The usual interpretation, which was fostered by subsequently reduced levels of incidents and political violence was that the government had successfully seized the initiative to force Shining Path to the brink of extermination. Another interpretation, however, with a precedent in similar sharp declines in Sendero-sponsored political violence between 1985 and 1987, was that SL had once again beaten a strategic retreat and was concentrating on rebuilding for the future rather than putting at risk its remaining forces. Should the latter view prove correct, a new spiral of Sendero-provoked violence could be expected by 1995-1996.

10. While it often seemed that SL shunned publicity and media attention, in fact the organization used the media cleverly and selectively, as in journalist visits to Sendero prisoners or to the UHV when SL dominated most of that area. SL also let the media further the party's desired image of power, capacity, ubiquity, and imputed responsibility for most violent actions whether its own or not. It also has a taste for the symbolic and spectacular, as in Lima blackouts and the display of a giant hammer and sickle on Guzmán's birthday or at the very moment the Pope's plane was landing. The shift in momentum from

Shining Path to the government since Guzmán's capture forced the guerillas and their supporters to adopt a different strategy. The media changed its focus to emphasize Sendero's vulnerability and its limitations, contributing to the guerrillas' loss of the psychological edge they enjoyed before the roundup of Guzmán and key lieutenants. To push Shining Path's cause, the small but vocal international Revolutionary Communist Party (RCP) community in Europe and the United States came to the fore, particularly in academic and political activist circles. Sendero tracts still found their way into the hands of certain independent Peruvian reporters and analysts. The debate within Shining Path itself over whether or not to support Guzmán's call for peace showed up in letters and broadsides, as well as in clandestine Peruvian and open European editions of Sendero's newspaper, *El Diario*. While key dates and events continued to occasion surges in SL activity, with the reversal of fortune the organization could not as easily use the independent media to advance its own cause.

11. Peasants individually and collectively are rational actors who operate in a context in which their options are extremely limited and in which they tend to be the subordinates in most role relationships. They will accept and work with whoever seems to provide them with the best available options at the time. Ironically, precisely because the peasants were more important to Sendero than they were to central government, in attempting to organize and mobilize the peasantry the insurgents frequently alienated them. They tried to impose a new set of relationships with which peasants were extremely uncomfortable because they seemed to limit their options rather than to expand them. These new impositions tended to occur after SL had established its credibility in an area and as the insurgency attempted to build its own "generated organisms" or support bases. The Peruvian government's ability to severely disrupt both Sendero's national organization and regional committees from late 1992 to early 1994 substantially reduced SL operating capacity at the local level. Military and police authorities increased their contacts with peasant communities and cooperatives, particularly by fostering the establishment of *rondas campesinas*. These occurred primarily in the most conflicted parts of the rural highlands, the declared Emergency Zones (EMZs), where military officials were in charge. With the reassertion of central government presence and declining rates of rural violence, substantial return migration began in late

1993. While pockets of Sendero support remained in these zones, the bulk of the peasantry there clearly concluded that the government had come to represent the best option once again. It remained to be seen, however, at what point real improvement in poor rural dweller well-being would occur.

12. Shining Path had much greater difficulty establishing itself in areas where a strong network of national or regional political or social organizations already existed, especially reformist parties or the church, which had been able over time to respond to some of the needs of local residents, peasants, or workers. By adapting its strategy to be more responsive to local concerns and to be less violent, as in Ate Vitarte and along the Central Highway, SL could make some progress. But its tendency to turn the strike into an instrument that works against the workers' material interests, or the peasant organization into an entity not related to production needs, often served to alienate those whose support SL was trying to win. Recourse to selective terrorism or intimidation then became a principal tactic used to move forward. With the substantial reverses experienced by Shining Path in late 1992 and 1993, the guerrillas' timetable for advancing to victory through such grass-roots organization and selective intimidation was set back considerably. Internal Sendero documents acknowledged the move back to a "strategic defensive" posture after having achieved, by their definition, a "strategic equilibrium" vis à vis the government in 1991. The "strategic defensive" mode required, for the moment, concentration on rebuilding the organization, training new militants, and defending against government incursion rather than on expanding local support bases. Local organizations, for their part, which grew up as neighborhoods and communities, tried to meet basic needs in times of crisis and represented a new grass-roots force to be reckoned with.

13. The left's disarray at the national level was counterbalanced to a degree by its continued success at the regional and local levels and by the strength of these grass-roots organizations. The dynamism of local leaders and groups continued to pose multiple challenges for Sendero because they were more moderate and more attuned to their constituents' needs. Sendero's reverses gave the left new opportunities to deepen local ties in settings of reduced political violence. However, the Fujimori government's centralizing initiatives made meaningful local activity more difficult. The key to success probably could be found in harnessing and channeling the large informal sector

— both political and economic — which grew up in the vacuum created by years of economic crisis and erosion of political party capacity as well. The prospect of meaningful national elections in 1995 could help revitalize and possibly reunite the left and its social welfare oriented programs.

14. The vast majority of Peruvians continued to prefer democratic governments rather than either a military or a revolutionary alternative, in spite of democracy's poor record and long-term economic deterioration. At the same time most Peruvians found the national governments of the 1980s increasingly unresponsive to their needs. Nevertheless, they persisted in supporting an elected alternative rather than turning to one more extreme. The "non-party" solution of 1990, with Alberto Fujimori's victory, generated tough and controversial economic and political decisions that finally restored a sense of stability and increased security even as they worsened individual circumstances for many. Continuing high levels of public support in opinion polls indicated that the majority of Peruvians supported what President Fujimori was trying to do and the results he has achieved.

These high levels of public support, given President Fujimori's authoritarian initiatives, including the *autogolpe* and military rather than civilian court trials, could indicate an easy victory for the incumbent in the 1995 national elections. In fact, however, even though a majority of Peruvians continued in 1994 to support the Fujimori administration, a substantial portion simultaneously opposed the President's reelection. This may have been because such a possibility was unprecedented in Peru. Constitutions before 1993 did not allow for immediate reelection of a sitting president. One reason the 1993 Constitution passed by so narrow a margin (52 percent to 48 percent) was because of popular disquiet over the immediate reelection provision. Citizens and their preference for democracy brought Fujimori to power, supported his drastic and sometimes authoritarian measures as necessary to save the country, and now may well send him back to his university professorship!

15. The Peruvian government did not take Sendero's armed struggle seriously for some time. This gave SL additional months, even years, to organize and to improve its military capacity. The elected civilian government beginning in 1980 was the first since 1963-1968 and was neither predisposed to call on the military to help so soon after its departure nor willing to admit that any organization could be acting to overturn an open democracy.

16. When the government did respond beginning in October 1981 with specialized police forces and in December 1982 with the military, it tended to use massive armed force as its major instrument rather than selective force combined with economic assistance. Sendero was beaten back in Ayacucho but did not lose its infrastructure or its key leadership, while the government committed many abuses in the course of restoring a tenuous control under military auspices, periodically punctuated by embarrassing SL actions against it.

17. Substantial government economic assistance to the main geographical regions of Shining Path activities was delayed by several years (as late as 1984 a military commander in charge of the Ayacucho emergency zone was removed from his post for complaining about the lack of promised economic aid). Economic assistance arrived during the first two years of the García administration and coincided with a regeneration of rural economic growth, decline of incidents and deaths in the area, and return migration. The economic crisis that began in late 1987 halted and then reversed these promising developments. The problems were so severe by 1990 that the Peruvian government could not even support basic services, much less continue its rural development program. Sendero activities and political violence increased, as did military and police human rights abuses. Economic shock measures further reduced government capacity even as they increased human misery in Peru. Although the drastic economic initiatives began to stabilize the economy in 1991 and 1992 and then to restore economic growth in 1993 in some sectors, new government resources were by and large still not available to rural Peru, even by early 1994.

In the absence of government assistance, many Peruvians responded by taking matters into their own hands — self-help organized by neighborhoods, soup kitchens provisioned by international humanitarian aid, local NGO assistance to new migrants and international refugees, and self-defense units sprang up to meet local needs. Rather than fall into Sendero's hands, most Peruvians bereft of government assistance took matters into their own. While government aid would have eased their problems, millions learned to cope without. Many of these millions supported President Fujimori; however, they were not indebted to him for specific services rendered or assistance provided.

18. In pursuing the war, government agencies sometimes did not act effectively on their own intelligence (for example, the March 1982 raid on the Ayacucho prison), and sometimes allowed institutional rivalries to interfere with effective actions (as between different intelligence-gathering agencies and between the police and military with Uchiza police station attack of March 1989). This is very likely a combination of the bureaucratic politics that affect government and its activities everywhere; of better career advancement possibilities in the capital than in the countryside, so that is where the better officers gravitate; of a continuing tendency to overestimate the ability of the center to deal with a problem at the periphery; and of the military's continuing institutional orientation, in terms of personnel, equipment, and strategy, on the Ecuador and Chile borders. Given the severity of the domestic security crisis in 1990 and 1991, significant shifts occurred. President Fujimori undertook a significant effort, quite successfully, to defuse tensions with Ecuador and Chile, which included state visits and a variety of bilateral agreements. By 1992, military forces began to be shifted from Peru's borders to be available for fighting the insurgency. In addition, adjustments in military field deployment requirements occurred at about the same time so that natives of particular areas could serve in their home provinces. Such adjustments substantially improved quality, morale, and intelligence-gathering capacity.

In another major shift, the Ministry of the Interior, which oversees Peru's police forces, created a specialized counterintelligence service, DIRCOTE, and gave it the autonomy necessary to pursue its counter-Sendero activities. This small organization (fewer than one hundred individuals) did the tedious intelligence-gathering work, totally out of the limelight, which enabled it to capture Guzmán, computer records, and many other leaders. With the crisis seen as past, however, government "politics as usual" reverted to form. Political criteria became more important, especially the issue of central control. DIRCOTE, a model of successful counterintelligence activity, saw its commander transferred, a reduction in its independence and scope, and other key officers reassigned to the country's National Intelligence Service (SIN). Social welfare budgets increased sharply in 1993-1994, but control remained centralized and disbursement slow. Increasing concern was also expressed over military corruption in drug-trafficking activities as the political violence threat receded and control was reasserted over coca leaf and cocaine paste producing regions — such as the UHV and the Apurímac Valley — formerly heavily influenced by Sendero.

19. Both Shining Path and the government have committed gross human rights abuses. SL views selective terror as demonstrating its power and inducing acquiescence and support. The government view is similar, but it is often much less selective. (In fact, Amnesty International concluded that the Peruvian government had the worst human rights record in the world in 1987 through 1991 in terms of "disappearances.") Government is supposed to uphold a higher standard as part of its claim to authority and legitimacy, especially in the context of a return to democracy. However, many of its own protectors, police and military, display a lack of faith in the system. In part this was because Sendero had a history of effective use of the legal process to get its people off. In part it was because the military forces did not feel they had been adequately supported at critical junctures by civilian authorities (for example, the police/military's response to the prison riots of June 1986) and in part it was because major portions of the central government, including much of the military, did not consider citizens of the periphery to be their equals. The immediate provocation for the April 1992 *autogolpe* was a judge's release of over two hundred convicted Shining Path militants for "good behavior," most of whom immediately resumed their guerrilla activities. President Fujimori's surprise move was strongly supported by the military; in fact, some leaked documents suggested that the armed forces actually had induced the *autogolpe*. In the weeks following, various government decrees sharply increased penalties for terrorism, from a maximum of twenty years to a life term without parole, and shifted jurisdiction for alleged terrorism from civilian to military courts.

Human rights violations mounted over succeeding months, including the chilling National Teachers University (La Cantuta) case in July 1992 in which army personnel abducted, tortured, and killed eight students and their professor. This case only came to light in November 1993 after detailed information on how to find the clandestine mass grave was leaked to a Lima newsweekly with close ties to the military. The pro-Fujimori majority in the congress elected in November 1992 violated the procedures for civil trial in the just-approved 1993 Constitution they themselves had drafted by legislating military court trials for the servicemen accused in the La Cantuta case. Convictions were forthcoming, but for lesser terms than those imposed on convicted Sendero terrorists and absolving any possible senior officer complicity.

At least part of the marked reduction in government human rights abuses in 1993 could be attributed to the shift in jurisdiction of terrorism cases to military courts and the efficient dispatch thereof — usually with guilty verdicts and long prison terms. However, the international human rights community and the U.S. government still had grave doubts about procedure and due process in Peru's administration of justice. Most Peruvians, nevertheless, felt that their internal terrorist crisis was so severe and the civilian court system so corroded that the drastic measures adopted were both justified and effective in giving them an increased measure of personal and collective security.

20. Racism (the view that one's own race is superior and has the right to rule others and the policy of enforcing that asserted right) may well be a key factor in the continuing inappropriate response of many of those in government to the emergence and development of the Sendero phenomenon.

> a. Many did not take the situation very seriously: "How can these people be capable of organizing against and attacking the state?"

> b. Government tends to meet the needs of the urban (mostly Spanish) population before the rural (mostly Indian) population.

> c. Police and military often use brutal force against peasants, mostly Indian.

> d. Government is slow to provide economic resources to assist these same people.

SL seems to have sharpened the historic differences between Peruvians that, until the 1980s, seemed to be slowly breaking down through economic growth, urbanization, migration, and education. Whether Shining Path returns in force or not, the racist legacy remains and will be very difficult to overcome. The pattern goes back to the Spanish conquest and has tended to be reinforced since independence by the rules and procedures of a central government dominated by non-Indian elites. Decentralizing initiatives of the 1980s — including regional legislatures which were to have been given substantial resources to be able to operate effectively, and municipal governments with new taxing power — were reversed by the 1993 Constitution and by Fujimori administration decrees. Restoration of peace and stability, real economic growth, effective distribution of social welfare, and the deepening of mass democracy should break down Peru's racist legacy over time. There is no doubt, however, that this will be a long and difficult process.

21. The center did not respond effectively when it had the chance. The continuing economic crisis then made it impossible to respond. The economic shock measures of the Fujimori government may well restore the economy in due course, but they ensured through 1993 that the focus was not on economic assistance but rather on a military response to Shining Path. This gave SL the opportunity to try to regain its organizational and operational initiative and to move forward with its long-term strategy to overthrow the established government of Peru. The *autogolpe* played into SL's hands by cutting off many institutionalized links between citizen and system and by delaying the restoration of economic growth by well over a year. However, DIRCOTE's intelligence coup turned the tide of the Sendero advance, which has been running out ever since. Fujimori's authoritarian approach to dealing with Peru's multiple crises proved by most accounts to be a success in the short run. Political violence declined, Shining Path was put on the defensive, weakened, and divided. Economic growth in some sectors finally returned in 1993 and was generally expected to be fuller and broader based in 1994 and 1995. Privatization and the fiscal rationalization of government moved forward, and new foreign investment increased sharply.

However, the long run was much more problematic. The political recentralization embodied in the 1993 Constitution reduced local government capacity to control issues most important to neighborhoods and communities as well as limited the role of the traditional parties to channel popular concerns within the system. Desperately needed social welfare programs had yet to be effectively implemented and, due to excessive centralized control, offered no guarantee that they would respond appropriately to the wide variety of local needs.

President Fujimori deserved credit for bringing Peru back from the brink of catastrophe, but could now be accused of trying to turn this success into a long-term authoritarian project for personal political benefit. Sendero had taken severe and multiple blows, and was at least temporarily marginalized as a major force in Peru's complex social-political-economic matrix. Even so, Shining Path has come back before and could well do so again.

Bibliography

Allen, Catherine J. *The Hold That Life Has: Coca and Cultural Identity in an Andean Community*. Washington: Smithsonian Institution Press, 1988.

Americas Watch (AW). *Peru Under Fire: Human Rights Since the Return to Democracy*. Human Rights Watch Books. New Haven: Yale University Press, 1992.

———. "Una guerra desesperada: Los derechos humanos en el Perú después de una década de democracia y violencia." Lima: Comisión Andina de Juristas, 1990.

———. *In Desperate Straits: Human Rights in Peru After a Decade of Democracy and Insurgency*. New York: AW, 1990.

Ames, Rolando (and others). *Informe al Congreso sobre los sucesos de los penales*. Lima: OCISA, 1988.

Amnesty International (AI). *Peru: Violations of Human Rights in the Emergency Zones*. New York: AI, August 1988.

———. *Caught Between Two Fires*. New York: AI, November 1986.

Anderson, James. *Sendero Luminoso: A New Revolutionary Model?* London: Institute for the Study of Terrorism, 1987.

Ansión, Juan, ed. *Pistacos: De verdugos a sacaojos*. Lima: Tarea, 1989.

Arce Borja, Luis, ed. *Guerra Popular en el Perú: El Pensamiento Gonzalo*. Brussels: Edición del autor, June 1989.

———, and Janet Talavera Sánchez. "La entrevista del siglo: El presidente Gonzalo rompe el silencio." *El Diario*, July 24, 1988, pp. 2-73.

Arguedas, José María. *El zorro de arriba y el zorro de abajo*. Lima: Editorial Horizonte, 1983.

Ash, Robert B. "The Rural Struggle in Latin America: The Case of Peru and Sendero." *RUSI — Journal of the Royal United Services Institute for Defense Studies*, 130:2, June 1985, pp. 39-42.

Béjar, Héctor. *Las guerrillas de 1965: Balance y perspectiva.* Lima: Ediciones PEISA, 1973.

Bennett, Philip. "Peru: Corner of the Dead." *Atlantic*, May 1984, pp. 28-33.

Berg, Ronald H. "Retribution and Resurrection: The Politics of Sendero Luminoso in Peru." Paper presented to the American Anthropological Association, Phoenix, AZ, November 1988.

———. "Explaining Sendero Luminoso." Proceedings from the Area Studies Symposium, *The Legitimacy of Political Violence? The Case of Latin America.* Occasional Papers Series 22, Amherst: University of Massachusetts, 1988, pp. 1-14.

———. "Sendero Luminoso and the Peasantry of Andahuaylas." *Journal of Interamerican Studies and World Affairs*, 28:4, Winter 1986-1987, pp. 165-196.

———. "The Effects of Return Migration on a Highland Peruvian Community." Ph.D. Dissertation in Anthropology, Ann Arbor: University of Michigan, 1984.

Biondi, Juan, and Eduardo Zapata. *El discurso de Sendero Luminoso: Contratexto educativa.* Lima: Consejo Nacional de Ciencia y Tecnología, 1989.

Blasier, Cole. "Social Revolution: Origins in Mexico, Bolivia, and Cuba." In Roland E. Bonachea and Nelson P. Valdés, eds., *Cuba in Revolution*, New York: Doubleday, 1972, pp. 18-49.

Bonner, Raymond. "A Reporter at Large: Peru's War." *The New Yorker*, January 4, 1988, pp. 31-58.

Boris, Jean Pierre, and Jan Theilen. "Testimonio de un Senderista." *Debate*, 33, July 1985, pp. 33-42.

Burgler, R. A. *The Eyes of the Pineapple: Revolutionary Intellectuals and Terror in Democratic Kampuchea.* Saarbrucken: Breitenbach Verlag, 1990.

Chávez de Paz, Dennis. *Juventud y terrorismo: Características sociales de los condenados por terrorismo y otros delitos.* Lima: Instituto de Estudios Peruanos, 1989.

Chen, Yung-fa. *Making Revolution: The Communist Movement in Eastern and Central China, 1937-1945.* Berkeley: University of California Press, 1980.

Comisión Investigadora de Grupos Paramilitares. *Una lucha cívica contra la impunidad.* Lima: Manuel Piqueras, 1990.

Committee on Governmental Affairs, United States Senate. *U.S. Government Anti-Narcotics Activities in the Andean Region of South America.* Hearings before the Permanent Subcommittee on Investigations. 101 Cong., 1st sess., September 26, 27, 29, 1989, Washington: U.S. Government Printing Office (USGPO), 1989.

Conley, Michael C. *The Communist Insurgent Infrastructure in South Vietnam: A Study of Organization and Strategy.* Washington, D.C.: The American University, 1966.

Cumings, Bruce. "Interest and Ideology in the Study of Agrarian Politics." *Politics and Society*, 10:4, December 1981, pp. 467-495.

Degregori, Carlos Iván. "A Dwarf Star." *NACLA Report on the Americas*, 24:4, December 1990-January 1991, pp. 10-16.

————. *Ayacucho 1969-1979: El surgimiento de Sendero Luminoso: Del movimiento por las gratuidad de la enseñanza al inicio de la lucha armada.* Lima: Instituto de Estudios Peruanos, 1990.

————. *Que difícil es ser Dios: Ideología y violencia política en Sendero Luminoso.* Lima: El Zorro de Abajo Ediciones, 1989.

————. "Del mito de Incarrí al mito del progreso: Poblaciones andinas, cultura e identidad nacional." *Socialismo y Participación*, 36, December 1986, pp. 49-56.

————. *Sendero Luminoso: Los hondos y mortales desencuentros y lucha armada y utopia autoritaria.* Lima: Instituto de Estudios Peruanos, 1986.

————. *Ayacucho, raices de una crisis.* Lima: Instituto de Estudios Rurales José María Arguedes, 1986.

————, and José López Ricci, "Los hijos de la guerra: Jovenes andinos y criollos frente a la violencia política." In Centro de Estudios y Promoción del Desarrollo (DESCO), eds., *Tiempos de ira y amor*, Lima: DESCO, 1990.

De la Riva, Carlos. *Donde nace la aurora.* Arequipa, 1961.

Department of State. "Peru," in *Country Reports on Human Rights Practices for 1983...1990* (inclusive). Reports submitted to the Committee on Foreign Affairs, U.S. House of Representatives and the Committee on Foreign Relations, U.S. Senate. Joint Committee Print. Washington: United States Government Printing Office (USGPO), February 1984...1991.

Desai, Raj, and Harry Eckstein. "Insurgency: The Transformation of Peasant Rebellion." *World Politics*, 17:4, July 1990, pp. 441-465.

DESCO. *Violencia política en el Perú, 1980-1988*, 2 vols. Lima: DESCO, 1989.

Díaz Martínez, Antonio. *Ayacucho: Hambre y esperanza.* Ayacucho: Waman Puma, 1969.

————. *China, La revolución agraria.* Lima: Mosca Azul, 1978.

————. "Ayacucho y las comunidades del hambre." *América Indígena*, 30, April 1970, pp. 307-320.

Dix, Robert H. "Why Revolutions Succeed and Fail." *Polity*, 16:3, Spring 1984, pp. 423-446.

Dollfus, Olivier. *El reto del espacio andino.* Lima: Instituto de Estudios Peruanos, 1981.

Equren, Fernando et al., eds. *Perú: El problema agrario en debate.* Lima: Universidad Nacional de San Cristóbal de Huamanga, 1988.

Farhi, Farideh. "State Disintegration and Urban-Based Revolutionary Crisis: A Comparative Analysis of Iran and Nicaragua." *Comparative Political Studies*, 21:2, July 1988, pp. 231-256.

Farnsworth, Elizabeth. "Peru: A Nation in Crisis." *World Policy Journal*, 5, Fall 1988, pp. 725-746.

Favre, Henri. "Sentier Lumineaux et Horizons Obscurs." *Problèmes D'Amérique Latine*, 72, 1984, pp. 3-27, also published as "Peru: Sendero Luminoso y horizontes ocultos." *Quehacer*, 31-32, September-October 1984, pp. 25-35.

Flores Galindo, Alberto. *Buscando un Inca: Identidad y utopia en los Andes*. Lima: Instituto de Apoyo Agrario, 1987.

———, and Nelson Manrique. *Violencia y campesinado*. Lima: Instituto de Apoyo Agrario, 1986.

García Sayán, Diego. *Tomas de tierras en el Perú*. Lima: DESCO, 1982.

———, ed. *Narcotráfico: Realidades y alternativas*. Lima: Comisión Andina de Juristas (CAJ), 1990.

———, ed. *Coca, cocaína y narcotráfico: Laberinto en los Andes*. Lima: CAJ, 1989.

———, ed. *Democracia y violencia en el Perú*. Lima: Centro Peruano de Estudios Internationales-CEPEI, 1988.

General Accounting Office (GAO). *The Drug War: U.S. Programs in Peru Face Serious Obstacles*. GAO/NSIAD-92-36. Washington: GAO, October 1991.

Gianotten, Vera, Ton de Wit, and Hans de Wit. "The Impact of Sendero Luminoso on Regional and National Politics in Peru," in David Slater, ed., *New Social Movements and the State in Latin America*. Amsterdam: Centre for Latin American Research and Documentation-CEDLA, 1985, pp. 171-202.

Goldfrank, Walter L. "Theories of Revolution and Revolution Without Theory: The Case of Mexico." *Theory and Society*, 7: 1-2, January-March 1979, pp. 135-165.

Goldstone, Jack A. "Theories of Revolution: The Third Generation." *World Politics*, 32:3, April 1981, pp. 425-453.

Gonzales de Oliarte, Efraín. *Economía de la comunidad campesina: Aproximación regional*. Lima: Instituto de Estudios Peruanos, 1984.

———. *Economías regionales del Perú*. Lima: Instituto de Estudios Peruanos, 1982.

González, Raúl. "Las armas de un general." *Quehacer*, 62, December 1989-January 1990, pp. 38-43.

———, "Coca y subversión en el Huallaga." *Quehacer*, 48, September-October 1987, pp. 59-72.

———. "Sendero vs. MRTA." *Quehacer*, 46, April-May 1987, pp. 47-53.

———. "De como Lumbreras entiende al Perú de Sendero." *Quehacer*, 42, August-September 1986, pp. 34-43.

——. "Gonzalo's Thought, Belaúnde's Answer." *NACLA Report on the Americas*, 20:3, June 1986, pp. 34-36.

——. "Puno: El corredor senderista." *Quehacer*, 39, February-March 1986, pp. 49-58.

——. "Las conferencias senderistas." *Quehacer*, 30, July- August 1984, pp. 19-20.

——. "Ayacucho: Por los Caminos de Sendero." *Quehacer*, 19, September-October 1982, pp. 36-79.

Goodwin, Jeff, and Theda Skocpol. "Explaining Revolutions in the Contemporary Third World." *Politics and Society*, 17:4, December 1989, pp. 489-509.

Gorriti Ellenbogen, Gustavo. "The War of the Philosopher-King." *The New Republic*, June 18, 1990, pp. 15-22.

——. *Sendero: Historia de la guerra milenaria en el Perú*, vol. 1. Lima: Apoyo, 1990.

Granados, Manuel Jesús. "Ideología del PCP Sendero Luminoso." *Socialismo y Participación*, 37, March 1987.

——. "La conducta política: Un caso particular." Senior thesis, Universidad de San Cristóbal de Huamanga, 1981.

Harding, Colin J. "Antonio Díaz Martínez and the Ideology of Sendero Luminoso." *Bulletin of Latin American Research*, 7:1, 1987, pp. 65-73.

——. "The Rise of Sendero Luminoso." In Rory Miller, ed., *Region and Class in Modern Peru*. Institute of Latin American Studies Monograph 14. Liverpool: University of Liverpool, 1986, pp. 179-207.

Hartford, Kathleen, and Steven M. Goldstein, eds. *Single Sparks: China's Rural Revolutions*. Armonk, NY: M. E. Sharpe, 1989.

Hawes, Gary. "Theories of Peasant Revolution: A Critique and Contribution from the Philippines." *World Politics*, 17:2, January 1990, pp. 261-298.

Hazelton, William A., and Sandra Woy-Hazelton. "Terrorism and the Marxist Left: Peru's Struggle Against Sendero Luminoso." *Terrorism*, 11, pp. 471-490.

——. "The Influence of Sendero Luminoso After One Decade of Insurgency." Paper presented to the International Studies Association, London, March-April 1989.

Hemming, John. *The Conquest of the Incas*. London: Penguin, 1983.

Hudson, Rex A., ed., *Peru: A Country Study*. Library of Congress, Federal Research Division. Washington: USGPO, 1992.

Huntington, Samuel P. *Political Order in Changing Societies*. New Haven, CT: Yale University Press, 1968.

Husson, Patrick. "Guerre indienne et revolte paysanne dans la province de Huanta [Peru]." Theses Université, Paris IV, Sorbonne, 1983.

Ideología, Revista de Ciéncias Sociales. Ayacucho: Universidad de Huamanga, Instituto de Estudios Regionales José María Arguedas, 1987.

Instituto de Defensa Legal (IDL). *Perú 1989: En la espiral de violencia.* Lima: IDL, 1990.

———. *Perú 1990: La opportunidad perdida.* Lima: IDL, 1991.

Instituto Democracia y Socialismo (IDS). *Perú 1990: Encrucijada.* Lima: IDS, 1990.

Instituto Geográfico Nacional (IGN). *Atlas del Perú.* Lima: IGN, 1989.

Instituto Nacional de Estadística (INE). *Perú: Compendio Estadístico 1987.* Lima: INE, 1988.

Inter-Church Committee on Human Rights in Latin America (ICCHRLA). *1989 Annual Report on the Human Rights Situation in Peru.* Toronto: ICCHRLA, 1990.

Isbell, Billie Jean. "The Texts and Contexts of Terror in Peru." Paper presented to the Research Conference, Violence and Democracy in Colombia and Peru. New York: Columbia University and New York University National Resource Center Consortium, December 1988.

———. "An Anthropological Dialogue with Violence." *COSP Newsletter*, 5:4, 1986, pp. 2-8.

———. "Images of Domination and Rebellion in Highland Peru." *Social Education*, February 1985, pp. 119-121.

———. *To Defend Ourselves*, 2d edition, Prospect Heights, IL: Waveland Press, 1985.

———. *To Defend Ourselves: Ecology and Ritual in an Andean Village.* Austin: University of Texas Press, 1978.

———, and Fredy Roncalla. "The Ontogenesis of Metaphor: Riddle Games Among Quechua Speakers Seen as Cognitive Discovery Procedures." *Journal of Latin American Lore*, 3:1, 1977, pp. 19-49.

Jenkins, J. Craig. "Why Do Peasants Rebel? Structural and Historical Theories of Modern Peasant Rebellions." *American Journal of Sociology*, 88:3, November 1982, pp. 487-514.

Karl, Terry Lynn. "Dilemmas of Democratization in Latin America." *Comparative Politics*, 23:1, October 1990, pp. 1-22.

Lam, Truong Buu. *Resistance, Rebellion, Revolution: Popular Movements in Vietnamese History.* Singapore: Institute of Southeast Asian Studies, 1984.

Lázaro, Juan. "Democracy and Human Rights Violations in Peru." Paper presented at the International Studies Association Meeting, London, March-April 1989.

León, Frederico R., and Ramiro Castro de la Mata, eds., *Pasta básica de cocaína: Un estudio multidisciplinario.* Lima: Centro de Información y Educación para la Prevención del Abuso de Drogas (CEDRO), 1989.

Letts, Ricardo. *La izquierda peruana: Organizaciones y tendencias.* Lima: Mozca Azul, 1981.

Lopes Ahedo, Carlos A. *Apuntes para una historia de la lucha por la tierra en Puno durante el Siglo XX: Tierra, la violencia y la paz.* Lima: Instituto de Apoyo Agrario, 1988.

Lynch, Nicolás. *Los jóvenes rojos de San Marcos: El radicalismo universitario de los años setenta.* Lima: El Zorro de Abajo, 1990.

MacGregor, Felipe, and Laura Madalengoitia, eds. *Violencia y paz en el Perú hoy.* Lima: Asociación Peruana de Estudio e Investigaciones para la Paz-APEP and the Fundación Friedrich Ebert, 1985.

———, José Luis Rouillón, and Marcia Rubio, eds. *Siete ensayos sobre violencia en el Perú.* Lima: APEP and the Fundación Friedrich Ebert, 1987.

Mallon, Florencia E. "Nationalist and Antistate Coalitions in the War of the Pacific: Junín and Cajamarca, 1879-1902." In Steve J. Stern, ed., *Resistance, Rebellion, and Consciousness in the Andean Peasant World, 18th to 20th Centuries.* Madison: University of Wisconsin Press, 1987, pp. 232-280.

———. *The Defense of Community in Peru's Central Highlands: Peasant Struggle and Capitalist Transition, 1880-1940.* Princeton, NJ: Princeton University Press, 1983.

Manrique, Nelson. "La década de la violencia." *Márgenes,* 3: 5-6 December 1989, pp. 137-182.

———. "Sierra Central: La batalla decisiva," *Quehacer,* 60, August-September 1989, pp. 63-71.

———. *Yawar Mayu: Sociedades terratenientes serranas, 1879-1910.* Lima: Instituto Francés de Estudios Andinos and DESCO, 1988.

———. *Las Guerrillas indígenas en la guerra con Chile.* Lima: Centro de Investigación y Capitación and Editora Ital Perú, 1981.

Mariátegui, José Carlos. *Siete ensayos de interpretación de la realided peruana.* Lima: Amauta, 1959.

Marks, Thomas A. "Peru's Fatal Distraction." *Soldier of Fortune,* 15:7, July 1990, 30-33.

———. "Terrorism vs. Terror — The Case of Peru." *Counterterrorism and Security,* 2:2, May-June 1990, pp. 26-33.

———. "The Guerrilla Myth." *Soldier of Fortune,* 15:5, May 1990, pp. 56-59, 65-68.

———. "Corner of the Dead." *Soldier of Fortune,* 15:3, March 1990, pp. 44-51.

Masterson, Daniel M. *Militarism and Politics in Latin America: Peru from Sánchez Cerro to Sendero Luminoso.* New York: Greenwood Press, 1991.

Matos Mar, José. *Desborde popular y crisis del estado: El nuevo rostro del Perú en la década de 1980.* Perú Problema 21. Lima: Instituto de Estudios Peruanos, 1984.

——— et al. *Dominación y cambio en el Perú rural.* Lima: Instituto de Estudios Peruanos, 1968.

Mauceri, Philip. *Militares: Insurgencia y democratización en el Perú, 1980-1988.* Lima: Instituto de Estudios Peruanos, 1989.

Mayer, Enrique and Marisol de la Cadena. *Cooperación y conflicto en la comunidad andina: Zonas de producción y organización social.* Lima: Instituto de Estudios Peruanos, 1989.

McClintock, Cynthia. "Peru: Precarious Regimes, Authoritarian and Democratic," in Larry Diamond, Juan J. Linz and Seymour Martin Lipset, eds., *Democracy in Developing Countries: Latin America.* Boulder, CO: Lynne Rienner, 1989, pp. 335-385.

———. "Peru's Sendero Luminoso Rebellion: Origins and Trajectory," in Susan Eckstein, ed., *Power and Popular Protest: Latin American Social Movements.* Berkeley: University of California Press, 1989, pp. 61-101.

———. "The War on Drugs: The Peruvian Case." *Journal of Interamerican Studies and World Affairs,* 30:2 and 3, Summer/Fall 1988, pp. 127-142.

———. "Why Peru's Alan García is a Man on the Move." *LASA Forum,* 16: 4, Winter 1986, pp. 9-12.

———. "Why Peasants Rebel: The Case of Peru's Sendero Luminoso." *World Politics,* 37:1, October 1984, pp. 48-84

———. "Sendero Luminoso: Peru's Maoist Guerrillas." *Problems of Communism,* 32, September-October 1983, pp. 19-34.

———, and Abraham Lowenthal. *The Peruvian Experiment Reconsidered.* Princeton, NJ: Princeton University Press, 1983.

McCormick, Gordon H. *The Shining Path and Peruvian Terrorism.* Santa Monica, CA: Rand Corporation, 1987.

Melgar Bao, Ricardo. "Las guerrillas de Sendero y la ilusión andina del poder," paper presented at the Latin American Studies Association Meetings, Albuquerque, NM, April 1985.

Midlarsky, Manus I., and Kenneth Roberts. "Class, State and Revolution in Central America." *Journal of Conflict Resolution,* 29, June 1985, pp. 163-193.

Molnar, Andrew R., et al. *Human Factors Considerations of Undergrounds in Insurgencies.* Washington: American University, 1965.

Montoya, Rodrigo. *Capitalismo y neo-capitalismo en el Perú.* Lima: Mosca Azul, 1980.

Movimiento Revolucionario Internacionalista (MRI). *Declaración del Movimiento Revolucionario Internacionalista.* London, 1984.

———. *A World to Win.* London, 1985.

Nieto, Jorge. *La izquierda y la democracia en el Perú, 1975-1980.* Lima: DESCO, 1983.

Noel Moral, Roberto Clemente. *Ayacucho: Testimonio de un soldado.* Lima: Publinor, 1989.

Oviedo, Carlos. *Prensa y subversión: Una lectura de la violencia en el Perú.* Lima: Mass Comunicaciones, 1989.

Paige, Jeffrey M. *Agrarian Revolution: Social Movements and Export Agriculture in the Underdeveloped World.* New York: The Free Press, 1975.

Palmer, David Scott. "The Revolutionary Terrorism of Peru's Shining Path." Paper prepared for the Ford Foundation-sponsored project, "Terrorism in Context," January 1990.

———. "Terrorism as a Revolutionary Strategy: Peru's Sendero Luminoso." In Barry Rubin, ed., *The Politics of Terrorism: Terror as a State and Revolutionary Strategy.* Washington: The Johns Hopkins University, 1988, pp. 129-152.

———. "Rebellion in Rural Peru: The Origins and Evolution of Sendero Luminoso." *Comparative Politics*, 18:2, January 1986, pp. 127-146.

———. "Peru." In Robert Wesson, ed., *Yearbook of International Communist Affairs.* Stanford, CA: Hoover Institution Press, 1983, pp. 121-123.

———. *"Revolution From Above": Military Government and Popular Participation in Peru, 1968-1972.* Latin American Studies Program Dissertation Series 47, Ithaca, NY: Cornell University, 1973.

Palomino, Abdón. "Movimiento campesino de 1978 y reforma agraria en Andahuaylas." *Allpanchis* (Cuzco), 11-12, 1978, pp. 187-211.

Pareja Pflucker, Piedad. *Evaluación de las elecciones municipales de 1989.* Lima: Instituto Nacional de Planificación, 1990.

———. *Terrorismo y sindicalismo en Ayacucho, 1980.* Lima: Empresa Editora Ital Perú S.A., 1981.

———, and Eric Torres Mendoza. *Municipios y terrorismo.* Lima: Instituto de Estudios Peruanos, 1989.

Partido Comunista del Perú (Sendero Luminoso). *Elecciones, no, guerra popular, sí.* Lima(?): Ediciones Bandera Roja, 1990.

———. *Bases de discusión*, Lima(?): Ediciones Bandera Roja, 1987. (Same document was published in five successive "special issues" of *El Diario*, from January 3 to January 8, 1988.)

———. *¡Gloria al Día de la Heroicidad!* Lima: Ediciones Bandera Roja, 1987.

———. *Desarrollar la guerra popular sirviendo a la revolución mundial.* Lima(?): Ediciones Bandera Roja, 1986.

———. *¡No Votar! Sino, ¡Generalizar la Guerra de Guerrillas para conquistar el poder para el pueblo!* Lima(?): Ediciones Bandera Roja, February, 1985.

———. *Desarollemos la Guerra de Guerrillas.* Lima(?): Ediciones Bandera Roja, 1981.

Pedraglio, Santiago. *Armas para la paz*. Lima: Instituto de Defensa Legal, 1990.

Peru. Instituto Nacional de Estadística (INE). *Censo nacional Agropecuario, II: Departamento de Apurímac*, Lima: INE 1972.

———. *Censos nacionales VIII de Población, III de Vivienda. 12 de julio de 1981. Resultados Definitivos*. Lima: INE, 1984.

Peru. Ministerio de Agricultura. *Estudio socio-económico de la provincia de Andahuaylas*, Lima: Dirección de Comunidades, Ministerio de Agricultura, 1970.

Peru. Senado. Comité Especial sobre las Causes de la Violencia y las Alternativas de Pacificación en el Perú. *Violencia y Pacificación*. Lima: DESCO and Comisión Andina de Juristas, 1989.

Peruvian Constitution of 1979. Lima: Diario El Peruano, July 1979.

Pike, Douglas. *Viet Cong: The Organization and Techniques of the National Liberation Front of South Vietnam*. Cambridge: M.I.T. Press, 1966.

Portocarrero, Gonzalo, and Patricia Oliart, *El Perú desde la escuela*. Lima: Instituto de Apoyo Agrario, 1989.

Pulgar Vidal, Javier. *Geografía del Perú: Las ocho regiones naturales*. Lima: PEISA, 1987.

Quintanilla, Lino. *Andahuaylas: La lucha por la tierra, testimonio de un militante*. Lima: Mosca Azul, 1981.

Ramos Solís, Factor, and Jorge Loli Cabana. "Historia del Movimiento Popular en Huamanga." Senior thesis, Universidad de San Cristóbal de Huamanga, 1979.

Reid, Michael. *Peru: Paths to Poverty*. London: Latin American Bureau, 1985.

Rojas Samanéz, Alvaro, ed. *Sendero de violencia: Testimonios periodísticos, 1980-1989*. Lima: Colegio de Periodistas del Perú and Concejo Nacional de Ciéncia y Tecnología (CONCYTEC), 1990.

Roldán, Julio. *Gonzalo, el mito*. Lima: Edición del autor, 1990.

Rosenau, William. "Poor Peru." *American Spectator*. 23:12, December 1990, pp. 16-18.

Rudolph, James D. *Politics in Peru: The Evolution of a Crisis*. Stanford, CA: The Hoover Institution Press, 1992.

Salcedo, José María. "The Price of Peace: A Report from the Emergency Zone." *NACLA Report on the Americas*, 20: 3, June 1986, pp. 37-42.

———. "Con Sendero en Lurigancho." *Quehacer*, 39, February-March 1986, pp. 60-67.

Sánchez, Rodrigo. "Las SAIS de Junín y la alternativa comunal." *Debate Agrario*, 7, July-December 1989, pp. 85-101.

———. *Tomas de tierras y conciencia política campesina: Las lecciones de Andahuaylas*. Lima: Instituto de Estudios Peruanos, 1981.

Schram, Stuart R., ed. *Quotations from Mao Tse-Tung*. New York: Bantam Books, 1967.

Schutz, Barry, and Robert O. Slater. *Revolution and Political Change in the Third World*. Boulder, CO: Lynne Rienner, 1990.

Scott, James C. "Revolution in the Revolution: Peasants and Commissars." *Theory and Society*, 7:1-2, January-March 1979, pp. 97-134.

————. *The Moral Economy of the Peasant: Rebellion and Subsistence in Southeast Asia*. New Haven, CT: Yale University Press, 1976.

Sendero Luminoso. "Develop Guerrilla Warfare." Pamphlet, originally published in Spanish in March 1982, translated and published by the Revolutionary Communist Party, n.d.

Shakespeare, Nicholas. "In Pursuit of Guzmán." *Granta*, 23, Spring 1988, pp. 150-195.

Shanin, Teofor. "The Peasants Are Coming: Migrants Who Labour, Peasants Who Travel, and Marxists Who Write." *Race and Class*, 19, Winter 1978, pp. 277-288.

Shugart, Matthew Soberg. "Patterns of Revolution." *Theory and Society*, 18, 1989, pp. 249-271.

Simon, Yehude. *Estado y guerrillas en el Perú de los '80*. Lima: Asociación Instituto de Estudios Estratégicos y Sociales, 1988.

Skar, Harold O. *The Warm Valley People*. Oslo: University of Oslo, 1982.

————. *Between Freedom-Fighting and Terrorism in Peru — The Case of Sendero Luminoso*. Oslo: Norwegian Institute of International Affairs, 1988.

Skocpol, Theda. "Review Article: What Makes Peasants Revolutionary?" *Comparative Politics*, 14:3, April 1982, pp. 351-375.

————. *States and Social Revolutions*. New York: Cambridge University Press, 1979.

Slater, David, ed. *Revolutions: Theoretical, Comparative, and Historical Studies*. Chicago: Harcourt Brace Jovanovich, 1985.

Smith, Gavin. "The fox and the rooster: The Culture of Opposition in Highland Peru." *This Magazine,* 19, April 1985, pp. 9-14.

Starn, Orin. "Missing the Revolution: Anthropologists and the War in Peru." *Cultural Anthropology*, 6:1, 1991, pp. 63-91.

Stern, Steve J., ed. *Resistance, Rebellion, and Consciousness in the Andean Peasant World, 18th to 20th Centuries*. Madison: University of Wisconsin Press, 1987.

————. *Peru's Indian Peoples and the Challenge of Spanish Conquest: Huamanga to 1640*. Madison: University of Wisconsin Press, 1982.

Tarazona-Sevillano, Gabriela. *Sendero Luminoso and the Threat of Narcoterrorism*. Center for Strategic and International Studies (CSIS), Washington Papers 144, (New York: Praeger, 1990).

————. "The Personality of Shining Path and Narcoterrorism." Terrorism Seminar Paper, Center for Strategic and International Studies (CSIS) Washington, D.C., February 29, 1988.

Taylor, Lewis. *Maoism in the Andes: Sendero Luminoso and the Contemporary Guerrilla Movement in Peru*, Working Paper No. 2. Liverpool: Centre for Latin American Studies, University of Liverpool, 1983.

Tello, María del Pilar. *Perú: El precio de la paz*. Lima: Ediciones Petroperú, 1991.

————. *Sobre el volcán: Diálogo frente a la subversión*. Lima: Ed. CELA, 1989.

Terrill, Ross. *Mao: A Biography*. New York: Harper Colophon Books, 1980.

Tewlow, Jeff. "Peru's Mistaken Path: History and Sendero Luminoso." Senior thesis, Vassar College, 1989.

Tuesta Soldevilla, Fernando. "Cartilla de Información Electoral," mimeo, Lima, May 1990.

————. *Perú político en cifras*. Lima: Fundación Friedrich Ebert, 1987.

————. *Elecciones municipales: Cifras y escenario político*. Lima: DESCO, 1983.

Universidad de San Cristóbal de Huamanga (UNSCH). *Libro jubilar en homenaje al tricentenario de su fundación*. Ayacucho: UNSCH, 1977.

U.S. Committee for Refugees (USCR). *The Decade of Chaqwa: Peru's Internal Refugees*. Washington: USCR, May 1991.

Vargas Llosa, Mario. "Inquest in the Andes." *New York Times Magazine*, July 31, 1983, pp. 18-23 ff.

Vásquez, Mario C., and Paul L. Doughty. "Cambio y violencia en el Perú rural: Problema del indio." *Socialismo y Participación*, 34, June 1986, pp. 115-123.

Washington Office on Latin America (WOLA). "Peruvian Government Shaken By Cayara Massacre." Washington: WOLA, 1988.

Werlich, David P. "Peru: The Shadow of Shining Path." *Current History*, 83:490, February 1984, pp. 78-82.

Wickham-Crowley, Timothy P. "Understanding Failed Revolution in El Salvador: A Comparative Analysis of Regime Types and Social Structure." *Politics and Society*, 17:4, December 1989, pp. 511-537.

Wiener, Hugo F. *Cambios en la estructura social del campo peruano*. Lima: Instituto de Apoyo Agrario, 1987.

Wiener, Raúl A., ed. *Guerra e ideologia: Debate entre el PUM y Sendero*. Lima: Amauta, 1990.

Woy-Hazelton, Sandra. "Peru." In Richard F. Staar, ed., *Yearbook on International Communist Affairs*, Stanford, CA: The Hoover Institution, annual, 1985-1991.

————, and Stephen M. Gorman. "The Peruvian Left Since 1977: Ideology, Programs, and Behavior." Paper presented at the annual meeting of the American Political Science Association, Denver, CO, September 2-5, 1982.

Periodicals

El Comercio, Expreso, La República, and *Página Libre* usually carry regular reporting of subversion-related incidents, as well as feature articles and interviews. However, the reader is advised to take provincial reporting with a grain of salt. Two weekly magazines, *Caretas* and *Sí,* provide more concise coverage.

Required reading on Sendero's thinking is *El Diario,* the pro-Sendero publication that switched from daily to weekly in September 1989. Especially valuable are the series of historical documents from Sendero's preinsurrection period. These were printed between 1987 and 1989. In late 1989, the government closed down *El Diario,* though it has continued to appear in clandestine editions on a weekly or irregular basis.

These sources may be supplemented by *Resumén Semanal,* a weekly summary of all newspapers and magazines published by the Centro de Estudios y Promoción del Desarrollo (DESCO) research center in Lima. *Resumen* carries a section on subversion as well as a monthly summary of incidents through 1990. A more detailed coverage comes from the monthly *Informe Mensual,* put out by the Instituto de Defensa Legal. The bimonthly *Paz-Tarea de Todos* provides a more analytical, peace-oriented writing. It is published by the ecumenical center Centro de Estudios y Acción para la Paz (CEAPAZ). DESCO also brings out *Quehacer,* a bimonthly journal that built its reputation on following Sendero's trail from the early 1980s onward.

Research Centers

The Lima research centers DESCO, the Instituto de Defensa Legal, Democracia y Socialismo-Instituto de Política Popular, and the Instituto Bartolomé de las Casas have ongoing programs on political violence. InterCentros, a grouping of centers, human rights advocates, and other concerned institutions, has a task force on political violence and pacification.

DESCO has a database that draws on its extensive coverage of political events and trends.

Human rights organizations also have databases, case studies and publications available. The main human rights organizations are the Comisión Andina de Juristas (CAJ), the Asociación Pro Derechos Humanos (APRODEH), the Comisión de Derechos Humanos (COMISEDH), the Centro de Estudios y Acción para la Paz (CEAPAZ), the Comisión Episcopal de Acción Social (CEAS, part of the Catholic Church's Episcopal Conference), and the Coordinadora Nacional de Derechos Humanos.

Another interesting area is video libraries. The Instituto de Apoyo Agrario and CEAPAZ have begun gathering raw material and producing videos. Of uneven quality, these videos do allow a visual account of some of the incidents in the past decade.

The Catholic University's Centro de Documentación also has an archive of original documents and pamphlets.

Glossary of Acronyms
with Spanish and English Expansions

AP (Acción Popular) Popular Action Party

APRA (Alianza Popular Revolucionaria Americana) American Popular Revolutionary Party

AS (Acuerdo Socialista) Socialist Accord Party

CAEM (Centro de Altos Estudios Militares) Center for Higher Military Studies

CAMBIO 90 Change in 1990 Party

CCUSC (Comité Coordinador de Imofocación Sindical Clasista) Coordinating Committee for the Unification of the Working Class — Central Highway

CGTP (Confederación General de Trabajadores del Perú) General Confederation of Workers of Peru

CL (Comité de Lucha) Committee for Struggle — Central Highway

CORAH (Proyecto de Control y Reducción del Cultivo de Coca en el Alto Huallaga) Upper Huallaga Valley Coca Cultivation Reduction Control Project

DINCOTE (Dirección Nacional contra el Terrorismo) Counterterrorism Agency of the Police Force

EGP (Ejécito Guerrillero Popular) Popular Guerrilla Army — Shining Path

EMZ (Zona de Emergencia) Emergency Zone

FER (Frente Estudiantil Revolucionario) Revolutionary Student Front — Marxist organization gradually taken over by Shining Path

FONCODES (Fondo Nacional de Compensación Social) National Social Welfare Fund

FREDEMO (Frente Democrático) Democratic Front Party

FUE (Federación Universitaria de Estudiantes) University Student Federation

GR (Guardia Republican) Republican Guard

IS (Izguierda Socialista) Socialist Left Party

IU (Izguierda Unida) United Left Party

MRDP (Movimiento Revolucionario de Defensa del Pueblo) People's Revolutionary Defense Movement — a Shining Path umbrella organization which includes the groups listed below:

> CLCAA (Comité de Lucha Clasista de la Avenida Argentina) Class Struggle Committee of Argentina Avenue — an important older industrial area near the center of Lima
>
> CLOTCC (Comité de Lucha de Ofreros y Trabajadores Clasistas de la Carretera Central) Laborers and Workers Class Struggle Committee of the Central Highway
>
> CTIM (Centro de Trabajo Intelectual Mariátegui) Mariátegui Center for Intellectual Work
>
> MBP (Movimiento de Bases Populares) Popular Bases Movement
>
> MCB (Movimiento Clasista Barrial) Neighborhood Class Movement
>
> MCP (Movimiento Campesino Popular) Popular Peasant Movement
>
> MFP (Movimiento Femeniono Popular) Popular Women's Movement
>
> MIP (Movimiento Intelectual Popular) Popular Intellectual Movement
>
> MJ (Movimiento Juvenil) Youth Movement
>
> MOTAG (Movimiento de Obreros y Trabajodores Agrícolas) Agricultural Laborers and Workers Movement
>
> MOTC (Movimiento de Obreros y Trabajodores Clasistas) Laborers and Workers Class Movement
>
> MPJ (Movimiento de Pueblos Jóvenes) Shantytown Movement
>
> MRPJ (Movimiento Revolucionario de Pueblos Jóvenes) Shantytown Revolutionary Movement
>
> SPP (Socorro Popular del Perú) Popular Aid of Peru

MRTA (Movimiento Revolucíonario Tupac Amaru) Tupac Amaru Revolutionary Movement

PCP (Partido Comunista del Perú) Communist Party of Peru — Moscow Line

PCP-BR (Partido Comunista del Perú — Bandera Roja) Communist Party of Peru — Red Flag — Maoist, Saturnino Paredes faction

PCP-PR (Partido Comunista del Perú — Patria Roja) Communist Party of Peru — Red Fatherland — Maoist

PCP-SL (Partido Comunista del Perú — Sendero Luminoso) Communist Party of Peru — Shining Path — Maoist, Abimael Guzmán Reynoso faction. Calls itself the PCP to emphasize its claim to be the only authentic Communist Party of Peru.

PIP (Policía de Investigaciónes del Perú) Peruvian Investigative Police

PPC (Partido Popular Cristiano) Popular Christian Party

PRODERM (Projecto de Desarrollo de Microregión) Microregion Development Project

PUM (Partido Unido Mariateguista) United Mariateguist Party

SINAMOS (Systema Nacional de Apoyo a la Mobilización Social) National Social Mobilization Party

SL (Sendero Luminoso) Shining Path

SNA (Sociedad Nacional Agraria) National Agrarian Society

SNI (Sociedad Nacional de Industrias) National Industrial Society

SUTEP (Sindicato Unico de Trabajadores de Educación del Perú) Union of Peruvian Teachers

UMOPAR (Unidad Móvil de Patrullaje Rural) Mobile Rural Patrol Unit

VR (Vanguardia Revolucionaria) Revolutionary Vanguard Party

Index

The Faculty of the University of San Cristóbal de Huamanga, Ayacucho, Peru, December 1962. University Rector Efraín Morote Best is seated, center; Abimael Guzmán Reynoso is seated, third from the right (in light suit); David Scott Palmer is standing, third from the left, between second and third row (without ribbon and medallion).